About the A

Robin Pritchard was born in Cou . 1984 he was ordained a priest in the Church of England. As well as being a Parish Priest in Norwich Diocese he enjoys writing novels. In 2010 he gained an MA in Creative Writing from the Anglia Ruskin University.

You may contact Robin through his Amazon Author's Page.

THE

URBAN

MYSTIC

Robin Pritchard

Chapter 1

<u>When God is far off, he labours too</u>

When God is far off, he labours too:
You hear the sound of His axe in the far wood;
Above the noise and other words too quiet for sound,
The bruising of the wood, crying, singing - some poor fellow.
Not you this time.

When God is close, he labours still:
You feel the pain of the sharp blade between your boughs:
Alone the noise and other prayers too loud for peace,
The binding of the sap to vine, weeping, hymning - some poor fellow.
Just you this time.

When God is still, the end has come:
You see the flames leap high and bright;
Anoint the noise, his only word too alive for life.
No wood this time, an instrument divine - some pure fellow,
With all his time.

The name is Gregory. His name, my name; he was chosen after all. He would be forever confused as to how they took him. Drugs? He certainly felt dopey when he woke up. There were no obvious bruises on his head but the rest of him had many grazes and scratches. A yellow purple swelling marked out his right elbow and made it difficult for him to bend his arm. At first he could not remember anything but then images of the morning came into his head. But was it that morning? Finally, the physical discomfort overcame him: he was lying on a stone floor and the cold was seeping into his left side. Somebody had put him in the recovery position. He opened his eyes and sat up. The room - he was clearly inside - was small and musty. A kind of stone flour smell oozed from the walls. There was something ancient and venerable about the place and in the distance he thought he could hear faint chanting. By the echoes and silences he could tell that the room, in which he lay, was part of a much larger edifice. He pulled himself up on a nearby chair and staggered to his feet holding himself against the stanchions of a glassless but be-curtained window directly in front of him.

Suddenly these curtains were ripped back and the light flooded in causing him a terrible shock in his befuddled state. A large black shape stood in front of him.

"Ah, good, you are awake now," said a male voice. It was not a question. At the shock of the noise Gregory staggered backwards and slumped against the far wall of the room. This second wall was ply board and only about two metres away from its counterpart: it was more of a cell than a room. "I am sure that you will quickly recover and feel better. I have been assured that the consequences," he said this in a rather nasal way, "will soon pass off." In fact he sounded as though his sinuses were permanently blocked. As if to underline this he sniffed at the end of the sentence.

"Am in hospital?"

"Good gracious no. You are in a safe place." It was said with such a confident voice that nobody would dare to question it. Gregory shook his head and sat down on the chair. None of this made any sense. That morning he had left the house as usual to go to work. Around the corner from his house he had stopped to buy his paper and sandwiches. Then he had come out of the shop... He slowly felt down his arms and torso. No he hadn't been run over or had an accident. This just did not add up.

"I appreciate that all of this does not make any sense to you, but the truth is we have acquired you."

"Acquired me? For why?" The words would not come out straight.

"We need your gift and we have chosen you."

"But?"

"Let me get you a cup of tea." It must have been on hand because he was back in seconds. "I expect you are very bewildered. We need you as an attraction here and so we have selected you. It is an honour." Gregory sipped the sweet tea.

"Couldn't you have advertised?" He sounded stupid. "I mean you didn't ask me."

"Well that didn't seem very relevant to us - to me," he corrected himself.

"So you just had me lifted from the street. Sorry who are you?" In some dark recess of his mind he knew that he was being too polite.

"I am the Dean here."

"And your name?"

"Just the Dean." The black shape appeared to swell with pride.

"Who is in charge?"

"I am."

A bile was beginning to rise in Gregory's throat that even the tea could not quench. His blood began to run cooler. "So you are telling me that you," he paused for a moment to select the right word, "kidnapped me and brought me here against my will?"

"Yes." The light was still behind this figure and so the only clues to the man's identity were from the voice. It was uniformly flat and matter of fact. "Well, we will have many conversations about this in the future but at the moment we need you to rest. I will come back later and explain it more." Gregory was still too shocked to protest. The figure disappeared from sight.

"How do I get out of here?"

"There is no way," came a distant reply.

"Where am I?" he shouted.

And the voice came back almost like a whisper, "St. Arburn's Cathedral."

Chapter 2

Gregory sat for a moment bewildered and with rising anxiety. The adrenaline was leeching out the effects of his kidnapping. He still had no recollection of how it had been achieved. Some determination rose in him and he stood up and began to look around. This cell, for that was what he now perceived it to be, was about three metres by two; it was simply furnished with an old leather armchair, a very small wooden table with chair and a wooden pallet bed. The fabric of the cell was dressed stone but with no ornamentation except for a vaulted ceiling. To his left were the glassless windows. They were not real windows being free of glass and very narrow: he would not have been able to fit much more than his head through the any of the six gaps. Now he knew the nature of the building he was in it all began to make sense. When he pressed himself up against the openings he could see the bare shell of the original sanctuary, now stripped of any furniture. The ancient reredos looked down on him sombrely, spotted with cavities for displaying the missing statues. It was clear that some ancient butchery had acted upon it, as here and there the remains of a carved hand or foot clung to the edges of the orifices. As he had noted before the other wall of his cell was ply board and, he presumed, covered a similar feature to the one he was looking through. It was so long since he had been in a cathedral that he could not visualise the geography of his position.

Behind him, when he turned, was a short narrow set of stairs. Halfway down was a door on the right with a second door at the foot of the stairs. This first door revealed a shower with toilet. The single tap ran cold in the basin. The second door was locked to him and there was not a handle or anything on which he could get purchase on the resistant panel in front of him.

He returned to the window. "Is there anyone there?" he half shouted pathetically. He wandered around his small enclosure once more, prying with his fingers in every nook or cranny to see if there was any give in anything. It was all solid and immovable like some ancient and beautifully crafted Inca ruin: the blocks of stone matched seamlessly with each other and the door and panel ran congruently into the stonework.

He stepped to the grill and shouted again. He was still acting uselessly. In between the shouts he could hear faintly the noise of a Hoover or floor-polisher. Gregory remained too numb to react to what was happening to him so he sat down disconsolately on the chair. As he looked around he noticed it was getting darker and he automatically felt for his watch. It was gone. Gregory guessed it was evening but as he did not feel hungry he was not sure.

The Dean returned. Gregory had not been aware of him at first and it was possible that the man had been observing him for some moments during his period of apathy. Now that the light was not behind him he could see him more clearly. The Dean was dressed in a long black robe that buttoned to the neck. There was a sort of cummerbund of the same material around his waist. He had short dark but grey flecked hair and could have been between forty and sixty years old. The skin on his face was sallow and he looked as though he had recently shaved: there was an oiliness to his lower jaw. Otherwise his features were sharp and his eyes moist but muddy.

"How are you doing now young man?" It was an observation rather than a question. Gregory found nothing more irritating to be called a young man when you were near to thirty.

"What time is it?" He was told, confirming his impression that it was early evening. "Where is my watch?" The Dean shrugged as if it was of no consequence. "I want to be let out now."

"That is not possible."

"Why not? The door cannot be jammed."

"No, of course not. We are just not going to let you out."

"Explain to me!" Gregory took a step forward.

"We have chosen you to be our mystic here at St. Arburn's. It was my idea to have one," he said conceitedly, "but the chapter readily agreed. All attractions are in competition against each other now and we need to keep our cutting edge. I believe we are the first cathedral to provide such an amenity." Gregory looked at him closely. "No we are not mad," said the Dean, scorching out Gregory's embryonic thought before it took root. With a change in tone the nasal sounds became less prevalent.

"So this is purely a commercial decision?"

"Not quite - we are all driven by financial concerns - but we believe that we offer the general public much more than that. We are always trying to bring added value to what we do. Our market research has shown that people of all age groups respond well to spiritual attractions."

"So I am to be a spiritual attraction?" The Dean did not answer. He looked a bit bored, as though having spent so long discussing and planning for this he could no longer be bothered to go over it again, not least for the person it affected most.

"It doesn't make much sense to me. Would you not have been better to actually employ a mystic? I am certainly not a mystic and have no aspirations to be one. Just let me go and we will forget all about it."

"I would be repeating myself to say, 'No,' but the answer is still, 'No,' and will continue to be so." At these words Gregory hung his head for a moment in silent contemplation of the floor.

"I want to see a doctor."

"Are you ill?"

"Yes."

"I think I will be judge of that."

"I am not a mystic," Gregory told him with some force. He moved forward and leaned through the bars.

"I think you are selling yourself short. We chose you after an extensive search. It was you poem that clinched it."

"What....."

"The one in that begins, "When God is....."

"Well there you go - I didn't write that." The Dean raised a quizzical eyebrow.

"I mean I did write it but I did not think it up - it just came to me."

"Quite, just like I say. And you have mediums in your family."

"Mediums? What the..."

"They show a spiritual sensitivity. Many mystics of long ago, long before the Great Eclectic even had occult powers."

"But I don't have any occult powers. I am not a medium. You're taking this all out of context. You may as well choose a monkey to be a mystic. It would be as much use. Anyway, whatever it is, you cannot make me do - it whatever it is. I refuse. There is no way you can force me to do it. Even if you starve me I won't do anything for you." Gregory was getting childish. His failing defence drove him back into the gloom of his cell. The Dean spoke more loudly to compensate and the nasal resonance returned.

"Yes, I understand the argument. Whatever force we use on you would be a waste of time - if you have not within you the natural gift of being a mystic. However, that is where you and I differ because I believe those talents are in there and we just need to tease them out. You see something that has not been lost over the years is discernment. Much has been lost in our great traditions - and conventional spirituality has shrivelled away - but this last gift remains an ability to see the way forward and the insight to choose our leaders."

"If you have nominated me as leader then obey me and let me out."

"That would not be protecting you from harm or giving you the opportunity to develop this skill that we all need."

"Sheer bunk. I don't need protecting. I am not a child. For God's sake let me out."

"'God,' such an old word. See, you really do cling to the old ways. You must be some sort of genetic throw back."

"What you have done is completely immoral. What about my family?"

"Morality, there is an interesting word as well. Morality is defined by the situation, by the need of the involved parties and by their individual characters."

"Morality is right and wrong."

"True, we have decided it is right to bring you here." The Dean began to gently rock on his heals as he demonstrated some unease.

"No it is wrong to bring me here."

"But we have done it." The rocking stopped suddenly.

"That does not make it right. Just because you can do something does not make it right."

"We think it does." His eyes were sharp with new conviction.

"Then you are corrupt."

"Perhaps you are corrupt and decadent for ignoring and

squandering a gift that can be used for the common good."

"You cannot make me do it. You must give up and let me go eventually."

"Maybe we just kill you," the Dean said, as if he had just thought of it for the first time. He shook his head slowly to himself. "No that would be immoral. Nevertheless, we have discussed the possibility of your refusal at great length and taken pledges that we will not let you go until you have proved yourself to be a mystic. I don't expect that you can see the implications of that at the moment but I assure you that we have prepared ourselves and are ready to suffer the consequences however painful they are for you or us."

"The only way out is to become a mystic? Maybe I will kill myself."

"That would be such a waste and we would not let it happen."

"What of my family?" Gregory's face reflected this hopeful thought.

The Dean paused or a moment, as if considering whether to speak the answer.

"We have been very thorough - your family think you are already dead. Your funeral is next week."

"You bastard!" Gregory launched himself at the Dean but he was standing to far back. Gregory poured out as much venom as he could think of. The Dean stood impassively and took it.

"This is all very natural and what we expected. You need to work through this grief and get to work."

Gregory began to sob. "Go away leave me alone." The child melted out through his tears.

He went to sit in the corner and a slowly encrusting numbness spread over his body. Suddenly a new voice shouted, "Food," and a paper bag fluttered into his cell. Whoever it was had obviously stood well back and aimed the bag through the bars of the cell window - for fear that the wild animal penned inside would grab them and drag them in. Outside he could hear large resonating thumping noises as though furniture was being dragged about or stacks of chairs moved.

In the bag were three stale sandwiches and a chocolate muffin. Gregory crumpled the bag up and threw it into the far corner. "No drink," he thought but then he remembered the tap in his toilet.

He sat quiet and still for a long while as the shadows lengthened and the cell become dark - there was no light fitting in there at all. But his mood did not match that of the Cathedral. It had become very noisy and he could tell by the sounds that an orchestra was preparing to play and that the building was filling up for a concert but nobody came near him. It never occurred to him to call out and he just continued to sit dumb until the cold seeping up from the floor impelled him to move. Just as he was standing up the lights went on in the sanctuary, making him jump as the cold halogen flooded his cell. He picked up his sandwiches and took a few bites of one before drawing the curtains and lying down on his pallet. Within minutes a deadly exhaustion swept over him and he fell into a troubled sleep to the strains of a classical concert.

Chapter 3

[A] The Urban Mystic needs to take time away from where she lives. This is not a contradiction. The Urban Mystic has been set aside to immerse herself in the mores of the society in which she lives. She is to be taken up in the physicality and spirituality of it all: the spiritual current and waves; the crashing surf of the place in which she dwells. Even so, in the weariness of the soul and at times we must all escape from the place the divine spirit has put us. He takes you away for retreat because he is a just and loving spirit. So you will come to the country, in much the same way as a hermit, who spends most of his ministry in the backwoods of beyond, comes to the city for a challenge, for a distance from the place where he lives and ministers, so she can reflect upon it. [All quotes from the book, ADAM AND THE BLACKBIRD IN THE CITY]

He had been on the boat a long time before he let them know he was there. Conditions in the sail store had become too un-hygienic for him to stay there anymore; you cannot urinate repeatedly and even crap in the corner of small space without it becoming too obnoxious to you. There would be all hell to pay when someone had to clear that up. It never occurred to him that they might make him do it.

Mr. Kertz was so livid that, when the sailor brought Greg before him, you could see the veins in his forehead swell dangerously. He hit Greg hard half a dozen times whilst the sailors held his arms and he swore a great deal. It was only when Sue cried out that he stopped and looked malevolently at her instead. She looked so beautiful and fragile that Greg's heart melted all over again.

"So it is you again. You have done a dangerous and

stupid thing by coming on my yacht. If it were not for the fact that I cannot be sure that you were not seen getting on, then I can tell you, nobody would ever see you get off. What are you trying to prove? That is not a question. You have become like some faithful doggy that drools every time you hear the word food but for you it is every time you see her." He almost spat it out. Greg noticed again that Mr. Kertz never used her name. By contrast, Greg always used her name: he was always rolling it around his mind. "You are a sick, useless, lustful little prick. I can tell you the fruit is mine and will never be yours. She knows where all this comes from and who lines her purse. It's business isn't it my little slut?" She winced." See she acknowledges the name. I have spoilt her for you for ever. Take him away. Lock him in a cabin!"

    Greg was only let out once in the next five days as the yacht sailed steadily south. And that was to prove to be sport for the sailors as they made him clean out the sail locker. Not once did he hear or see Sue.

    On the sixth day the weather turned and by the evening he was feeling quite claustrophobic and very sick as he was catapulted around his small cabin. In the middle of the night the ship lurched out of its regular rhythm and he heard a hiss travel past his outside cabin wall. Then a sickening judder and metallic scream. Their forward motion became limp and soggy and the boat slowed to a halt. A primitive fear gripped Greg as he began to realise that the cabin might become a watery grave.

    After pounding on the door for a few minutes and shouting, it was opened and a pale faced sailor said cryptically, "Time to go home." He had a struggle to get onto the deck, fighting against the motion of the boat, and when he got there it was almost deserted. As the ship reared and plunged he saw the lights of another smaller boat some distance off. He waved and hallooed to it before it dawned on him that it was going away: it was the ship's launch. They had left him to his fate. The sailor, who had released him from his cabin, was at his elbow, shouting over the howl of the sea and wind. Unable to make himself heard he gesticulated for Greg to follow. With tremendous difficulty they hauled themselves up to the small bridge. There inside lay Sue. She lay limp and still, her pale blue top and skirt was spotted with her own blood from a deep head wound. As she lay at an unnatural angle he could see a deep bruise forming over her left hip and spreading up diagonally into her abdomen.

He took her in his arms and kissed her. She opened her eyes and murmured. The sailor was tugging at his arm. "Boat, boat," he cried.

Later when they were thrown by the surf onto the shore he had no memory of how they had launched the dingy or how they had come to be there. Some miracle had freed them from the sinking ship and had brought them to safety. It was early morning now and the sun shone watery over the long beach and crashing waves. He picked her up tenderly in his arms and carried her into the adjacent forest. He stumbled forward for a while until, in the gloom of the forest, he spotted a mossy bank by a gentle stream. Even here, despite all his difficulties, he could not but smile to himself at this romantic Shakespearean setting. If only Titania would come with her magic and heal his love.

Greg slouched down on the bank and cradled her in his arms. "My beloved," he whispered into her left ear and her eyes flickered as if in response. "I only know corny things but maybe if you can wake up and hear them they will seem a little magic to you." She stirred slightly. "I've dreamed of a moment like this ever since I first saw you. I was just completely unsettled by our first meeting, it was as though I knew that I was incomplete and that together we would make up one new whole. You are just so spectacular to look at. Your hair, your eyes." He caressed her hair as he spoke and kissed her eyes. "Your lips." He kissed them, they tasted salty and when he looked at them he could see that their embrace had smeared blood from the corner of her mouth onto her bottom lip. An unnatural chill passed up his spine when it caught his attention. Then he heard some shouting on the beach behind him and the sounds of someone crashing around in the jungle at some distance off to his right. It distracted him momentarily so that when he looked back at her he found her eyes were open. What they were saying he had no idea. Was it a smile?

He could not be sure.

"Would you like a drink?" he pressed but the only answer was for her eyes to shut slowly - trembling as they did so. She must have relaxed because she became heavier. Then there was a gentle sigh from her lips and he just knew without anyone telling him, that she had breathed her last. Her skin looked paler, her beauty beginning to fade. "It must have all been in her soul," he said to himself. Then he began to cry and huge drops, as big as berries, fell in self-pity from his eyes.

"How touching," a voice said behind him. It was Mr. Kertz. "I knew that I would find her with you. A dog always returns to its vomit. What amazes me about you is the spectacularly ignorant way you have doted on this creature. She was a whore and nothing more." Greg did not turn to look at him, he heard him light a cigarette and felt his throat catch at the first whiff. "Come on let us get her back to the beach - the bursar is a bit of a doctor - he can patch her up."

Very gently Greg released her body from his grasp. He slid it onto the bank where it lay like a human sacrifice. He contemplated her for a moment and then turned to face Kertz. Mr. Kertz who now looked a little discomforted, his face showing a slight blush. Greg only felt a cold calculating hatred for the man who stood there.

"Steady on, we can make her well again." Kertz stared at the motionless body and began to suspect the worst. He did not dare ask the question for fear of how it would provoke Greg. His left hand began to move to the pistol which he kept in his trouser band behind him.

"Why did you leave her on the boat?" Mr. Kertz shrugged. "Did you have no feelings for her at all?"

Sometimes non-violent people dream of a moment of absolute rage when they strike out. They wonder what it will be that provokes them to the point. They see themselves pivoting gracefully as, like a trained athlete, they bring the whole force behind that one murderous lunge. When it happened for Greg it was not like that, forty percent of the force must have been dissipated in his unfitness and poor technique but the results were still awesome. The forward drive of his fist completely crushed the man's nose and sent cartilage splinters into his own knuckles. The carry forward took him completely onto Mr. Kertz as they both crashed backwards into the undergrowth. When Greg got to his feet he cried out in the sheer pain and terror of what he had done. On the ground in front of him lay the man, his head, twisted at an unnatural angle, following the contour of a large boulder that pushed it off centre. Greg saw the gun lying by his hand. He turned away, picked up the girl and carried her carefully back to the beach, his bloody hand leaving a trail of drops on the crushed vegetation behind them.

[J] The Urban Mystic is drawn to crowds. She stands with them. If they are working she adds solidarity and support to what they are doing. She handles and touches things. She dwells, spends time. She drinks in atmospheres. She thinks hard about what she sees.

One of the problems for the Urban Mystic is that there is too much of everything. And her sensitivity can be overawed - overcome by all she sees and does. And therefore she must be aware of this danger. She is like a war artist. She appears to be unemployed but she is there nonetheless doing a valuable work. Yet the picture she draws, the things she records are of the spirit. She is so sensitive that noises make her jump. She must keep her sensitivity sharpened and heightened in order to hear and see what is going on. She feels drawn to be in certain places - to stand, be, reflect and contemplate. There are no monastery walls for her. She has left them behind.

Chapter 4

Gregory shook himself and raised his hands to his head. Later when he sat up he shivered. He had not been warm enough and he was now chilled. When he felt strong enough to stand up he jogged about for a minute and slapped himself. There were no obvious signs of vapour in the air when he breathed but it was definitely turning autumnal in this large building. There must be no heating, he decided. It was quite dark in the cell so he pulled back the curtains at the window to catch any gleam of light from the high Presbytery windows.

His system was sluggish and he felt quite poorly so he fetched himself some water in the plastic beaker provided and sat in the chair to drink it. Slowly his mind woke up and the torture began. His mind, once more free of distraction, began to run on in the most uncomfortable way. He had always been quite an analytical person but nothing would work at the moment.

After what seemed like hours of growing anxiety, when his body had begun to twitch in sympathy with his internal workings, he heard a door open in the far distance and some lights clicked on supplementing the dawn's rays. It had to be somewhere between seven and nine he reckoned. "Hello anyone there?" he shouted. No answer. If they were that well prepared, he thought, they must have a plan of how to deal with him. What did he know about cathedrals and their daily routine? He shrugged. He knew about monasteries from school but that was history. He could even remember visiting a cathedral on a school trip as a very young child and being impressed by the size of it all. But now. There wasn't one anywhere near his home and he must be about 200 kilometres from there now. He was vaguely aware that, since the end of the Great Eclectic, most churches, and several of the cathedrals, had been turned into private residences. Only the few that had historic resources continued and became tourist attractions, or centres of historical education, or whatever. But people did not travel very much now with the tensions. Clearly this one supported itself by selling itself in some way; the concert last night and now him - the attraction. He had never been one to ask for advice but he felt the lack of it now. Here he was facing some test and he needed help desperately. Gregory knew he must escape, that he could not cope with being there and if he was made to stay he would break down. He would wait until it was fully light before making his plans, even so the anxiety continued to grow.

At some later time another bag of sandwiches came through the window but when he rushed to see who had thrown them he could not get a sight of them. Every so often he would shout ineffectually for someone to come, without a response. At first he did not feel up to eating anything but after a while he forced himself and then, when his blood sugar rose, he made to act. What he did not know was what resources they had to repulse him or recapture him should he get free from the cell. He did wonder whether it would be best to wait until night. It was clear to him that the first job was to conduct a meticulous search of his cell. And he was just about to do this when the Dean arrived. He was looking smug.

"I expect you are beginning to think how to escape today," were his opening words. "However I must warn you that it will not be possible." He sounded incredibly smug. "We have various responses in place should you try," he continued, "and we have provided you with a servant to see to your needs." It was almost as if he wanted to be congratulated. Gregory intuitively saw that evil had to be narrow-minded if it took the part to be greater than the whole. The Dean turned and waved to somebody who was out of Gregory's eye line to come forward. "This is Bailey." Bailey was a small man but lithe and muscled with a military bearing. He had short brown hair and Gregory guessed him to be about forty years old. He was unsmiling with heavy lidded eyes that made his blinks short and unspectacular.

If Gregory could have laid hands on him he could easily have overpowered him, due to his diminutive stature but the cage of the cell supplemented the physical strength that this man lacked.

"It will be useful to have a servant, especially an obedient one. Someone who will fetch and carry for me. Someone who will follow my orders?"

The Dean actually grinned. "That's the spirit - a sense of humour. No, he is to obey my orders and help you to settle and to do your work."

"Am I to be fed properly and given warm clothes and heating?"

"Within reason." He meant when you can be trusted.

"No visits from my family," he noted bitterly.

"No - I agree that was quite deplorable but in the circumstances expedient."

"This work of mine, when am I to begin? What is it you require of me?"

"I don't expect you to start yet. You will be feeling too raw - but in time, when you have come to accept your position, we will discuss it."

"You surely cannot expect me to accept being a prisoner?"

"I think you have developed a too modern understanding of personal freedom. In past ages the majority of people had to accept a curtailment of their freedom in order to serve the community."

"That is easy for you to say." Gregory picked at a blemish on his face in agitation.

"Don't you think that I myself do not make sacrifices to keep this grand edifice of spiritual understanding alive."

"No I think you are free to do as you please, whereas I am not. You have chosen what the greater good is without any reference to me. I don't believe that what you are talking about is the greater good."

"Oh I think as you spend more time here, and soak in the atmosphere, you will change your mind." There was an unctuous look on his face.

"Impossible." Then Gregory asked quietly, "How is it that you intend to stop me escaping?"

The Dean looked at him coolly. In the pause another voice, a female one, called out from some distance away. "Who have you got there? Who are you talking to?"

The Dean turned away speaking as he went. Gregory heard him begin to reply, "It is all right honey..." and the rest was lost. Bailey moved to take the position of the Dean and looked malevolently at Gregory.

"Are we to be friends then?" But Bailey did not answer or respond in any way.

The Dean came back, pushing Bailey out of the way as if by an invisible bow wave. The dog obeys his master, thought Gregory.

He looked cross. "There - you have upset my daughter now and I must go."

"My question," insisted Gregory.

"Can you imagine that someone who would go to the trouble of bringing you here alive, for a particular purpose, would not use every means at their disposal to keep you here and safe. Use your imagination." And finally, "Bailey will help you to understand." Gregory felt a chill in his bones and a surge of anxiety. The Dean left and Bailey took his place again.

"Are you married? Do you have children?" No answer. There was no warmth to this stationary brooding man that Gregory could hope to use any emotional arguments on. He tried to ask him several other questions about the Dean and the daily routine of the Cathedral: when he was to expect a meal next but to no avail. Eventually, Bailey turned on his heel, and although he did not salute there was the merest smidgen of such a response there, as he walked away.

Gregory sighed and sat down. Then almost immediately, as if his whole body was filled with a leaden dread, he dragged himself to this feet. He must search his cell. In the bathroom he tested every fitting. There was no chain on the toilet: the cistern was behind the wall and Gregory surmised it flushed itself regularly like an urinal. He applied his full force to the taps and sink and toilet bowl but they were all stainless steel and absolutely immovable. He realised that he must be careful not to compromise his own safety. Even if he did a dirty protest they would just leave him, he suspected.

The rest of his cell also proved uninspiring for escape material: he reasoned that he could smash the small amount of furniture he had and maybe find a nail, or piece of wire, but there was not a key hole to pick on the door at the bottom of the stairs; even if he tried to scratch way the wall it would be a long and laborious process and they might well hear him. It was not knowing how they might stop him that frightened him most. He returned to his seat for reflection. The morning was stretching on and, from the noises he could hear, it was clear that the Cathedral had visitors. What day was it he wondered? He must ask, he told himself. Inspired he stood up and called through the window, "Bailey." He said it a few times before Bailey appeared. "What day is it?" Impassively Bailey walked way.

Suddenly a real heaviness came upon his heart: the first touch of grief for his family filled his soul and he began to cry. He came back to the window and cried out "Help me. Help me. I am being held against my will. Please call the police." Then he said it again louder, and again, this time shouting. When he paused the noises in the Cathedral had stopped. He shouted more and more until his voice became hoarse.

When the first bucket of cold water drenched him it was a double shock because he had not even noticed Bailey deliver it. He must have been shouting with his eyes shut. Water filled his mouth and nose; he choked and the coldness of it made him shudder with pain. Gregory was speechless. "You bastard!" he shouted at Bailey. Bailey grinned back at Gregory with a look of evil humour. Gregory felt absolutely outraged and continued to shout. "Help! Help! I am being kept a prisoner by the Dean. Please tell the...." Before he could get it out another bucket came. Not so much a shock but a spur to his determination. Nothing would stop him now he decided. He continued to shout and scream alternating from imprecations to cries of help. He encouraged his listeners, wherever they might be, to call the police on his account. He screamed out the story of his kidnap. And still the buckets came. Bailey must have had someone to help him as he only disappeared out of his sight for seconds before returning with another bucket. The cell was awash with water and the damp made the stonework smell of wet rock. There were standing pools here and there, where the floor was uneven, but most of it had poured down the stairs and run under the door of the cell. He could hear men shouting and the sound of brushes and pails through the plywood wall.

After about ten minutes he stood back panting. His heart was beating fast and his chest hurt with the pain of it and the shouting. But still the buckets came. They were treating him like a tenacious spider in a basin. They displayed a barbaric determination to wash him away. In the end he took refuge in his toilet cubicle and there he began to shiver with the cold and stress. He took some of his clothes of and wrung them out. He felt insane with fury at his treatment. Never in his whole life had he been treated with such contempt. Suddenly the Cathedral organ sprang into life playing loudly and wildly. He nodded to himself - to cover up his noise. He would give them noise he said to himself.

He came quietly out of the toilet and checked if the coast was clear. The deluges had stopped and Bailey was not in view. He picked up his chair. It was a superior sort of high backed waiting room chair, quite tall for elderly people. It had four good legs on it. Gregory repeatedly crashed it on the ground until something gave inside it and the legs become loose. He continued to strike it on the floor taking out his venom in some gestalt way on this piece of lifeless furniture. In time he pinned it to the ground with his foot and having weakened it was able to wrench of one of the legs. He now had a substantial club. The organ continued to play without pause. He didn't recognise the music but it had a similar frenzy to it as he himself felt. "Keep going," he said to motivate himself. He was determined to break out. The most vulnerable point was the window. It was broken into six slim glassless apertures. It was ecclesiastical shaped with some ornamentation. But the best thing about it was that it did not look very strong.

He hit it hard with his club and the jolt shuddered up his arm. The blow made a large unpromising dent in his club. He began to hit the stone work rhythmically but not as hard as the first time. The stanchion began to crumble and chip. He felt exultant. In order to brace himself he curled his hand around the upright between the first and second aperture. It was a mistake. Bailey who had come up obliquely hit the back of his knuckles with a hard leather strap. Incredibly, taking into account the force of the delivery, it did not break the skin but the force bruised the bones inside. Gregory gave out the most horrible animal scream and withdrew his hand. The tears burst from his eyes and he dropped to his knees and held the hand up in front of him. He did not know what had happened at first but when he looked up he saw Bailey withdrawing with the weapon in his hand. There was an cruel look on his face. Gregory wept afresh with pain and outrage. He began to tremble with the shock and his whole body went cold. His heart must have slowed because he felt really ill. He lay down on his soaked bed and whimpered. They were black moments for him

In the end he had to get up because he was so cold and he needed to move around. His hand looked mangled and the pain was appalling but he took up his club again. This time he kept his hand well clear and a weather eye out for Bailey. Afresh he pounded away at the stanchion. They tried a few buckets of water but he just jeered. By hitting at the top and bottom of the stanchion he hoped to break a chunk out. And when it came loose and he was able to wrestle it free he gave a cheer. But it was short lived for he discovered that there was a thick metal rod behind it which had been hidden by the bulk of the stone. In anguish he threw the broken piece of the stanchion to the ground and fresh tears came to his eyes. He felt the bar and checked behind the other uprights. It was the same all along. He collapsed on his bed in despair and the organ stopped.

Another bucket of water came on him as he lay on the pallet. Most terrifyingly of all was that Bailey said nothing. Maybe he was dumb, judged Gregory.

Over the next few hours he battered way at the plywood wall to little avail. In time he reasoned that it would be possible to rub a hole by friction but he guessed that they would probably frustrate that plan by patching it from the outside. In any case he suspected there was another window behind it and thus more iron bars. In addition, he decide that although in time he might be able to work a screw loose from the chair, the likelihood of using it as a tool to get through the walls was remote.

But by now he had a new problem, he felt very poorly and even though he had stopped his attempts to escape every so often more water came. They must be punishing him.

The drenchings continued intermittently during the day. Each time he laboriously stripped off the wet clothes and wrung them out. There was nowhere for him to rest: he had to keep moving anyway and the pain in his hand was appalling. It had swollen to twice its size. Every so often he would weep with the stress and fatigue. No food either. That night he was left alone and it became the worst he had ever experienced. If he had been hardened by long years of frugal living and physical exercise he would have coped better. However, he was a product of his age and spoilt by easy living. During the dark hours he paced around his cell occasionally lying on the bare pallet: the mattress was ruined, once he tried to sleep standing up pressed against the wall. By the morning his nose was running and he felt shivery, his throat was hoarse and sore from the screaming.

He was left alone for the morning despite feebly calling for help. Still no food. He felt frustrated with himself that he could not rise above this physical torment but it was not his calling to endure such and survive. His constitution was too weak. He felt hopeless about his cell, he could not see that there was any way that it would ever dry out. They had broken him already with very little effort. By the evening he was delirious and sometime later he collapsed.

Chapter 5

He felt their hands and heard their voices but he could not move. "This is badly done Bailey. You've gone too far. It was obvious that he had stopped and was controlling himself. You were only supposed to use sufficient force to diminish the noise. You knew he couldn't get through the bars. And his hand - what have you done to it? If it is broken and we can't call medical help he could get gangrene or anything." There was a pause. "I hope you know what you are doing. Make sure you get the air out of the syringe this time or we will end up with another body on our hands." He felt the prick and the rough hands. "Sit up a minute." This was directed at him. "A pill to make you better." Something was thrust in his mouth and hard hands held his nose. As he fought for breath he swallowed the tablet. "Right let's get him out of here. No. I'm not touching him. I hate flesh especially wet dead flesh. The spirit must always be better. Nobody would want flesh surely? Get a verger to help you. Watch him carefully. When he wakes another tablet and another injection. Then back in here. I expect this cleared up in the meantime and dried out or he will never get better." During all this Gregory never heard Bailey or the others, if there were others, reply. "Use your initiative. New furniture. Get one of those industrial heaters in here and give it a blast. Must I do everything?"

[L] It may be that he sees these sensitivities as a personal curse because they hinder his life in the world and disable him from the victorious life he may want to lead. He may be full of fear and anxiety. The most sensitive are the most susceptible to disease and break down.

When Gregory woke up he was very groggy and very weak. He was back in his cell on a dry bed with fresh clothes on. His hand was bandaged. He stretched and pulled himself up slowly avoiding the bad hand. When he turned to the window he saw that someone was sitting outside. It was the Dean. "Good show," he said, "here is some food." He held out a bag and put his hand through the bars.

When Gregory made no move to take it the Dean threw it onto the end of the bed. Since the previous meeting the Dean had changed his clothes to a grey suit, black shirt and clerical collar.

"It has been a bad do and I have reprimanded Bailey for taking it too far. But at least you know what we're capable of. If you draw attention to yourself in that way again then regrettably we will repeat the whole thing. But I expect, judging by the effect it has had on you that you would not want to play that again." It was a rhetorical question. Gregory lay in silent assent. The Dean drew himself more upright and looked keenly at him.

"Now your work must begin."

"Did you have one of me - a mystic - before?"

"What gave you that idea?"

"I heard you say it when I was ill."

"No you're mistaken. We did try to hire a mystic but it didn't work. He did not seem to be able to apply himself in the way we wanted. Altogether bogus. Not motivated at all. But you are different - I sense that. I know we can work together and make St. Arburn's great again. It always was a centre of spirituality and now it can be once more. This thought made his face brighten and smoothed out some of his facial lines.

Gregory spoke, his voice was still sore and it came out as little more than a whisper. "You must be completely insane to think that." The Dean looked genuinely hurt.

"Well we could debate insanity."

"Yeah go on let's do it." The Dean looked at his watch.

"I've got time. Maybe you're insane and this whole thing is just a figment of your imagination."

"I wish I could imagine you don't exist."

"Not possible I think. Anyway I expect that madness is when you lose control of your imagination," there was a pause, he was really enjoying himself, "and mysticism is when you truly gain control over it. Don't you think?"

"Pass."

"Mysticism is the full use of all your creative powers and all your spirit given gifts to their ultimate limit. Thus the more powerful your imagination, the greater the possibility of inspiration."

"I have little imagination."

"I disagree, your perpetual anxiety proves you have a

sensitive spirit."

"Spirit and imagination are different."

"Umm. To you." Gregory distrusted the Dean.

"Maybe you are insane, criminally insane - and Bailey - and the others whoever they are. You must have control over quite a few people."

"Yes, my staff are loyal and trust me. I hope you will come to as well in time. Anyway, you are distracting me. What is madness anyway? Sanity is only an artificial construct. Society declares that people within certain limits are normal." He held his hands up to indicate his point. "If you fall beyond that," He demonstrated with his hand, "then you are declared insane." Gregory could see that the man was pleased with himself: he was inflating and deflating like a medical respirator with the flow and ebb of the conversation.

"It can't be that clear cut."

"Of course not there are grey areas at each end." He raised his hands again.

"I don't think you are hearing me," Gregory pursued with as much vehemence as he could, "I don't want to be here and I don't want to do what you want. That is never going to change."

"You are being silly - everything changes. Would you rather be alone? Are you ready to make a start?" Gregory was exasperated. He shuffled uncomfortably on his bed.

"There is some connection missing here. Tell me, explain to me, what is it that you require from me. What is a mystic? What was mystic?"

"Half of that is irrelevant. Who cares what one was. I want you to be a mystic for now. Yes, there were men and women in touch with the divine. They disciplined themselves, sometimes quite severely, to transport themselves into trances and the such like to tempt God to contact them. What we want from you is to be a mystic for today, for now, for St Arburn's. I want - we want you to be a channel for direct communication with the divine spirit. Our congregation is hungering for a new relevant knowledge of spirituality for themselves. They want a role model to emulate, and a go between, so they can question them." Gregory shook his head in despair.

"Surely you are the Dean - that's your job?"

"You are so simplistic. I have never seen my role as a clerical

Dean. If I am honest I have similar longings to that of my congregation. Life can be very empty you know with my responsibilities."

"So you are going to make my life empty. You take away my friends and family." Bitter tears sprang to Gregory's eyes. He could not help himself, he felt weak and maudlin. The Dean got to his feet.

"Now now you must not feel sorry for yourself - this is a great calling. You are unique to this vocation and I have every confidence in you."

A voice in the distance called, "Daddy can you come."

The Dean stood fixedly, spearing Gregory with his eye and pointing his finger at him told him firmly. "My daughter." It was meant as, "Don't go there."

The Dean disappeared. "Wait," Gregory called. There was a forlorn look on his face.

"Tomorrow," came a distant voice.

```
[S] The object of these notes is to
enable the reader to live easily and without
regret in the urban environment.
```

Gregory felt very weak and when he opened his sandwich bag he found a small bottle of penicillin and attached to it a scribbled note as to how to take them. There was a damp smell lingering in his cell, nonetheless, there had obviously been some heating on for a while to make such an improvement. He had a new chair and bed with more blankets and he could see a thin pile of clothes in the corner. They were his original clothes now laundered. He was wearing a very old-fashioned track suit and, he guessed without checking, someone else's underpants. They were too small.

He dosed on and off for the rest of the day. There were no visits, bar the sudden appearance of a food bag that an unknown person chucked through his window. Then unfortunately he was wide awake and it was the middle of the night and he felt very frightened. It may have been the tablets, he had never been very good with medication, but his spirits were low. Given the choice he would never have entered such building after dark and now here he was incarcerated in one. "Anyone there?" he asked fearfully. Surely Bailey, or one of his cohorts, were around somewhere. He reasoned that there must be a night watchman, unless Gregory himself was he.

Like any large building it was far from silent. First of all his ears hissed, later he distinguished vague creaks, scratching, scamperings and low sonorous booms. He kept away from the window for fear that something nameless would come through the openings and get him. He hid down under his blankets and shivered with fear. In the past he would have taken himself in hand and made himself get a grip but, at this juncture, there were no psychological resources in him to do it.

He began to think of his old life. His last parent had only died a few months before and he had only begun adjusting to the empty house. His older sister was married and lived some distance away and he did not see her often. Gregory had been the one to stay on at home, drawn into the carer's role as first one and then the second of his parents had become long term ill. His dreams of college had gone in the daily struggle and for the last ten years he had worked in a local warehouse moving from the till to stacking the pallets and working the forklift truck. He had not had much in common with his workmates, they thought he read too much: his unfulfilled brightness distanced him from their more worldly concerns. He had made do with his hobbies, a few night classes and the telly as over the years he had maintained his on-call duty to his parents. It would be easy to think of him as some sad case who had been blackmailed by dominant parents into a perpetual childhood but it had been more from grace on his part than their demands. They would have excused him many times if he had left them - but as he did not leave - they remained affectionately grateful to the end for his kindness. And there had been women but his conscience would not let him take any of them further whilst he was thus encumbered, and most were not prepared to wait. He was too old-fashioned for them in his filial duties. He was tall, with a rugged care-worn handsomeness, yet quite slim and un-athletic. He had been a sickly child.

Who would have gone to his funeral, he wondered.

The night passed slowly and he fell into short bouts of troubled sleep waking from them frequently with a start. With the dawn his mood lifted. Gregory knew that if he was to escape he must be much more subtle about it and he decided to go along with all their machinations until he could form a new plan.

In the morning the Dean reappeared. Gregory, remaining without a clock, did not know the time. Before the Dean could open his mouth to say a cheery welcome Gregory said, "I need a watch."

"Oh is that wise? Surely the time will drag too much for you?"

"I need to organise my day," he replied simply.

"Are you feeling better?" Gregory did not reply. "I know it is very early days for you but I suggest you make a start on your work. The sooner begun ...," he said banally.

"You must be more direct as to what you want me to do. Are there any books I can read on the subject or holy words to help me?"

"You were asking that yesterday. It is clear that you have not yet realised how unique and important you are. There was no chance involved in your choice. We have had our eye on you for some time. You filled the criteria absolutely." These conversations were not easy to stage: if Gregory hung too far back in his cell, although this discomforted the Dean, making him peer furtively into the gloom, it did not allow Gregory to be dominant. In turn the Dean declared his discomfort by standing as someone more used to sitting and sounding forth from behind a desk.

"You've been watching me?"

"Yes."

"For how long?"

"Oh, a month or two."

"That's irrelevant. Have you no scruples - no conscience? I know that society is decaying but what you have done is completely immoral." Gregory was drawn nearer as he began to engage more fervently in the conversation, nervously pushing his hair from his eyes.

"You're still not seeing the whole picture. Now do you want me to explain?" Gregory was silent. "We need someone who is intelligent but untutored. Someone unconnected with any other spiritual quest and someone with proven or suspected spiritual sensitivity. In other words we did not want you to come with any baggage to the task."

"This is plainly ridiculous, surely someone with natural qualities still needs to be trained. Your argument does not make sense. You expect me to become a qualified mystic without any training."

"There is nobody to train you. Only the divine spirit."

"So let me get this right. I am being tied up as a kind of sacrifice - like an animal tethered in a clearing - hoping that the divine spirit will come along and take me."

The Dean grinned, a deep smile of pleasure. "Splendid! I knew you would get it. I defended your choice to the others."

"What others?"

"Oh the chapter," he returned quickly. "Anyway you are not without resources. Look at how we have provided for you so far. A cell!" He moved his arms about. "To give you solitude and freedom from distractions. If you reach out to it the spirit is bound to respond."

"Do you believe in this divine spirit?" A change came over the face of the Dean.

"Of course I do," he said firmly.

"What happens if he is not as you expect him to be? The Dean did not answer. "So I'm to sit in this cell for ever waiting for something to happen."

"Mostly yes, it is an experiment.

"I am an experiment? You're the torturer!" Gregory stared intensely at him, a hot rage flushing his face.

"No, that is too harsh. I know that this is an old fashioned term but I am more in the nature of a spiritual director."

"Surely you should have gone there first. Mentors are always more experienced."

"Nonsense, if unmarried priests can comment and encourage marriage so can a non-mystic be a confidant and a motivator of a mystic."

"Crap. You must give me something to read or I will go mad."

"Hmm." Gregory was going to ask by what criteria they would judge that the experiment had been a success or not, but the Dean continued before the question was formulated. "You should know that the congregation are very interested in you. Many of them have very deep spiritual needs and in due course they will want to consult you. They will want their money's worth," he threatened. "So we don't want to disappoint them do we? Over the next day or two we are having a temporary screen made for this window. Then every day for an hour it will be put in place here - a bit like an old fashioned confessional - then people will come and consult with you."

Gregory gave a deep sigh. "You are completely insane."

"We shall see. I have faith and at the moment my faith is stronger than yours. You may lean on it and let it carry you through."

"You can't make me do it."

"It will disappoint people if you don't do it. Anyway you may find their stories interesting."

"I want better food, vegetables - and hot food - and clean clothes."

"All in good time. Few people will come near you at the moment. You're frightening them. Anyway you are not safe to have a knife or..."

"Fucking afraid of me! How come I have to take all this shit for other people's emotions when I am the one suffering most. It's bloody unfair." But the Dean was gone, he was not interested in Gregory's feelings about the situation at all. "Fuck! Fuck! Fuck........." The interview had tired him so he lay down and drifted into a bad dream.

Chapter 6

I pulled back my bedroom curtains and looked outside. "My God, my God, what a beautiful car!" I was bursting to get out to it. We had only finished it the week before and now, in its new paint job, it looked great. I had paid for a professional spray: not one of those dull back street ones with thick paint and matt shine. The paint on it was thin and crisp with the sparkle of a new car about it. And it was new a new body at any rate. You see my friend, Geof, who works as a mechanic sometimes, had seen it in the yard of a garage where he occasionally works. Anyway, at his instigation, I bought it as a write-off and then, with his help, bought a new body from the factory and swapped all the running gear over. A big job I can tell you. Geof has an old shed, a barn more like, in his mum's garden and we did the engineering there. You should have seen the block when we swung it out and across to the new frame. It was only a year old and not a leak on it despite the shunt - and the wonder! Nobody can see that and not feel the wonder of it. It just dropped in as though it was meant to be there. What a slog though. We killed ourselves, all through the bad weather, every night and weekend. We nearly had hypothermia in that shed I can tell you. Geof got jealous in the end: even he had not seen how good it would be. He almost cried when I drove it away. Pathetic! I've had to promise to help him do one next and I gave him extra money for his trouble.

That morning I went out straight away. I couldn't see when those feelings for the car would wear off. There on that damp morning, in the weak sunshine, my car wore its dew like a royal robe. It deserved that attention from the nature. I had brought a shammy leather and I wiped it off before the sun dried it in streaks. I remember I was really feeling good that day: I had a drive ahead of me, all the way up north to collect my girlfriend. I love driving at the best of times but to drive for a purpose is more authentic. I just love to plan the route. Let me tell you, "don't go up the motorways!" What is the point of having such a car and just driving it in a straight line? No way. You need inclines and curves to show it off and feel it respond to the road. You want to see the look on people's faces when they think, "How did he get it up that steep hill, why did he take it up there?"

When it was dry I hugged the car then, at the back, leaning into the cool metal and feeling its shock through my clothes. It was so arousing. I felt the blood flow everywhere. I stood back and admired it again from the offside. The thing is I am not so pleased with the nearside. The front door doesn't fit properly. You see we used the original door first and it must have been buckled in the crash. But even going to the expense of new one it just never hung right. There was an imperceptible line that broke that wonderful smooth skin. Damn! Nobody else could see it and Geof reassured me a hundred times that it did not matter. The trouble was, if I was not careful, I could always see it and it obsessed me. I have trouble like that - things on my mind - back and back they come. Sometimes you can only get rid of them by doing them.

I loved the lines of the body, especially the back. They'd taken the shape from that popular model in the fifties, and updated it, but you could still see the ghost of the curves there. Wonderful! I almost skipped back inside with the joy of what lay in front of me. I took two minutes to pack: I would be away for two nights so I washed and shaved quickly. Then I was out there again in the morning sunshine like a gourmet in a five star restaurant.

The lock tweeted as I fired the key at it and I slid into the driver's seat. Leather I tell you! Me with a car with leather seats, I didn't believe my luck. The engine started and settled into a smooth hum immediately and I watched with renewed fascination as the dials swept up to their resting positions. I felt like a pilot. Then I put it into drive and I was away. The gear box was one of those dual automatic-cum-manual things so you can swop back and forward. Besides I always like to pull away that first time in the morning, in automatic, and hear the whoosh of the auto-changer.

First stop was the trucker's cafe half a mile away. When I am on my own I generally eat breakfast there, and I needed to feel that I was on my way that morning. I parked my beauty where I could see her and went inside with my maps. This was the first bit - the prologue to the journey - after the opening bars of driving to the cafe. I would savour it.

I took a couple of Idelmadol from my pocket and swallowed them. They were good and helped me to drive with concentration. "None addictive," the bloke who gave them to me said. They weren't cheap and he warned me that this present lot was a bit different to usual - better. He told me, "They have some blue in them." He was right because when I held the gelatine capsule up to the light I could see the odd blue speck in them. "It's OK I had two yesterday and I am still here!" You have to have a bit of trust if you take drugs or you never would.

I worked for a time, after I had eaten, on the maps but my attention was constantly caught up to the car. The car driver's end of the cafe was empty except for me but the far end was full of truckers. Their lorries, which did not interest me, were around the back.

I did not notice the door open but a female voice suddenly made me look up. "Can I sit here?" she said. I looked up cautiously and glanced around the cafe puzzled. "It's no smoking," she said, "I like to sit by the window." I was itching to get back to my maps. "Look at me!" I obediently looked up again. She was pretty. "I would like some company. Is that OK?"

"Sure." She sat down opposite me and sipped her coffee. I turned to my map again.

"Pay me some attention."

I gave her a heavy sigh. "Where have you come from?" I did not mean it literally but she told me anyway. I looked at her more closely. Mmm, yeah, she was nice. She had large hands with strong bony, sinewy wrists and a really nice body. When she bent forward I could see her breasts over the top of her blouse and they made me smile inside. Her face was firm with a tight crop of short hair. She had a little eye liner on and muddy coloured lipstick. There was tattoo peeping out of her neckband on her right shoulder. It was impossible to say how old she was, but I judged, by the cares in her face, she was over 20 years old. She looked straight, with no slyness in her manner, and I liked what I saw.

She put down her cup, then put her hand out and rested it on my road list. Swiftly she swung it around on the table and looked at it. I slipped it from her fingers. "I need a lift," she said. I nodded to the truck drivers. "They will want to be paid," she responded enigmatically.

"Maybe I will. Where are you going?" She told me the name of a northern city. "No way! You just saw that on my list."

"No. It's true. I am doing a visit north."

"I am not stupid you know," I said.

"Am I the sort of girl that would sit with stupid man?" I had laughed.

"OK can you give something for petrol?"

"For that thing?" she said. "You must be joking, you'd need a mortgage to fill it up."

"True." I wondered what to do. "OK." I made up my mind swiftly. It must have been the Idelmadol making me bold. "We'll give it a go, but I might kick you out anytime."

"Are we going on the motorway?" she asked.

"No! And if you want to you better go with the truckers."

"No I hate motorways."

"Me too."

"I just need the loo," she had said, draining her cup and getting up.

I strolled out to the car and rested against the door. She came out promptly and I let her in. In her hand was a leather grip. She turned and put it behind my seat. Disappointingly, she was quite unfazed by the luxury of my car. "Rich kid," I had thought. We crawled out of the city and headed north on the A---- There had been a companionable silence to begin with and I was enjoying the driving so much I had kind of blotted her out.

"Can we have the radio?" she had asked.

"No," I had replied curtly. She had sighed. We drove on a bit longer. "I like making up stories," I offered eventually.

"Oh yeah," She had shown an interest. "Like what?"

"Well I make up kind of stories in my head and then I

work on them every time I am going on a journey."

"Such as?"

"Well the current one is about this guy......"

"I like science fiction," she had interrupted. "Aliens and adventures in space or aliens coming to earth and freaking everyone out."

"Well this one is not science fiction."

"Tell me." We came to a roundabout and turned onto another A road.

"It's about this photographer. He goes out one night and, in a night-club, sees this really beautiful girl. He kind of recognises her from school, a couple of years before him, and he wants to take pictures of her and also go out with her. He really fancies her. Looks crazy but it turned out that she has this really rich sugar-daddy figure who is paying for her to go to college in return for sex."

"Look I've heard this one," she said.

"That's impossible!" I said angrily, "I just made it up!"

"No it's been on the telly."

"No way!"

"I tell you. I have never seen it on the telly!" I was getting mighty riled.

"Well you must have done. It's stuck in your subconscious and then you've dredged it up and you think it's new to you. There aren't that many original stories out there anymore. Like music, they just recycle all the old tunes."

"You're making me bloody angry! I tell you this story is my own invention!"

"Keep your hair on. I am only joking you." He knew she wasn't. She was fearing he would kick her out of the car. "Look just cool it. I didn't mean anything by it. It's your story and unique to you. My mistake. Sorry." We drove on a bit further in silence. "Go on tell me some more," she begged at last putting her hand on my knee for a few seconds. "Have you got anything relaxing," she requested. I did not answer at first. I looked at her, she was taking her jacket off, slipping it between the seat belt and turning and showing off her figure. I took the bottle from my pocket and gave it to her.

"Try one of these. Just one." She unscrewed the cap

and took two before I could stop her, swallowing them down without water. "Damn you." She put her seat back and settled down. "Go on tell me your story." I decide to humour her and see what effect the drugs had on her. I was used to them. She should not have had two. It could be interesting.

"Well," I began, "it needs writing down of course. But there is this guy Greg."

"What's your name?" she interjected. I told her. "He is a bit like you," she said.

"Yeah maybe."

"What you want to be like?"

"No. He's not got this car."

"Shit no," she ejaculated. "How come you've got it?"

"Look do you want to hear this story?"

"Sure." she pouted.

"He's been to college and done photography then worked in a commercial photography company for a while, but now he is freelance and wanting to build up his own portfolio thing. And so he is always out scouting to look for models."

"Wants to be a glamour photographer does he? You bloody men are all the same. Your big dream is to take pictures of nubile women with their clothes off and then have them afterwards." I coughed hard. "Sorry. Go on."

"No more interruptions or you're out," I said. She put her fingers to her lips. "No he wants to take portraits." She made a face and I chose to ignore it. "So one night he goes to this night-club, and almost as soon as he has got through the door he sees her there dancing on the stage by herself. It was still quite early, few punters there, so he could get a clear view of her. It was only those dedicated girlie dancers who get up at that time. The men have not had enough to drink yet. He bought himself a shot, greeted his friends but keeps himself looking at her all the time. At one point she looks towards him with one of those impassive faces that says that she had noticed him looking. How do girls know that? Don't answer that! She is a lovely dancer all - smooth and articulated. A dream body and lovely flowing hair, old-fashioned but suits her, and gives her a timeless kind of quality. He can see other men looking at her and decides he better act before they do.

He puts down his drink and without explaining to his mates what he is doing he walks up to her. They give him a cheer. 'Don't mind them,' he said to her.

'No I won't.' He settled in to a dance with her but he felt awkward beside her more expert offering. She wouldn't meet his gaze. Demure and that. Eventually she slows down, half way during a song, and makes to walk off.

'Would you like a drink?'

'No, but come and join me at my table with my friends,' she says. Greg follows her like a sheep, watching her as she walks, drinking in all her grace. When they get to a table at the back in the darker bit of the club, he is surprised to find it mainly full of older men in suits."

"Mafia!" the girl in the car jumped in.

"Nah! You're getting ahead of it. She goes up to a slick looking older man, in a rich suite with manicured hands, and sits by him. She gesticulates towards the photographer to come and sit at the end of the row. The older man puts his arm around her shoulders and she smiles shyly at her new companion. 'Another waif and stray I see,' observed the man to his neighbours and they laugh coarsely. 'You are going to have to stop doing this Sue,' he remarks to her. 'You can't be left alone for ten minutes without arousing some of these young bucks.' Greg felt uncomfortable he was not sure what was going on or why he was there."

"So, they don't speak again and he goes home and shoots himself."

"For God's sake, just shut it. You don't have to ridicule it." I was getting hot under the collar again. This was supposed to be my private moment driving the car and fantasising: this stupid woman was spoiling it. "You're gonna have to go."

"No. No. Please!" she pleaded, "I was impressed by your story - jealous actually. I couldn't believe it. It was although you were speaking with someone else's voice. It went through me. You're good really. You look too rough to have this sensitive side." Her words hung in the air for a moment. I wasn't sure how to respond to them. Maybe she was winding me up. I couldn't be bothered to pursue it.

"OK."

We drove on. I was doing what I do best - smooth and sure. Drawing up to each car or lorry ahead and then accelerating hard past and on. Life is like that, so it seems to me: always going forward, merciless, letting your own pace dictate your progress; driving around obstacles. You can't give too much for other people's feelings. When you are in a car travelling fast there is only time for your own response.

"Look I need the loo again," she said. "Can we stop soon? There are some services up ahead. Please." I hate stopping so soon after I have got going but I had no choice. I made up my mind to leave her there, so parked near to the garage, but she asked me to go with her.

"She must have second sight," I thought.

Chapter 7

[Y] The Urban Mystic sees lonely dark streets at night, quiet residential roads in the day. The hustle, the bustle, traffic that whizzes to and fro. The after dark night clubs. He compares all these different environments and he walks in them all at times listening and walking with the divine spirit. Being aware of his presence at all times.

A pocket watch appeared three days later, but rather bizarrely someone - Bailey he presumed - had removed both the sweep and the second hand. He had no idea whether it was right or how he would tell its accuracy, but he thought he could write down when his meals came and when dawn was, until he realised he had no paper. "I need paper and a pen," he shouted into the ether. Maybe they had a microphone somewhere just out of sight which communicated to a guard room. Gregory made up his mind to organise his time in some way. After a shower and a change of his clothes he felt so washed out he had to sit down and rest. Thoughts and bad feelings pressed into his mind in a worrying way mingling all sorts of frustrating thoughts scampering about his brain. They were all disconnected thoughts about being a mystic - he couldn't help himself even though he completely rejected the idea - but because he was a completer, and also constitutionally obedient, he knew that he would attempt to do it. Then there were all sorts of plans to escape, all impossible, and the real hope that someone might come and rescue him - plus great fear and anxiety.

About two hours later there was a sign of movement outside his window and he could hear a number of people coming. It was the Dean and some workmen, with Bailey hovering in the background. "We are building your confessional today," he announced. There is no point talking to the workmen - they are all profoundly deaf. It is one of our charitable works," he offered by way of explanation. "And we have led them to believe that so are you. So don't attempt to interfere with them." It was as though he was reading this out. "Best not let Bailey use water on you - like last time - it would be regrettable. And we don't want to do that again do we? Or worse. We have bought him a new toy haven't we Bailey? Show him!" Now Gregory could see that Bailey was hiding something behind his back. He brought it out with a flourish, it was a short ugly looking stick with a prong on the end. Gregory was not very impressed, not knowing what it was. "It is a cattle prod," explained the Dean, "and you won't like it. Don't make us use it on you."

"I would like some paper and a pen."

"Splendid," said the Dean. During all this the three men had stood looking quizzically at Gregory in his incarceration. The Dean turned to them and signed something to them. They started and became busy very sharply. There was a lot of fear in their eyes. Poor bastards, Gregory thought.

"And another thing - the Cathedral is being reopened today." Gregory looked puzzled, he thought it had been opened all the time. "We have had it shut for a few days in respect of you - which has been a sacrifice. In other words be grateful. We have lost a lot of revenue over it and we need to make it up with your help."

"Don't tell me," replied Gregory, with a flash of inspiration, you are going to charge them to see me."

The Dean put out his arms; he looked quite beatific and turning to Bailey said, "See, didn't I tell you we have a sharp one here."

"Are they are all going to be deaf as well?" The Dean smiled.

"Of course not - but they are very vulnerable and simple people and we are trusting you not to take advantage of them. That would be cruel." Gregory felt so exasperated.

"How about putting me in the subgroup of people that you ought not to be cruel to."

"You know we can't do that because you are special and have been called to live a different - a sacrificial kind of life."

"Only by you." There was no point arguing with him; he was deficient in some way. Gregory looked at Bailey and he could see that he was itching to use the cattle prod.

When the Dean had gone the three men, with their eyes averted, worked swiftly. They measured the windows. When one of their hands came near him Gregory grasped it but the man shook himself free and looked at Bailey. Gregory let go. They fitted a kind of shield in front of the window with a letter box in it coinciding with the gap in the middle aperture. He couldn't see how it was fastened but it made his cell very dark and oppressive and he was glad when it was taken away.

During their work he had heard a bell ring throughout the Cathedral and the sound of doors in the distance. At first the noise of workmen had covered it up, now he could tell that a lot of people were coming into the Cathedral. Not one came directly into the Presbytery, nonetheless he could hear their voices through his opposite wall. He went down the stairs to his outside door and banged on it for a few moments and shouted, "Help," through it even though the only response was some laughter.

He heard a man say in an unusual dialect, "Read the notice honey. It's the mystic and we are not to mind his strangeness or his ranting when the spirit grabs him."

"Poor man," a female voice replied. He returned to his chair. The nearness of such sympathy and his own inability to experience it filled him with a profound loneliness.

He looked to the roof of his cell and asked quietly, "Is there anyone there?"

In what he took to be the afternoon a sheaf of paper roared through the window and a pencil clattered to the floor breaking its lead. These sudden apparitions frightened him and made his heart race. If it was Bailey who brought them, he walked as silently as the dead. With some effort he managed to sharpen the pencil on the wall and then wrote his guess at the time on the paper and the event. At various times during the next hours he heard amplified voices in the distance and some music, the organ played for a while. At another point he was sure a guided tour went by because he could hear the drone of the guide. In the evening there was another concert far away and some chanting. Finally a bell rang and the noises died away. The next day was the same. Gregory still felt weak but his growing anxiety, and at times the hard beating of his heart, robbed him of any relaxation. He decided that he must start some exercise in the near future. A deeper gloom was settling upon him. There was not enough light, or variety, or distraction to prevent the slow fall into depression.

He must have slept in the next day for he had not even heard the bell when the Dean woke him. "It is our Sabbath tomorrow," he announced, "and some of us will be using the Presbytery. However, today you may begin your public ministry." It sounded like a treat for good behaviour. "In an hour and for an hour we are to let the congregation speak to you." Gregory scratched his head.

"You are forgetting I am not a mystic."

"No matter - any calling must be validated by the other ministers and by the general congregation. As they take to you, and I am sure they will, it will strengthen your resolve to fulfil your calling."

"Where do you get this old language from? Who are the congregation?"

"Well some are friends of the Cathedral - they pay for special privileges - and the language - well it is appropriate to draw on the heritage of this site and bring old sensible words back into use."

"Rather quaint." The Dean looked cross at the criticism.

"Not at all they best define what we are trying to do."

"Which is what exactly? To make money?" he added as an afterthought.

"Of course we couldn't exist without that. I have a staff of forty to provide for and all their dependants and, of course, our charitable work in the deaf school. As to the other, I am not going to tell you yet because you are part of what we are trying to do."

"Fuck you," said Gregory. It was becoming his liturgical response to the Dean.

Shortly after the Dean had gone his three deaf drogues came and fastened the screen in place, which made it difficult for him to carry out his new plan. He wrote out, several times, his name and address on the paper he had been given. He hoped to be able to pass them to his customers.

The Cathedral sounded quite full. In ten minutes he heard a rattle on his cage and he looked out. It was the malevolent Bailey with a middle aged women who came and sat down on a chair in front of his post box. She looked nervously at Bailey but he stood implacably close. "Go away Bailey," Gregory commanded, "this is private." Bailey hesitated, looked briefly off stage left, before sauntering away. "Is he out of ear shot?" Gregory asked the woman. She looked around shyly and then nodded back at him. The slot was bigger than a normal post box at about a quarter of a metre by two thirds.

Gregory drew his chair up and sat down. It was a pleasant surprise to find that it was at the correct height and he could see and hear easily, yet maintain a degree of privacy for himself. He sat and waited. The woman said nothing. "Well," he said tersely. It would be one thing to hear some juicy secrets but if it became like extracting teeth he would soon lose interest. There was a catch in her throat.

"It is my husband," she began.

"Did you know that I am a prisoner here?" he interrupted. Gregory just did not have the patience to consider anyone else's pain when his was so strong. "I have been kidnapped and brought here against my will. My family think I am dead." She looked startled but nodded slowly.

"I know - we have been told that. It is on a notice down there." She pointed off.

"Well, what are you going to do about it?" he queried. "Whatever your petty little problem is." He was losing his temper. "It cannot be anything like mine. Here," he said and thrust out one of his prepared pieces of paper. She would not take it at first and he had to shake it under her nose. "Can they see," he hissed.

"No," she replied in a monosyllable.

"Take it to the police, please! I don't mean to be harsh but I am not who you think. I am not a mystic and I can't help you. Please do me a good turn and get me out of here." He was pleading. She eventually took it surreptitiously and slipped it into a pocket. She looked beseechingly at him. "Yes?" He took a deep breath. "All right tell me."

"My husband is terminally ill," she began again. He sighed.

"Sorry, sorry, I don't know what you expect me to do." This was exasperating.

"Give me a word."

"I'm not clairvoyant."

"Some comfort?" He shook his head but did not know whether she could see him. She reached her hand out to his, which was resting on the lip of the slot. "Pray for him - please - I am desperate. I could not bear to lose him." Gregory got up and walked away. It was kindling his own grief.

"Go away now and go to the police for me." He had not realised it would be this difficult. His assumption had been that it would be entertaining but it was going to be downright depressing.

There was no way he could not cope with this.

But there was not time to think. Somebody new was knocking on the partition and saying, "Hello." It was a mentally disabled young man. He grinned sheepishly at Gregory but kept looking away at someone else. "My mum," he volunteered at last.

"Yes?" No reply. They sat staring at each other for a few moments and then the man stood up and walked away. He was followed by half a dozen other people who professed to various ailments and all who asked him, like a bad recording, for a blessing, or a word, or a prayer. It must give instructions on the notice he decided. He steadfastly refuted all their claims on him and gave the more intelligent and sympathetic ones a piece of paper.

Then, judging by her build, a young woman presented herself in front of him, but he could not be sure in his assessment as she wore a deep hooded jacket which was pulled far down over her face.

"Yes?" again his terse enquiry.

"How are you?" she asked in a melodic voice. "Are they treating you well?" Gregory was flabbergasted.

"Are they hell!" he responded without thinking.

A voice shouted from behind her. It was the Dean. "I told you, I told you." he said. "Come away at once." She got up and moved away. The Dean appeared. "My daughter - Little - I have warned her not to come near you." He was red in the face. This was worth noting, thought Gregory, something that rattled him.

"How old is your daughter?" he enquired. The Dean scowled and walked away.

"Get on with your work." Next came a powerful young man in work clothes. There was something ugly about him. He could have been Bailey's son, Gregory judged.

"I want you to put a spell on someone and make them like me."

"It is no exchange for charm," he replied flippantly.

"What?" asked the man in a surly voice.

"Perhaps you should explore other avenues before you turn to an unfair advantage like magic," Gregory stated.

"Don't be smart. I've paid good money to come and see you - so do as you're told."

"I think you are mistaken about my powers. I am a prisoner here," he began on his special explanation but the man interrupted him.

"I am going to tell you her name," he told Gregory softly. "Come closer so I can whisper it." Gregory obediently leant forward so his head was close to the slot and because his head was turned sideways so as to present his ear he did not see the man's hands snake through the aperture. It was only when he felt them on his throat that he began to react. But it was too late. The man had a grip of iron. Then he was shouting and swearing at Gregory about it being a waste of money and shaking him at the same time. The pressure on his throat was enormous and Gregory could feel himself beginning to black out: he had not breath even to scream. In the background, there was shouting and a commotion. Cathedral staff were trying to wrestle the man to the ground and when he let go of Gregory he collapsed onto the floor of his cell. His throat felt bruised and he panicked at his inability to swallow. There was need to rest for a moment on the floor before he could think about picking himself up. Next the door at the foot of the stairs began to open: it was Bailey with the cattle prod and following hard on his heals the Dean. They stood frozen for a moment then Bailey lunged forward with the prod. Gregory held up his hand to ward it off but it caught him on his exposed wrist. There was a jolt and a pain gripped his chest. Although he was half way to rising his legs collapsed and he fell back to the floor, once more, writhing in a new sort of pain.

"You imbecile," screamed the Dean. He threw the bits of paper, that Gregory had distributed, back at him. They fluttered in the air. Bailey lunged again with a mad look on his face. There was spittle at the side of his mouth. This time the prod struck through Gregory's shirt on his right breast and made him jump and writhe on the cold paving stone. He began to cry and scream with pain. He felt trapped and as terrified as a hunted animal. The Dean was still shouting at him. Gregory knew intuitively that this was something to do with his daughter but there was no let up. Bailey had gone berserk and was pursuing him with feral vigour. Gregory tried to kick the prod away with his feet but the shocks kept coming and now Bailey was using his feet as well. "You witless creep," the Dean was incandescent and did not call his hound off. "Did you really think that we would trust you with real people? They were all my staff. It was simply a dummy run. Don't ever do that again. Whatever your feelings are you must treat other people with respect." Any impartial observer would have found the scene completely bizarre. The blows kept raining down until Gregory stopped moving and slipped into unconsciousness. Even then Bailey kicked him viciously in the ribs before they both withdrew.

[F1] It is a bit presumptuous to call oneself a mystic, nevertheless, everything in the spiritual life is presumptuous. It is presumptuous to say you have been called or to have a godly ambition. Godly ambitions rest on the initial call of God, a gentle breeze of the Spirit, a climate of faith without arrogance and the confidence to be able to say, "The divine spirit spoke to me today, he told me to do this."

Chapter 8

When Gregory woke up he vomited on the floor - there was fresh blood in the mess. His whole body was numb with pain. He must have been unconscious for some while because he was also frozen with the cold from the floor. His now frail body was a sorry sight. The previously injured hand throbbed with sharp pains. When he came to look there were burn marks on his flesh from the prod and his clothes were scorched. Gregory wondered why his heart had not stopped. There were bruises forming here and there in great blotchy patches. Later when he washed his face the water turned red with blood. Without a mirror it was difficult to see where he was hurt but by touching he could tell he had a swollen lip and a cut on his chin. A deep gloom settled on him. The Cathedral was busy around him but when he looked for his watch he found it was broken, so he could only guess at the time.

After a further difficult night he awoke to the Cathedral Sabbath. Through the haze of his pain he was vaguely aware of different activity in the Presbytery adjacent to his cell. He was to weak too call for help. The service lasted about an hour and a half and at one point when he dragged himself to look out of the window he saw the Dean with a phalanx of acolytes mumbling and bowing to the old wooden table in front of the expurgated reredos. There was nothing on the table save a bunch of flowers, a closed book and some small wooden like objects that he could not make out. The Dean was dressed in a richly embroidered cope with pictures of flowers, trees and animals on it. When he turned around there was a symmetrical pattern on the other side like a maze and the sun and moon stood proud on the raised collar. One of the acolytes was swinging an incense censor and the pungent smoke made Gregory cough and sneeze when the draft drew it into his cell.

Along the far wall, on a wooden bench, sat a row of hooded monk-like figures. He could not see their faces but by the shape of them, some were women. The incantations made no sense, he guessed they were in Latin but after this short reverence for the table and its dressing, the procession withdrew and the rest of the service went on in the distance of the main Nave. There were songs but he could not make out the words and the congregation obviously joined in with some of them. At other times the choir sang religious music. He derived no solace from any of this intrusive litany and he wondered if the congregation had. Gregory guessed, analysing the noises before and after the service that there must be a large crowd there.

There was no food that day but then he wanted to die anyway. Even more so when, on the evening of the second night, Bailey came to visit him. He was sitting resting in his chair near the window, to catch the failing light, when he was thrown violently to the floor by the touch of the prod on the back of his neck. Bailey had crept up on him and zapped him. The electricity made it difficult to stand up and before he could react Bailey reached through and did it twice more once on his shoulder and once on his left buttock. Later he surmised that Bailey was trying to get his testicles. He was paralysed and twitched on the floor. Whilst he was thus prone the door opened and Bailey came into his cell. The man was an evil menace and without a word he gave Gregory a good kicking. There was no space left untouched except his face. Just before he passed out he wet himself.

Gregory began to shut down as a person. He was too sensitive to be able to offer much psychological resistance to this process: anxious thoughts increased and he became nervy and twitchy. Gregory was fed that day but his appetite had forsaken him. He moved his chair away for the window and kept a watch preparing himself as much he could for the next attack. Once or twice he saw Bailey hanging around and in the distance he heard the Dean's voice. However, he was no match for this incarnate mix of wickedness and sadism for when he dozed in his chair that evening the prod reached across and got him on the arm. His cell was not wide enough to protect him. The only place he would have been safe was behind the outside door but he could not endure to live down in that well. Two more prods followed on his twitching body until he writhed continually again, then, at the dreaded sound of the key in the lock, his heart fell. He tried to gather his limbs into a tight ball but they would not obey him. There was no way he could protect himself so he cried in frustration and fear.

This time Gregory did not pass out but he could not move for quite a while and when he did it was only onto his bed where he shivered and whimpered through the night. A clinical depression began to sink upon him. It has always been the curse of the constitutionally anxious to court depression and now it came on him with force but there was nothing in his personality or circumstances that could resist it. He longed to die and began to think of how he might speed up the process. His bowel turned to jelly. He could not eat but neither could he truly wake up. A boil developed on the back of his neck. For the next two nights he endured the kicking. Bailey did not even bother to stun him the last time. Gregory was sitting in the stair well when he came and Bailey simply opened the door against him and slammed it on his legs repeatedly until he crawled out of the way.

The next night he was left alone and the following morning the Dean came with a torch. He shone it on Gregory and inspected him. As it happened, Gregory was lying on his pallet with his shirt ridden up showing the mass of bruises on his torso.

The Dean disappeared and came back with Bailey: he was pulling him by the ear as you would a naughty schoolboy. "It seems that Bailey has exceeded his brief," the Dean said starchily and threw Bailey to the ground. Gregory hauled himself to his feet to see Bailey's expression. He lay partly crouched on the floor looking up at the Dean. The grimace was not repentant but proud and wicked. Whatever power the Dean had over him he better not let it drop, conjectured Gregory. Then turning to Gregory. " This unfortunate episode will not happen again. Either way." Bailey stood silently and slipped away. "You will behave with our pilgrims - if you can offer no solace - you will say nothing or give them a blessing or say that you will pray for them." It was if the word, 'will', was underlined. "Is there anything you need to recover?"

"A new watch and some pain killers if you insist on killing me in here - but best of all would be to let go." This time the Dean did not try to cajole him.

"I am a patient man," he said, "but only stoic in order to get my own way." He exited.

Gregory did not know whether he could trust the Dean's control over Bailey. Anyhow it all seemed pointless: the infinite sadness and terror of his depression had a grip now and he did not know how he might shake it off. With his usual daily timetable denied him and without all the pleasant upbuilding relationships it seemed impossible. He sat in his chair and like a wound began to fester. Bad thoughts and gloomy scenarios ran obsessively through his mind. He tried to shake them from his head but they would not go. Once again he spoke quietly to the air of his cell, "Is there anyone there?"

[H1] The Urban Mystic has to deal with the uncertainty of her own life. She has to put aside ambition. She tries as hard as she can to put away all her material and emotional longings: even her desire for power and the impure sexual thoughts she experiences. She tries to live a perfectly committed life with God so that her sensitivity is not destroyed in any way.

The following evening there was a concert and for a short while he was able to lose himself in the music.

The next day they put the screen up and he had some visitors. To the first few enquired, "Do you work here?" and when they denied it he sat and listened. Well he pretended to at any rate. Their problems and difficulties made no impression on him and he had forgotten each preceding sentence by the time they started on the next. "Yes," he would pray for them and he ended, "Bless you." It was like responding to a sneeze. He was hoping it would soon be over and he kept his new watch in front of him. When the hour was nearly up a young woman appeared before him. Gregory sensed intuitively it was the Dean's daughter. "You are Little," he noted. She blushed.

"How do you know that?"

"I'm a mystic," he answered with an attempt at a grin. It was the first warmth he had felt for a long while.

"I don't think so. I am sure it is just because you have a good memory."

"Caught out," he said. "I don't think you should be here," he went on "I seem to remember that you father forbade it."

"He is not here today."

"Won't the other staff tell him?"

"No I don't think so - only Bailey - but he rarely speaks at the moment."

"What made him stop?"

"Nobody knows. The staff are very afraid of my father."

"And you?" She didn't answer but looked plainly at him. Gregory came nearer the slot so he could see her more clearly. She looked as if she was in her early twenties but it was difficult to judge her build as she was sitting down. Once more she wore the hood and he could only see the tip of her nose, her mouth and chin clearly. She had good skin and a clearly defined jaw. Her voice was lilting and melodic but he could not place the accent. She was slim and he could tell from her wrists that she was athletic and spare. He thought how lovely her hands looked. They were placed demurely on her lap. She was not demonstrative as some are when they talk but she played with her rings and the fingers on the opposite hand. There was some tension and unhappiness there in these restless movements. They had lapsed into silence.

"It is very good of you to do this," she said. This puzzled him and for once he decided not to tell her he was a captive. "I hope you are getting paid a lot." Was that bitterness or irony, he did not know. Gregory did not respond. "It's all right I know," she told him and slowly, tentatively lifted her hand and put it into his cell. He took it and put it against his face. It was cool and smelled of soap. He was overwhelmed by this small act of kindness and he began to cry. The tears ran onto her hand but she did not withdraw it. She must have been able to feel them run over the back of her hand and drip onto the floor. He cried noiselessly but deeply. After a while he gave her back her hand but she did not wipe it and he could see the tracks of his tears on the pale skin.

When he had regained some composure he asked, "Do you work here as well?"

"Yes," her voice was bright: she had clearly been moved by his tears but was trying to be cheerful for his sake. "When I was a university, during my second year, my mum died." There was catch in her voice now. "So I came home to look after dad and never left."

"Did you get your degree?"

"No - a certificate only - special case and all that. Now I work in the office over there," she pointed away from him. "Separate building."

"Are we making a profit?" he asked sarcastically.

She nodded, "We are a going concern." He was itching to talk to about her dad and to ask whether she could help him, unfortunately, her quiet demeanour seemed to forbid it at that time. They lapsed into silence again.

"One minute," a voice called.

"How much has this cost you? She told him and he winced.

"I can't think of anything to do," she explained, "my father's word is absolute here." She looked about her. "And the police are in his pocket. He gives them special privileges." He wanted to interrogate her but he hung on her words. He wanted to argue with her that surely there was something she could do yet he remained mute. All he could do was to make his request.

"Will you come and see me again?" She nodded, stood up and walked away.

Gregory's heart felt sore and he found it very difficult to pay any attention to his last customers. He was heartily glad when it was all over. When the screen was gone and he was alone he played these precious moments back through his mind and they gave him some small ease for the rest of the day.

The Dean was back the next day and called briefly to say, "Well done - glad that things have settled down." And then went away well pleased with himself.

During that morning's session of pilgrims he was visited by a young lady with peroxide hair. As soon as he saw her she looked familiar but he could not place it. Her first few words also rang a bell but the mystery did not last long. "I am the Dean's daughter."

"I don't think so," Gregory responded immediately, "I have met her already." Gregory immediately regretted his words for fear that it would get Little into trouble. He drew himself near the slot to have a good look. She also was sitting close and as he looked down, he had a view straight into the cleavage revealed by her low cut top. He did not respond openly to what he saw but with a sheepish and inward surge of pleasure.

"I don't see why Little should have all the fun," she said. "Now we have got you at our mercy. That's my name by the way." She had course features, yet was not unattractive. Her clothes were too slutty to suite Gregory's taste. A younger sister he decided.

"And what is you spiritual difficulty?" he questioned. He found it difficult to take his eyes from her chest, at first assuming that she did not perceive his interest. But it soon became apparent that she knew and was teasing him: she kept leaning forward in the chair and she caressed herself by smoothing her clothes. He was immediately embarrassed and made himself sit back.

Her eyes flicked with triumph at his reaction and he acknowledged that she had scored a victory over him. If she had been ruthlessly bold and crude she could have asked, "Don't you like what you see?" Instead she purred, "It must be difficult for you stuck in there all day, being a man." There was an emphasis on the last word. He knew intuitively that she was offering herself to him. It was such a casual invitation that he was both horrified and aroused at the same time. He remained mute. "Come on, it cost a fortune for this." Whether she was talking about her time with him or her clothes he could not discern. Neither could he begin to analyse what motivated this behaviour in her, nevertheless, he knew intuitively that if he did not respond appropriately that she would quickly turn against him and there would begin a new torment. He knew that there could be nothing more dangerous that to irritate the adolescent daughter of the Dean and his blood ran cold. He would become like a spider caught by a sadistic schoolboy. Bailey would be no match for the machinations of this girl.

"Well I'm very flattered that you have come to see me but really I am only here to listen - besides which I have taken personal vows for the time I remain in this cell." He was trying to play her game by not being too explicit.

"Bollocks," was the answer. "I know we kidnapped you and you don't want to be here."

"Haven't you got a boyfriend?" he began to probe.

"Maybe," was the coy answer. "Maybe more than one - but that doesn't stop us being special friends." It was there once more, that old and long used sexual look, full of promise.

"Look, someone might see us and then you would get into trouble."

"You're joking - if we are seen you would get into trouble. Corrupting my morals," she said with relish.

"Mercy." The Dean spoke behind her. "How can I keep you girls from this poor man. I've told you too much about him. Now run along."

"But I've paid money," pouted the girl.

"Go and ask for it back and say I told them to give it to you."

"Is her name Mercy?" Gregory asked stupidly.

"Yes it is," replied the Dean. She was in no mood to leave, so the Dean took her by the shoulders turned her around and gave her a little push and an unfatherly pat on her bottom. The Dean watched her go with an unctuous look on his face. He turned back to Gregory "I do not want you to see them again."

"I don't think I can stop them."

"You must discourage them."

"Why should I - I found them entertaining." The Dean was beginning to colour. "You may have forgotten that I am a prisoner here and I am not able to curtail, or even enjoy my own freedom, so how do you expect me to have any influence over your daughters. In fact, I think you have brought this on yourself. You seem to have made me irresistible to them by what you have done to me."

"Nonetheless, when they come I wish you to refuse to speak to them."

"They came for spiritual council. Am I to refuse them? Surely they are as much in need of that as anyone?" The Dean was very cross; there was a flush on his cheeks.

"These are completely inconsequential reasons. I repeat that I will expect to hear that you have refused to speak to them." Gregory shook his head.

"What will you do if I refuse? Will it be water, or electricity, or starvation, or neglect, or some worse abuse this time? Why not kill me completely then they will have nothing to draw them here or anybody to reply to their questions."

"I will ensure that they do not come to you again." the Dean said to himself.

"I suppose it raises the question as to how much you are to make me suffer to achieve your aims," observed Gregory. He was surprised by his own question. Somewhere in his pain of bereavement something more intellectual must have begun to grow in the darkness. The Dean was looking about him as though he had forgotten something and was about to depart. "Did you hear my question?" pursued Gregory quietly. The Dean turned to face him, there was different expression on his face that Gregory could not recognise. Had he too recognised this changed tone in Gregory's voice?

"Your suffering is worthwhile for the common good."

"The common good being, 'What is good for the Cathedral?' Do you mean the building?"

"No the Cathedral is bigger that the building. The fabric is of course very beautiful and it is worth preserving. It has a long history, not least as being a place of the numinous, where the divine spirit's presence has been experienced in the past." As the conversation became more serious the Dean tilted his head to one side as if first receiving, from another source, and then repeating the words he spoke.

"Very sad it is only in the past. So is it worth preserving?" Gregory stepped up to his window and put his head through. He reached through the adjacent aperture and swept the hair from his forehead. He scratched the bristles on his chin.

"It is worth trying to rediscover such tokens of excellence again," was the Dean's answer.

"You intend me to be the vehicle for that?"

"Yes."

"Wouldn't history have taught you to start with someone of learning and experience rather that a uneducated person like myself?"

"Well you are not unintelligent or we would not be having this conversation at all. I would be repeating myself to explain the reasons why we chose you."

"Yes, that puzzles me - they don't seem to me very intellectually satisfying reasons. Logic and rationality would have made me make an entirely different choice." The Dean put his head on the other side. This blossoming of an incisive mind was a surprise and a delight to him; a shy smile crossed his lips.

"You want me to admit that your choice was not purely rational?" There was pause. "I am prepared to admit that now you are being more reasonable." A touch of the old condescension. "I am not an ignorant man. I spend time in contemplation myself - and self-examination. I have, to a degree, some self-awareness. You are right, a purely logical decision may well have come up with a different choice. There is a missing factor which influenced me. I like to think of it being the divine."

"You are saying that God brought me here?" he used the very old-fashioned blasphemy once more.

The Dean nodded, "whatever you understanding of that word, and I prefer its modern equivalents, "there was input from outside."

"And it is that that has made it justifiable in your mind to treat me so badly?"

"You know I never thought of it in that way - even so I can go with that. There is a sense in which the responsibility for our direction of you is excusable if we can pass on the responsibility to the divine spirit. At any events," he went on quickly, "I hope that your suffering will prove to be the catalyst for the Cathedral becoming more what it should be and cathartic for you."

"Let me get this clear in my mind. You are saying that the physical Cathedral is a kind of memorial to a past spirituality and also a focus of the corporate life of the pilgrims that come here." The Dean nodded, he was looking quite intense as if he was finding the conversation stimulating. "And my suffering," continued Gregory, "is an involuntary sacrifice to propitiate the loss of that former spirituality?"

"Well, well, well," said the Dean, "where has all this come from? Confining you to this cell is having a positive effect on you."

Gregory gave his liturgical response and went on, "Well I am sorry to disappoint you Dean but I think it's a crap idea. My suffering is just that - my suffering - and meaningless in the context that you have described it. If it is anything it is a predictable consequence of your cruelty to me. If the divine spirit has any goodness in him then he will find it as distasteful as everyone else except you and Bailey." The eyes of the Dean sparkled.

"This is not some sort of game of chess in which you can outwit me. I hold all the cards and what is more, I'm not in some minute sub-group of evil essence. I am a good kind father, and I was a loving husband, and I have done my best for my staff and this cathedral for twenty years, and even these plans I have now are for its own good. I could easily find many people who would justify my actions - even judicially."

"So what! Even if you found ninety nine out of a hundred people to agree with you, it can never be justifiable to punish one person and to sacrifice them. You are a megalomaniac and a sadistic one at that. The divine spirit is more likely to look benevolently on you and your work if you let me go".

"Nonsense. Ninety nine out of one hundred is a good majority. Are you saying that it is never right for one person to take and make decisions for another? If you were a sick child and I your parent then I would be expected to make decisions for you and applauded for doing so. If you needed a painful operation, which given a choice you would refuse, yet which I knew would cure you, then of course I would overrule you. If you were insane....."

"Rubbish," shouted Gregory. A drip of sweat rolled slowly down his right cheek.

"You just don't want to hear it," persisted the Dean. "You are a clear case of irresponsibility and juvenility because you will not accept your calling - your true function - therefore it becomes imperative for responsible, clear sighted and thinking people to correct you."

"Punish me you mean." Gregory was beginning to feel tearful. He did not have much psychological power inside himself. The Dean was sensing his victory and battled away powerfully. Gregory no longer wanted to hear the words: his embryonic intellectualism was growing weary of the battle.

"I am convinced," continued the Dean," that the decisions we took on your behalf were unequivocally right: not only for the good but for the common good as well."

"Well only because you say so. It is easy to take that position when you are out there and I am in here. Might is right." It was all Gregory could say, he was done for. He slunk away to his toilet cubicle leaving the Dean wanting to justify himself more. The Dean tutted to himself and walked away. He did not look as triumphant as he felt. He looked diminished and old.

Chapter 9

Gregory was crestfallen for the rest of the day, he had been exhausted by this first attempt to defend himself intellectually. The only high spot was that he was given his first hot meal. It was brought to him by one of the deaf carpenters. The man had at first drawn attention to himself by making some grunting noises and then, rather tentatively, approached with the plate held out at arm's length. As soon as Gregory began to take it, the man had let go and it was only by a quick lunge that Gregory caught the plate. Yet this movement had frightened the man at the same time - he obviously thought Gregory was going for him. He jumped back as though scalded.

A hot meal was bit of a misnomer: the food had some residual warmth in it, which in turn saved him any discomfort from the fact that they had not provided him with any cutlery. There was no concert that night and although he could hear some noises in the distance it was obvious that the main body of the Cathedral had shut. He had begun to distinguish amongst the other sounds the faint sound of the bolts going home in the main door. In the evenings, before sleep overcame his senses, he returned to creating some fantasies for himself to pass the time: this was a sign that, now some time after his abduction, his mind was beginning to assert itself. In addition, Gregory had begun a calendar, as a typical prisoner, by scratching on the wall.

He was sitting motionless in the gloom when he heard footsteps approaching. He knew it could not be Bailey as he always appeared without a noise. He turned to his window and saw Little standing there. This time she was not wearing her hoody and he could see her face. "Hi," she said and, "you look amazed. Shall I go?"

"No, no, come nearer - get a chair. How have you managed this?" he asked shakily. "Your father…"

"My father and I have come to an understanding." He waited for an explanation but none came.

"So you are allowed to come here freely now?" She nodded. "Great." Suddenly he was overwhelmed by self-doubt; this was just curiosity on her part. She might never come again. She was young, she would get bored.

"What are you thinking?" He flushed slightly.

"I am just very grateful," he replied quickly.

"Unfortunately, my father being the Dean, has also agreed to Mercy coming to see you." Now she coloured. "Of course," she continued in a flustered way, "you might not think that is such a bad thing." Gregory could tell she needed some reassurance otherwise their relationship could be over before it began.

"No," he began, "she seems a bit too dangerous for my liking." Little sighed and relaxed.

"I'll get a chair." She was gone some time and he began to worry she would not return. "Bailey was being obnoxious," she muttered on her return.

"He has not hurt you has he?" he asked.

"No he wouldn't dare. How are you bearing up?" she enquired.

"I am trying not to be gloomy," he shrugged. Gregory sensed that he ought not to be too depressed in front of her or he would become a burden.

"Why are you here?"

"Don't you know?"

"Some. Tell me your side." He told her briefly.

She listened attentively and when he had concluded said, "It's monstrous. It makes me not know my father. How could he do this to another human being? I've been thinking about how I can help you."

"Don't get yourself into trouble." They sat quietly for few moments and he looked at her. She allowed his gaze to fall on her without flinching. She had shoulder length natural dark blond hair with a centre parting. Her face was on the whole well-proportioned but her nose was large for her face. She had a lovely mouth with neat red lips and a pale complexion. She had one or two spots on her face but she looked clean and well-groomed and he knew that she would smell nice if he could get close enough.

"Shall I look at you now," she said with a grin.

"Sure but I am not at my best," he responded, "prison diet and lack of sunshine have quite faded me away, only a beard to show for it." It made him feel good to attempt a joke. "Your dad thinks that my suffering will attract the divine spirit to bestow his blessing on St. Arburn's."

"What bloody rot!" she hissed. "How on earth can he think that - he is an educated man. History shows that unwarranted suffering is just that. It is not beneficial to be poor, ill or imprisoned. I can't believe it can do the human soul any good to suffer such hardships at the hands of others." She was getting worked up. "The bastard. I have told him to let you go but he refuses."

"It is true," he said, "I cannot feel any benefit from my suffering - it's making me sour and vengeful. I told him that the divine spirit is more likely to stay away than endorse what he is doing here but your dad doesn't see this," he looked around his cell, "as unwarranted suffering. He sees it as self-inflicted." Little reacted physically, she shifted to the edge of her chair and blustered. Gregory ignored her and continued, "Your dad feels that this is my own fault for not recognising my own gifts and talents - and that if I did I would have come and volunteered for the job - and he would not have had to lock me up. I would have begged him to let me stay." She was holding her head and shaking it as though she did not want to hear the words. "I suppose if that were true, then maybe the voluntary sacrifice of someone is different from a forced sacrifice. What do you think?" he asked.

"Yes, I can see that if we submit to the difficulties that life has thrown up, and learn wisdom and patience from them, we would become better people at least in achieving more maturity - by that we would deal with future difficulties more calmly - but whether the divine spirit is satisfied by such sacrifice, I don't know."

"What do you think the divine spirit is?" was his next question. She composed herself to answer and was on the point of opening her mouth when Mercy appeared.

"Coo, look at you two love birds. My turn now Little!" she said viciously to her sister. "You can't monopolise this feeble creature, dad says. I am to get my turn."

"He only agreed because he knows that you will soon get bored. I see you have come to plague him." Mercy was wearing a short tight dress which hugged the contours of her blooming body.

"Sod off sister." Normally this kind of banter may have been considered affectionate but Gregory could see that there was no sense of that here. "I would never have let them capture me," she said to Gregory.

"Well that just shows how cravenly ignorant you are," riposted Little. She was on her feet now. Gregory wondered whether it might come to blows. Mercy was larger than Little and heavy but Little looked fit and athletic. Gregory looked from one to the other, there was nothing similar about the sisters at all he decided. They did not look like siblings. "I will leave her to your mercy," said Little and walked away.

"Pathetic." said Mercy scornfully.

"Will I see you again?" asked Gregory but there was no reply. Either she had not heard or was too upset to respond.

"Hmm let's have a look at you," said Mercy. She showed no fear and came right up to the window and rested herself into the aperture. Gregory backed off. It would have been so easy to take her by the throat and strangle her, but what good would it do, he would still be imprisoned. They would kill him and torture him for that. Now she was tormenting him. As on the previous occasion she got her message over by the simple expedient of a direct come on. However, this time it was goading and crass with less subtlety. Some men would not even have paused at this invitation. She held Gregory fixed in her stare. Even if she had spoken it could not have added anything to this challenge.

"No." This was intolerable. He felt a primitive need to defend his sexuality. "You shouldn't flaunt yourself like this or suggest such an invitation." She did not deny her offer. "Of course there is part of me that would want to....." He left what unsaid and regretted his honesty immediately. "But it would be a very bad idea."

"Why? Nobody would know."

"Why are you offering yourself to me like this? What is in it for you?"

"I just know about men," she said. Gregory guessed she was not lying.

"Do you want counsel about it?" he asked. She threw back her head and laughed. "How old are you?" he inquired.

"Twenty." He could tell it was a lie.

"Seventeen then," he said.

"That just makes it more dangerous doesn't it?"

"Don't you have a boyfriend?" He had asked her this before and not got a straight answer.

"No, I've got several," she said. Gregory's mind was working fast. Possibly Bailey was around and he could call for help although he recognised that was quite a wimpy thing to do. Still he needed to repulse her in such a way that she would leave him alone.

"You may have a disease," he said provocatively. It had been the first thing that came into his mind. He would rile her somehow. His mind was clicking with the stress: he had no reserves for this kind of conversation. Inevitably it would be a mistake to stoop to her crudity.

"Not possible."

"Some diseases are hidden," he pursued her. She shrugged. He had never come across anyone quite so rapacious before.

"Do you want to go with me or not then?" It was so self-abusive he could not believe it. Maybe he should just use her, but he could not make himself do it. It would be against his essential nature: he wanted love and sex, not sex on its own. He wasn't occupying any moral high ground, it was just him. She stood back to give him the full effect once more. It did not look very attractive. There was no allure to it.

"What does your father think of your behaviour?" There was a slight movement in her shoulders but her voice was defiant.

"Why the shit should I care what he thinks. I'm a grown up."

"Not really," he said gently.

"He is hardly living a moral life himself."

"Why is he promiscuous?

"No - I mean keeping you here.

"So you admit it is wrong thing to do?" She did not answer. Then an insight came to him. "Has your father ever shown a sexual interest in you?" He may as well have slapped her. She took a step back.

"You have a disgusting mind," she spat at him. "What is it you get off on ? Is that what you do all day - think of having sex with children? You absolute pervert! Pervert! Pervert!" she screamed. "If you think I would let anywhere near me then you are a...." She could not think of a bad enough word to describe it. Mercy bent over, picked up the chair, and threw it at the window. Gregory stepped back in alarm. This was not the reaction he had expected. "I'm going to get you sorted," she continued to scream and blaspheme. Then, "Bailey! Bailey!" But he did not come so she was forced to go away shouting for him. The noises changed, she must have found somebody because he could hear a kind of explanatory tone in her voice. There was no response. It must be Bailey he concluded. Then she was back with the cattle prod and Bailey in attendance. She lunged at him through the window but he stepped back and avoided it easily. She tried several times but Gregory continued to duck. Then Bailey stepped forward and wrestled the implement from her hands. She collapsed to the floor and began to weep. Bailey grabbed her by the hand and dragged her up and away. Bailey did not turn back but yet Gregory could see from his profile that he was smiling. He was enjoying Mercy's discomfiture.

"Mmm," thought Gregory, "anyway he isn't such a loyal lap dog to the Dean after all. There are some politics going on here that maybe I can exploit."

He had only just settled down to rest in his chair when he heard voices coming towards him, however, only the Dean appeared. "Deary me," he said like some tutting geriatric. He looked tired but his eyes were menacing. "What have you done to Mercy to upset her so? I should not have to be dragged here at this time of night to deal with you. I knew no good would come of letting them talk to you. They are both too head strong. What did you say to her?" he repeated. Gregory did not answer at once but scratched his head. He knew he must take advantage of all these moments of stress to push forwards and weaken his captors.

"What did she say I said to her?"

"I wouldn't be asking if I knew," he blustered.

"Maybe she wants it to be a secret?"

"I think she is too upset to tell me at the moment - so we must clear it up for her." Gregory was trembling a bit, he did not know whether to tell the truth or whether he had the courage to stick in the knife and look for an advantage. He went for it.

"She offered to have sex with me and I refused." The Dean shook his head in amazement. "

"Absolutely preposterous. Mercy is a charming innocent young girl."

"How old is she by the way?"

"Almost eighteen, but that is irrelevant."

"She doesn't dress innocently," Gregory observed, "in fact she dresses very provocatively. Perhaps you should have a word with her. Little shows a good example."

"I can see you have never had children," the Dean began condescendingly. "It is well known that adolescent girls model out provocative behaviour, particularly to their fathers who are safe."

"I am not her father," noted Gregory, "and the truth is she did offer me sex."

"Yes - but that would have been impossible - you being in there and she out here. She has been naughty to tease you like this. I will put a stop to it. It is another case of it being safe for her to experiment because she knew you could not harm or get to her."

"She came very close. I reckon she was willing to let me touch her."

"You are being outrageous, I do not believe a word of it. I must insist once more that you do not see her."

"And further more I must repeat that it is not my job to restrain her. I may ask her to leave but I cannot make her. That is your duty."

"Quite. You know I see your game now, you are trying to upset me on purpose and .... I am not Othello and you are not Iago." Gregory noticed the interesting choice of imagery. "I understand you must have sexual fantasies, stuck in their on your own, but don't draw my daughters into it," the Dean said condescendingly. "You will need to take to chastity as you do your other callings. Good night."

Gregory spent a twitchy wakeful night stuck with the sexual fantasies of a grotesquely bloated Mercy, and Little was nowhere to be found.

```
     [I1] In the city the Urban Mystic does
not only confine himself to the major
thoroughfares. Although he does spend a lot of
time there he takes opportunities to walk or
cycle down all the byways, side-roads and the
residential streets. He watches the churches,
reads the notice-boards. He tries to be there
at different times of day so he can encounter
all there is to experience. He also drives in
a car when he can and takes public transport
and buses so as to be with people. He observes
```

them closely and sometimes his scrutiny can cause anger or distress because they can wonder what he is staring at.

Chapter 10

When we got to the entrance of the toilets she said, "I want to use the gents - they are cleaner. Go and look if there is anyone in there." I went in dutifully. When I appeared back in the doorway and shook my head, she pushed past me into the toilet. She grabbed me by the hand and pulled me after her. It was a total surprise: I had not seen that coming. I actually felt reluctant. I didn't want to lose the edge in my driving. Once we were in there she became all coy. Either she had changed her mind or she was just giving me mixed messages. Eventually after a bit of banter she drew me to her and we began to kiss. It wasn't very ardent and I was not trying too hard either. She pushed me against a cubicle door and when it gave way pursued me in. It was grim - it stank in there and we were both trying hard to get passionate. I slammed the lid down with my foot. Then it became weird and she became forceful. She told me to take my trousers off. I should've known! "All the way, all the way," she insisted.

Now she was kissing me hard and helping me. "You take your clothes of soon," I urged her. But she was fighting to help me so I couldn't concentrate on her. I sat on the seat and did as I was told. Then someone came in to the urinals and we had to stand very still. There was no sign of her joining me. She just stood and pulled faces to try and make me laugh out loud. Then she was posing herself like a model and playing with her hair. I tried to touch her but she swipe my hand away flirtatiously. Even so I kept looking at her and began to get turned on by the danger of it all.

When we were alone again, all of a sudden, she said, "back in a minute." She struggled out of the cubicle banging the door against my legs and dragging my trousers out on the end of her foot. The door slammed leaving one leg protruding under it and as I lent to recover my trousers they disappeared from under the door.

"Shit!" I heard her laugh. I swore deeply and gingerly opened the door. She was gone so I fetched them back in. I dressed slowly, still shocked by her ferocity: more anger rather than arousal on her part. I was humiliated. As I left the washroom I put my hands in the pocket for the car keys but they were not there. A hot flush crept into my neck. I returned immediately to the cubicle - there was no sign of them. "Fuck!" I thought, "It's that bitch. She's taken them".

    The car had gone I saw immediately as I ran outside. This was a very bad moment. My heart swelled with the loss, I became rigid with anger. I felt the sweat moist between my legs. I was jacked up to a high pitch of nervous response and that damned teaser had run off with my sweet car. Great waves of panic ran over me and I looked around the car park for what to do or who to tell. I saw a lorry driver mounting his cab and ran over to him. I explained briefly what had happened: he was delighted, he told me to get in. We set off painfully, slowly, the lorry grinding and accelerating up through it gears. As we swung into the slip road back onto the dual carriage way I could see my car beginning to pull into the traffic. She must've got stuck at the end of the slip road. My joy drew off erratically and I cursed her for the way she was treating it. I urged the driver to hurry but he just hunched his shoulders.

    After a few moments he said, "Do you want to ring the police? They can easily intercept it." He proffered his mobile.

    "No, not yet." I was keeping my eyes on my car. She was not going very fast and although it would be impossible to overhaul her, the straight road with the long running dips and troughs made it easy to follow her progress. After about fifteen minutes some more services were signposted and we saw her pull in. I urged the driver to hurry once more but he just drove calmly on and pulled in to the services for me. I was out of his cab without a thankyou before he had stopped properly and began to pull off straight away. I sprinted to the car, wrenched the door open and grabbing her by the hair dragged her out onto the tarmac. I felt like kicking her and would have done so had not a man come up behind me and put his hand on my shoulder. I turned to shrug him off but he was big and hard looking.

    "That's no way to treat a lady," he was enjoying himself.

I let go of her hair, she squirmed away from me and got up, brushing the gravel from her clothes. "Is there a problem?" the man questioned her. She looked from him to me. I must have been red in the face; I was breathing hard fit to murder her.

"I just played a joke on my partner - a practical joke. I pretended he could have sex with me and then I stole his car for fun." A crowd was gathering. I felt the man's arm relax he was smirking. "And he didn't find it funny," she said tartly.

"Make them kiss and make up," another man said, probably a friend to the first.

The man shook me and asserted, "You heard him." She puckered up in a travesty of a screen kiss and the man, without releasing me, pushed me forward and bent my head to her lips with his free hand. Our lips touched briefly. "Now both of you get in the car. Make up and bugger off." He gave me one final shove. "I will be watching," he put a thick finger to his eye.

I nodded to the girl to get in the passenger seat. I slipped through the driver's door and we drove off. There was no way but to go back on the carriageway and therefore no chance to stop to get rid of her. "Look," she said, "there was no chance you would let me have a drive."

"I may have."

"What your precious car!"

"So you took it!"

"So what. I waited until you got in that lorry. I made it easy for you to follow me."

"I should have called the police."

"Why didn't you? No big deal is it?"

"It is to me. Nobody drives this car but me."

She swore a few times. "I gave you a bit of excitement. This was the least you could do."

"I would have settled for petrol money," I replied. "It was no big deal," I taunted her with her own words. She was silent for a while.

"Anyway I'm not getting out anyway. Not yet. I need to get to............." She mentioned the northern city again.

"Well tough shit. I'm not going there anymore."

"Of course you are," she said defiantly. Another pause.

"Look let's be friends." I grunted. "Tell me some more of your story."

"Not yet!" I was calming down and vacillating about how and when to get rid of her.

"Can I put the radio on?"

"No!"

"Then tell me some more story - in that other voice you have." I acquiesced: I like my own stories.

"When Greg gets home that night he can't get Sue out of his mind."

"So he did what men do best."

"Damn you!" She looked worried that time when I looked at her.

"I can't help it. I'm just getting into it."

"I swear one more word and I'll kill you," I said menacingly. "Whose doing who favour here? This is my car and I'm giving you a lift. This is my story. Shut up! Shut up. Shut up. Shut up." She put her hands up in a supplicant gesture. "Greg decides he needs to find her and get to know her. So the next day he goes in search of her. He knows that she was at school with him, but in a lower form, so he rings around his old school friends and eventually manages to track her down. He gets an address: a friend's brother's girlfriend is studying at the same college as her which means he gets the name of the college.

Later that day he gets on a tube and goes to the campus. There are more buildings than he thought, so he doesn't know how to find her, except to camp outside until she appears. Though it occurs to him that she mightn't come every day. Meanwhile there he is standing outside, dithering as to whether to go in and chance asking the office staff when a big Merc pulls up, then he sees her come out of the entrance hall and get in. She does not see him, but he is wetting himself as to how to follow her, when fortuitously a taxi drives past. He manages to hail it and they trailed behind. The Merc drops her off at a typical student-type house and Greg gets out himself. He has no idea where he is or what to do next. Anyway....."

Suddenly, I was becoming unsatisfied with my story

and irritated by this woman being in the car with me. "They start a relationship. Her older lover finds out and threatens to kill Greg. He takes Sue away on a cruise and Greg stows away in the man's yacht. There is a shipwreck and Sue is mortally injured and dies in Greg's arms and ... well that is how it goes."

"You lost interest in your own story."

"I got tired of you being with me," I told her.

"That's cruel." I was approaching a roundabout so I checked my map and took a right up a B road which began to wind into the open country.

"Look, tough and all - I think you ought to get out now."

"Well the least you could've done was drop me on the main road not up some poxy deserted country lane. I don't do rural. Keep me until you get back on a major road then I will get out. Promise."

"OK. See I can be reasonable."

She began to talk to me about her early childhood but it was boring. My thoughts were still on my tale. I had got embarrassed telling her because I thought she was laughing at me. What she did not know was that I was always good at creative writing at school. Why should I tell her? This nonentity I had picked up.

"Your story," she began again. I sighed. "You haven't got enough interest in their intrigue. It's about love, as usual, unrequited love and death, and funerals, and things, but it needs to have some deeper plot. I did English at college you know."

"Really," I responded scornfully.

"Yeah. I never finished it but I did the first year. I could help you."

"I don't think so," I said. It didn't put her off.

"This girl needs to be a lost twin and her sister is on her trail - but the original girl - what did you call her?"

I told her, "Sue."

"She is hiding herself, because really what she is doing with this old guy is a kind of prostitution, and she knows her family will be ashamed of her. And this other sister has seen a picture published of her, taken by the photographer, so she breaks into his flat and discovers that he is a thief as well: he had been stealing vintage photographs and selling them on the black market. Then this older guy, he is up to no good either, but in a semi-legitimate business way - loads of money. So you get a tension between these two bad men and the poor girl lost in the middle of it."

"I don't like it," I said sourly. "It isn't my story." I began to drive faster.

"Shall I tell you my story?" she offered.

"If you must."

"Well it's set in the future and it's about an invincible alien that falls to earth: a purple man. First of all he is found by this guy and, although he is invincible, he is relatively benign. When the man takes him home to his girlfriend the alien takes her off him."

I interrupted, "How is he invincible?"

"He can't be crushed, or cut, or anything like that, or shot - nothing can touch him."

"Not convincing. I mean, perhaps they could bury him, or imprison him. Or if he is very light they could blow him away: attach him to a rocket and send him into space."

"You are being too scientific; it is a love story."

"Nevertheless people notice these inconsistencies and they lose interest."

"What do you suggest?" she asked with a sarcastic tone to her voice.

"He would have to be very heavy or he would need to be able to change his weight, mass. So normally he would be our weight, but if they tried to make him do something he did not want to he could make himself heavy and they would not be able to shift him."

"Is that possible?"

"No Derr!! It doesn't have to be as long as it is consistent within the story. And he would have to be immensely strong, so if he lifted his arm up, for instance, they could not stop it and he could use that as a lever. You could say that the alien was impervious to X-rays so that nobody knew what he was like inside. Then that..." I was thinking it up as I went along, "that the government tried to kill him off at first and that they tried all kinds of things. You could describe how they tried to kill this alien by poison and burying it alive. Perhaps at first they didn't know about its weight and that they decided to move it by helicopter until it suddenly got heavier and brought the machine crashing down. Or they tried to blow it up with a nuclear explosion. Pause! But it returned and irradiated all the scientists. All sorts of clever stuff once you take the idea to its logical conclusion."

"Anyway it is a romance," she persisted. "He steals the man's woman."

"Is she a slag like you?" I said cruelly. I was still pissed off with the way she had treated me."

"No, she's a virgin."

"Not like you then."

"No not like me. That would make it more poignant if her bloke is waiting for his first go with her and the alien steps in and gets her pregnant first go."

"Has he got the right anatomy for it?" She punched my arm. It wasn't in jest, she was getting riled now.

"You are just crude. Now who's taking over who's story?"

"But you don't mind!"

"I do actually. What makes you think that you could treat me like this? I did something fun for you."

"My heart bleeds." She scrunched herself up in her chair and distanced herself from me. I was getting angry again and I increased the speed one more click. She noticed and I saw her fingers move to clench the seat. I was being stupid but it was her fault she was she was making me. Why had I picked her up? It was stupid. I took the next corner, a left hand bend, too fast and the tyres screeched slightly but the car went around like a dream.

"Slow down. Why have you speeded up? My dad used to do this. Stop it. I hate it. You will get us killed."

"Don't you trust me?"

"No, I don't know you."

"I should've known you," I replied quickly, remembering an older meaning. She swore at me.

"Let me out!"

"I thought you wanted to go up north?" I was goading her.

"Not with you."

"You begged me to keep you." I was enjoying myself and that thrill of scaring her. A lovely swooping stretch of road opened up in front of me. There was no other traffic ahead or behind, so I put my foot down. A couple of miles ahead, there was the beginning of a wood growing on both sides of the road, and I could see that the road bent to the right just past the entrance to the wood. I was up to a hundred in a few seconds and glancing at her I could see how terrified she was. I was enjoying myself. She was too paralysed to speak. The speedo kept climbing, without any perceptible change to the big engine, which was still turning over lazily. With half a mile to the bend I eased off the accelerator and let the momentum begin to slow. The bend did not appear very steep and I intended to take it fairly fast but, as I drew near, I now appreciated that I had misjudged it and the bend was tighter that I had thought. Because I was going too fast I braked in preparation for the turn. I was bracing myself against the steering wheel but she slid forward. Then, as the car continued to slow, and just before I was about to put on the power again to come out of the bend, her door swung open, back on its hinges, and she fell out. I still do not know why her seat belt did not hold her. It worked perfectly later when I tried it. I was so busy steering the car that I only caught a glimpse of her out of the corner of my eye as she shot ahead of the car, catapulting into the ditch at the side of the road. "Hell's teeth!" I shouted to myself before stamping on the brakes for an emergency stop, slewing the car to a halt a hundred metres down the road. I was trembling like a leaf and the blood was pumping a monster headache in my temple. I got out of the car and staggered back to the bend. There were still no other cars around.

When I got to the ditch, I picked my way slowly forward, scared to even look into its maw. There she laid, her head skewed and her body lying in a very undignified way: her rump in the air showing the knickers under her short skirt. I licked my lips. She was obviously dead. Nobody's neck did that. Still no traffic. I panicked and ran back to the car. It was ticking over gently unaware of its part in the tragedy. The passenger door was stiff and broken like a bird's wing: bent forward past its normal resting place. It took some strength to push it back but in the end it did close drunkenly. The line of that side of the car was completely spoilt now. I got in and drove off. It was five minutes before I met another car and as soon as was practical I turned off that road to make a detour away from the accident.

    I don't know how I got to my girlfriend's; the whole idea of this being a pleasurable adventure was gone. The journey had become the worst nightmare ever. The plan had been for me to stop in a travel lodge and to get there early the next morning. Now I could not stop and the only anodyne to my tortured mind was to keep going. I made myself take the worst roads as punishment.

    Late into the night I stopped in a transport cafe and, after forcing some food into myself, slept in the car for a few hours, tossing and turning with the continued horror of it. When I got under way again I scoured the radio channels for some news without success. They may not have found her yet I told myself.

Chapter 11

As the days past Gregory determined to listen more carefully to the pilgrims. There had been no space in his heart for anyone else's problems until now and it had only taken one kind word from Little to awaken his sympathy and lift his mood. He could not help it, he was that sort of person. The pilgrims had not been getting their money's worth. In fact he was hard pushed to remember any details of what they had told him, even the more salacious ones. There had been precious few attractive people or personalities coming to his post box slot and even when they did, there had been nothing in him to listen. But now as his wounds healed, and his mind began to clear, he was surprised by the re-emergence of a long lost boredom, and little by little these intrusions in his day became a welcome diversion. He even suggested to the Dean that he might be prepared to serve two hours a day instead of the one. The Dean, although secretly pleased, pretended to Gregory that he was concerned that it would distract him from his work as a mystic. Gregory felt no nearer understanding what it was they required of him. He determined to talk to Little about it should she reappear and the Dean as well.

One morning his first client was an attractive woman in her thirties. She wore expensive clothes, there were gold rings on her fingers and her scent was heady and rich. "Yes?" it was his standard beginning but spoken more kindly. This was an improvement as generally he had been impatient and short with people. She would not meet his gaze. Gregory was never sure how much they could see of him so he could not tell if this was significant. She began to sob quietly, not an unknown occurrence: these interviews seem to provoke tears in many people. It was these waterworks that usually irritated him most: how dare they cry when he was suffering more than them? But now there was a small voice inside that was saying, "Yes I can do that, I have some love to share."

He sat patiently waiting for her to speak. It went on so long that he began to think she would run out of time. Unusually, this had never bothered him before because the fact they were shunted off every five minutes was a relief to him, but today his curiosity was aroused. "Can you tell me?" he asked gently. The tears continued. Eventually the attendant came and touched her on the shoulder meaning, "time's up".

At this she did not seem startled but looked up and said to Gregory, "Thank you, it has meant a lot for me to cry with you today. I will come back." Gregory was pleased for her, nevertheless, this intense listening, for that is what it must have been, had left him drained so he reverted to the old indifferent ways with the rest of his list.

The next day she was first in the queue again and seemed a little more composed, though as she spoke the tears ran again. "It will seem so silly to you," she offered, "but my heart is broken because I cannot have a baby. My partner and I have tried for six years."

Gregory could not stop the unbidden thought come into his head, "I bet I could give you one straight away." Now he was feeling better his libido was rising. Yet outwardly he nodded and encouraged her to go on. She talked about her partner and her love for him and their hopes for a family. When there was a pause Gregory asked, "What is it you want me to do?" This was a strong response for he generally followed the Dean's given instructions to bless them and to promise to pray.

"I would like you to talk to the divine spirit for me." He hoped she could not see him raise his shoulders hopelessly.

"Don't you think if I could do that I would ask him to get me out of here?" he thought. He surprised himself by saying, "Of course I will." At this her face relaxed and a shy smile came. She looked directly at him and putting her hands through the slot took his hands, which were resting nearby, and drew them out to her lips. She kissed them both passionately and deep thrill coursed through his body. That smile had made him catch his breath; he knew that he was suddenly infatuated with her. "If only she had been Mercy," he thought wryly.

As she went she told him that she would come back for an answer. That cooled his ardour a bit.

"In a month," he called after her. But he did not know whether she heard him.

Unfortunately this flush of passion put him in a bad mood for the rest of the session and he vowed to himself that he must guard against opening up his heart to the pilgrims. He regretted the offer he had made the Dean. "Best to be on my own than to feel again," he thought. It would be a torture to see her again or Little.

On a subsequent afternoon he was restless, even his newly self-imposed hour of exercise did not calm him and he wandered to and fro disconsolately around his cell for much of the time. He had never really felt the need of much human physical contact until now, when it was completely denied him. In addition, Gregory was fretful and puzzled as to how these pilgrims should have such confidence in him; he felt it was quite misplaced, knowing keenly his own unworthiness and lack of purity or anything approaching the sort of holiness he felt they were demanding from him. At times that afternoon Gregory cursed himself sharply for his terrible betrayal; that poor woman was telling him about her troubles and her love for her husband and he was silently lusting after her. The images would not go away and the misery continued. When he tried to indulge himself with serious thought about her, his mind unbidden invented daydreams which simply made it worse. The harder he tried to make her real in his imagination the worse it became. In the end he threw himself on his bed and determined to distract himself by constructing a safe daydream for himself.

```
[K1] Being mystic is a calling and with
all callings one can ask God for it.

[Y1] When the Urban Mystic is invited to
speak publicly he always speaks first of the
divine spirit.
```

It was difficult at first to imagine himself somewhere else. His time in the cell had somehow swamped out the rest of his life. He had become 'After Confinement' rather than 'Before Confinement'. Gregory determined that he would go on a visit in his imagination, somewhere that he knew, somewhere beautiful and natural, somewhere he could breathe and think and where he had previously experienced calm. He drove himself to Wicher Fen. It was not a place he had been to very often but his few visits had developed in him a love for its flat wildness. Gregory was trying so hard to get it right that he even made himself visit the toilet in the car park and with his eyes closed felt the damp cool walls.

It was almost impossible to get the weather right. At various points on his journey it reflected all the vagaries his country's weather could offer. It was warm when he wanted it to be warm and cold at other times to refresh him. His own emotions drove the meteorological engine. He even wondered if it were quite unnatural to give himself such an intense imaginary experience and pondered whether there would be the equivalent of a succubus that he would bring to life and draw into himself by the strength of his own wilful wishes. The museum and entrance building were variously empty and then full of people. It was impossible to tell if anyone was actually there. At any rate they did not see or respond to him in any way.

Then he was through this human vestibule and he stepped onto the walkway, and then into the wood, and finally he was among the trees. On real visits Gregory had been boringly predictable and stayed on the marked paths, but now at the earliest opportunity he cut into the woodland and hid himself from view. As he walked, he stumbled over roots and hummocks, such was his intense wonder at all the sights and smells of the pathway. He kept looking up at the sky which was full of clouds or, moments later, dull and overcast. The trees rose and fell changing from Spring to Autumn in seconds. And there was snow, and rain, and scorching sun from which he could only escape under the branches. His imagination was hunger-driven for any stimulation from the natural world and his soul brought out all of its storehouse. Finally, he slumped under a tree with his back against the trunk. As the wind stirred its top branches the tree nudged him in the back. Had he dreamt that? Then he slept to wake, with a start, two hours later. There was Mercy in his cell with him - no it was only a mark on the wall. "Hello Mercy," he said. But she did not answer or at that moment have the power to move him.

```
[D2]  The Urban Mystic is there to pose
the question to which there may be no
immediate answer.
```

One day, after his lunch, the Dean came to see him. "Are you sure that you want to step the pilgrim visits up to two?" The man seemed much calmer and he had brought a chair with him and sat down by Gregory's window. If he had wanted Gregory could have reached out and touched him. There was a companionable silence for a few moments. "Are you beginning to understand now?" enquired the Dean. The previous question was forgotten in the quietude.

"Not a clue," said Gregory. Even if he was beginning to get something, the Dean was the last person he would ever admit it to.

"I believe that a mystic has a natural gift for communication on the spiritual level," began the Dean. "That in itself it is partly genetic - in the same way that some are born to be a good listener and have had the kind of sensible upbringing that has allowed them to develop such a gift. Then on top of that is the divine given bit. He - God ," the Dean said the word with some distaste, "has - well I mean can - opened up a special channel for some people to hear him better. Of course on top of that some people have a spiritual sensitivity as well but they don't always have the discrimination to use it for good. They never had or they have become polluted."

"Is the spiritual world good or bad?" asked Gregory.

"It must be both I suppose."

"Where does evil come from?" The Dean paused at this question and rolled his eyes back. He answered with more of his own. "Does it just spring from the heart of personkind spontaneously or is it learned from other evil people? But then how did that all start? Or is there an evil spiritual tide in the world that perverts or encourages our own evil propensities?

"Perhaps there is not evil and good in some endless battle. It could be that it is all just a kind of grey," offered Gregory.

"Then we would all be the same and it could not explain how we end up doing bad things, despite a perpetual nagging but unobtainable desire to do good all the time. If it was grey than we could never be able to describe any action as absolutely good or bad - any action would be a mix of one or the other."

"Isn't that the case?" asked Gregory. He did not really mean the questions he just wanted to keep the Dean talking; the more he knew the more power he had.

"No there are good actions, perfectly so - and good people."

"Such as?" The Dean did not answer. "Is there a good spiritual personality and a bad one then, or is evil and good a force in the ether?" The Dean smiled.

"That is for you to discover for yourself." Now the Dean was grinning; yet it was not a warm encouraging grin one that affirmed you - it was sly and triumphant.

"So where am I in all this?" asked Gregory.

"Well," replied the Dean, "I think you have natural gift and a given gift - but I am not sure whether you have the will or the discernment yet to use both for good."

"Maybe I never will be able to."

"Arrh ha, that is where the divine spirit comes in. He will give you the power to use it positively."

"So am I to expect some lightning bolt to hit me and make me good?"

"No I don't believe you will ever become totally good, rather, as you communicate with the divine spirit and draw near to him, you will begin to become good."

"Holy?"

"If you like."

"Then surely we should all be doing that. Isn't that the purpose of this Cathedral to help us all to become as you say?" It would have been normal for somebody faced with such a question to display some conscience but the Dean continued impervious to the implications that the question posed to his own morality.

"Yes. But not all are leaders, most are followers."

"You are a leader surely?"

"An administrator and ...."   And what he would not say.

"If I become holy would you follow me?"

"I would not need to because I believe that I am already walking in the same direction. Have I not brought you here? Your glory will be mine."

"Good may come out of this bad thing you have done," said Gregory. "But if all you say is true, then surely there was a better way for me, that did not involve my imprisonment?"

"Too deep," was the dismissive reply.

"How can that be too deep for you, when you have just been talking of good and evil? Surely you must apply your knowledge to specific situations."

"Like yours?"

"Certainly."

"We are in the eye of the storm here Gregory all is still and calm. We are at the point of tension between two opposing forces, one slip on either of our parts and we will fall to one extreme."

"Are you suggesting that in this little universe, you have created for me, there is neither good or bad at this time?"

"You said it. Great things happen at the most inopportune moments."

"What does that mean?"

"This is a cusp, Gregory, for you and me and our country." Gregory sighed. "You still have not told me how to do it or shown me an example I can follow."

"There isn't one, it has all been lost - you must explore it on your own."

Gregory respond liturgically.

"And you have begun, I know, I can see it."

"Well tremble then," shouted Gregory so fiercely that the Dean started and got to his feet and walked away.

```
[E2] The Urban Mystic recognises that she
is a work of art in herself. She is within
herself loved and maintained by the divine
spirit.
```

He could smell Little before she appeared. "My God, Fish and chips!" he exclaimed. "That is the most wonderful present anybody has ever given me." Gregory snatched them out of her hand. "And they are hot. Brilliant! I have not had fish or a hot meal for weeks." He began to wolf them down.

"Slowly!" she urged him. But it was no good he could not control himself. Little started to giggle and then laugh out loud at his antics. The fish was steaming still and he kept burning his fingers and lips. At one point he had to let it fall back out of his mouth because he could not cope with it.

"It's better than sex," he declared and then blushed which made her do so also.

"You are going to have to comb your beard out," she observed. He shrugged.

"They won't trust me with an electric razor, let alone a wet one." He sat back with a slump. "I feel really sick now," Gregory said.

"I have no sympathy. I told you to eat more slowly. You are not used to so much food at one go. Have you lost weight?"

"I have no idea." He asked her what the weather was like and she told him. They were avoiding the subject of Mercy. "I hope Mercy is not coming again," he said.

"Yes - I hope so too," she said quietly.

"And the world - what is the rest of the world doing?"

"Well you have missed the referendum."

"Oh yes of course, I knew that was coming. Who won?"

"There is a recount because it is so close to the majority required - but the media are predicting that it will be city states." Gregory had no real interest in politics: as long as he was not taxed too much and all the basic amenities ran well he was satisfied. And even when they didn't, he always naively thought it was the utility that was at fault rather than the government. If the people who desired decentralised government wanted it to reach its own natural conclusion it did not bother him.

"Well it won't make much difference will it," he was not asking a question. At this Little's mouth almost dropped open. This insignificant physical movement triggered a response in the depths of Gregory's brain. He looked with a new interest at her. The physicality of her presence overcame him. It was as though she had snapped into focus in his mind. 'You are lovely,' he thought, 'really lovely.' He wanted to kiss her eyes.

She had noticed this dislocation in his thoughts, apparent from a subtle change in his looks, and knowing intuitively that it was for the good paused for a moment before saying, "You don't care do you?"

"No." She shook her head in amazement.

"It's not just another sort of local government you know. This is about sovereignty."

"Calm down," he replied. There was a sudden fear that this new conversation would upset their growing friendship. "Of course I care, it is just that I have no interest. I am a kind of dyslexic when it comes to politics. My brain cannot think clearly about it." This partly mollified her.

"You realise that if it goes ahead each city state will want its own militia?" Gregory sat silently for a moment and pondered this.

"How will that matter? At the moment the army is split into regiments anyway."

"No - don't you see - if we get city states it will mean there are boundaries - and boundaries that may need defending."

"Naw, it wouldn't come to that."

"Don't be too sure." This was an uncomfortable thought to him; although he was a provincial lad, he had travelled abroad on occasions and seen border crossing with armed guards.

"Where would be our City State? Based here at St Arburn's?"

"Yes. And going out to..." Little mentioned several places within fifty miles of the city. And they say the government will be at the old corn exchange next to the Cathedral."

"But who will run it?" Then a horrible thought. "Will your dad be involved?"

"He could well be. He always used to joke that, come the Revolution, the church would take back its traditional role at the centre of power. You don't realise the influence he has beyond the Cathedral."

"But surely there will be safeguards - there will need to be some sort of central government to deal with international issues?" He was dredging his brains to remember what he had heard on the news before his kidnap.

"Yeah, but I fear it will open up greater opportunities for corruption." He smiled at her; it had all got a bit heavy. She returned his smile. Gregory put his hand through the railing, and when she reached out to take it, he withdrew his so her arm had to follow his back through the railing. He pushed the chip paper into her hand and forced her fingers to close around it. "You cad sir," she teased and threw it back at him. "Actually I better take it - I don't want to get you or me into trouble."

"Your dad seems to think that my coming to the Cathedral is significant."

"Like a holy event," she added.

"Yes, some sort of dislocation, a spiritual one. He seems convinced that something significant will come from it."

"Do you feel that?" she asked.

"You know what I really feel at the moment - it's guilt. I have never known that before. I have always been a scrupulously honest person and when I have done wrong or made mistakes I have tried to own them and then - forgotten about them. But now I feel guilty that I am not getting on with it and feeling bad about the way my own personality and inner drives seem to get in the way. It all feels hopeless and I am wallowing. Then I get flooded with anger and rage about the way I am kept here. I am a turmoil of emotions."

"That is inevitable - you are being abused." Little spoke these words with compassion: Gregory had invaded her thoughts and she had come to worry for this awkward, intelligent, tortured creature imprisoned in the cell before her.

"Do you feel that my coming here is significant?" Some colour came to her cheeks she dropped her head.

"I can't tell."

"Come on tell me," he pleaded. "You had a thought there and now you won't tell me."

"You are embarrassing me. Stop it." She looked sternly at him.

"Oh, I see," he acknowledged but they both knew that he didn't.

"If you could become mystic then that would be significant. The pilgrims are starting to derive benefit from visiting you."

"Pah, I am just providing a kind of cheap counselling service," he snorted.

"It's more than that. Dad has got a board at the back where people can stick testimonies to what you have done for them."

"Wow, can you bring them to me?"

"Not yet, I don't want to make you big-headed," she said sharply. "And there is poster about you now - outside."

"No way." Gregory was human and he found this news gratifying. "It is not mystical is it though? No communication with the divine."

"Conceivably the spirit has something to say about city states." Little observed.

"You could be right." They continued to chat for a few more minutes. Gregory asked her about her childhood and he told her something of his. She looked at her watch, she was about to go when, not able to help himself, he asked. "Mercy. Why is she like that? It is kind of unnatural. She seems disturbed - lost innocence kind of thing." He dribbled to a halt. Little was looking upset. She did not say anything. The silence stretched to minutes and Gregory, transfixed by the emotions that were beginning to emerge in the face and physicality of Little just let it happen. She sighed a few times and wet her lip. It was as though she was going to try and speak but when she tried a shudder of emotion caught in her throat and a tremor her body. Little tried to communicate once more but the force of this apparent emotion prevented her. Deeper convulsions wracked her slender body and then the tears began to run. He was getting used to this: he seemed to be the repository of tears. It had surprised him, the spectrum of emotions that the pilgrims had presented to him; some were very angry, although not physically so like his first encounter, but nevertheless they ranted and raved at him and the divine spirit, raising their voices against the usual sepulchred hush of his part of the Cathedral. Others were very matter of fact and came out with a shopping list of requests. Some were for very mundane things but at other times they excelled themselves in their greed and avarice. Finally there were the tears - bucket loads of them. A veritable ocean of salinity cascaded from their cheeks onto their laps and the floor.

    He had once stood up and looked down at the chair on which the pilgrims sat and was puzzled not to see quite a puddle there. Little, however, did not cry much in terms of volume but there was an animal force behind it as if they were the tears of a deep wound. Gregory turned on his, 'I am here to listen to you', pilgrim's mode and composed himself for a long wait. Minutes passed and then with a quivering sigh she began to speak once more, quietly and interspersed with the sort of hiccups children have when they have cried hard.

    "I love Mercy but she has become something different. I don't recognise her now. I am about five years older than her so when mum died I became a kind of surrogate mum. Well, I suppose I had fulfilled that role even before that. For a while it was quite touching the way she clung to me but then subtly it all began to change and she became the monster you see today. There is nothing I can say that she does not challenge and argue against. I can never get her to see my point of view or hear me in any way. There is no give in her, no submission. Even things that would not normally be a matter of debate in a family become an instant battle ground. And her morals, as you have seen are terrible. She has become a real slut with a reputation to match."

"Doesn't your dad notice? He seems almost to condone it."

"Yeah he's still in the, 'she's my little girl' syndrome and indulges her like crazy. I suppose he is compensating for a lack of mum but he won't listen to me when I ask him to be more firm with her. I find it is so upsetting and whenever I think about it, it hooks up my grief for my mum. Sorry for the tears."

"No it's OK. I am used to it now." She was beginning to calm down. "I don't suppose something has happened to her - an event? You know." He did not want to use the words that would open up the issue of abuse. "It's just that I read somewhere, in a colour supplement, about how children, who have an inappropriate attitude to sex at an early age, sometimes..." Gregory's voice dried up. She was looking at him strangely, not wanting to hear what he was saying.

"What are you saying?" she asked directly.

"Nothing really," he fudged the issue. "Just wondering."

"No, No, I am sure I would know." She was still looking puzzled.

"There are no weird uncles or anything?"

"We shared a room for years. No I am sure not."

Gregory did not dare to say, "What about your dad?" His own motives, he knew, were not pure. There was a part of him that would want to take revenge on the Dean and create a rumour even if it were not true. He had malicious thoughts and, such was his need to punish the Dean, he would sacrifice Little's peace of mind for it. He changed the subject. "So why are you called Little? What is your proper Christian name?" Gregory looked expectantly at her and noticed the way her hair was sticking to her forehead. She was still hiccupping occasionally after her strong emotion and her face looked moist with tears and perspiration from her grief. Her weeping had washed the few faint lines from her face and she was transformed in her appearance to that of a young girl. It did Gregory good to look at her.

"Huh, I don't like it - so you will have to keep guessing."

"Lucretia? Morticia?" She laughed.

"So I am a ghoul am I? My real name is Susan, however I'm called Little because when I was young I had a fall and apparently I kept saying over and over again, 'Poor little me,' as a kind of response to the shock. For a while they would tease me with, 'Poor little,' then more affectionately it became Little.

"Mmm," a voice said behind her. It was the Dean.

"Had he been listening," Gregory wondered. He coloured. Despite his appalling treatment by the Dean there something incorruptible in Gregory that made him respond to the worst people with some core respect. He felt uncomfortable at his accusations, he felt angry with himself that he was embarrassed and frustrated, that he was not much stronger in his determination to seek revenge. He saw Little push the fish and chip wrapper under her chair away for the Dean.

"Fish and chips," noted the Dean.

"Don't start dad," she warned him. "I am doing no harm and the poor man needs some company. And, he is helping me spiritually," she said with an ironic laugh.

"Well anyway," the Dean looked a little unsure of himself. He had a brown envelope in his hand.

"Do I have to go now?" Little asked.

"No. I have this for our friend." That stuck in his two hearer's ears.

"I hardly think he can be called your friend, dad."

"Perhaps you better go then," he said sharply. She bent down, picked up the wrapper and walked behind her father. From there she grinned over her dad's shoulder back towards Gregory and pulled a face. Gregory kept a straight face in response, so Little shrugged and walked off.

"See ya," she called back.

The Dean became business-like. "You wanted a book," said the Dean. "Here is what remains of our black book - It may be of some use to you." He passed it between the first and second stanchion.

The Dean was becoming more confident with him, Gregory observed. Not keeping the same distance. Standing nearer and making himself more vulnerable. "Good," thought Gregory," I am lulling them into a false sense of safety. He wondered if the Dean carried a key on him. It would be possible to grab the Dean and to pull him partly into the cell. If he could imprison him then it was imaginable he could persuade them to let him go in return for the Dean's life. Would he have it in him to hurt or kill him, he pondered? What would Little think? Gregory took the envelope without comment.

"Well I had better go," said the Dean. Gregory did not contradict him.

With the Dean gone he feverishly tore the paper off the packet. What lay inside was disappointing. It was not really a book but the wreck of a book. In its original form, he could tell from the binding, it must have been two centimetres thick but now only a few pages remained and these had been largely scored through with black ink. What remained were isolated sentences or very short paragraphs because the text had been so annotated by some brutal censor. On some sheets there was only one such verse standing out amidst a full page of deletions. There were no more than fifty pages altogether. He felt very disappointed and, not bothering to examine it more closely, he went to lie down on his pallet. Gregory frequently made stories up for himself to pass the time and he filled them out and motivated the characters with as much details as he could imagine. Yet he did not feel like that now - he would return to Wicher Fen.

This time he went to one of the bird hides that he remembered in reality, and sat down on one of the hard wooden bench seats. It was quite dark in the shed and it smelt of damp wood. Leaning forward, he twisted the toggles at the end of his observation window and swung it up, pinning it back with a second set of toggles. In front of him was a large pond, fringed with trees that hid it from the public footpath, which curved around the eastern edge. A breath of fresh warm air wafted in through the aperture and he settled himself down to watch. There were not many birds about, nevertheless he did not really mind. He was not an ornithologist. If he had been asked to describe what he did at such places it would be to say he watched and drank it all in. Gregory felt the peace of it begin to invade his soul. Slowly he let he gaze hose around the scene, stopping occasionally to notice some details: a bent flower, or a ripple in the water, or the sunlight shimmering through the leaves. It was idyllic. He stood up and, strolling along the length of the bench, opened all the other viewing ports until the sunlight flushed through the shed. Returning to his seat a sigh escaped his mouth. "So lovely." Even the noises brought calmness and contentment.

"Excuse me." There was someone peering through his cell

window. Immediately Gregory was annoyed. He was vulnerable and exposed here in his cell and he resented this intrusion - he had been miles away - literally.

Then he recognised who it was and his attitude softened however he said in a low voice, "You shouldn't be here."

"I know - please don't tell on me." She looked behind her nervously. It was his fantasy woman - the woman who wanted desperately to get pregnant.

"What do you want?" he asked.

Breathlessly she began, "I know that you said to wait a month but I have been coming to the Cathedral every day and praying in front of the ...." Gregory did not know what that was but felt too tired to ask. "I just feel different since I spoke to you - and you promised to pray for me and now I don't know." She held out her hands in front of her breasts. "Something is happening," she continued, "my breasts are sore. Sorry!" She could see his embarrassment. "Isn't it good that the results of my pregnancy test come tomorrow? But I have a good feeling and I wanted to tell you. I couldn't wait. Thank you."

"That's OK," he sounded a bit doubtful.

Then she was about to start on social chit-chat but suddenly realised that that was probably not done with a mystic. Instead, "Aren't you a bit young to be a mystic?"

"No."

"Shouldn't be asking you that - it seems too personal." She was getting herself confused and embarrassed now. "Anyway I'll come and tell you when I know."

"Great."

"Erm." She did not know how to leave.

Gregory got a grip on himself and casting his eye around he cell caught sight of the black book. "Look," he said thinking quickly. "I have got a line from the black book here for you."

"Oh, yes thank you." She was showing polite interest.

He quickly fumbled with the pages and turning it to the light let his eye scan down the page. There was nothing that seemed relevant at all, he was beginning to feel really stupid when his eye hesitated at a verse and he read out quickly,

"I was to them like those
who lift infants to their cheeks.

I bent down to them and fed them."

"That's interesting," she observed doubtfully.

"Shall I write it down?" he asked.

"No, I will remember it. What was it again?" Gregory repeated it. She rehearsed the phrase a few times to herself.

"Got it," she smiled.

"Hopeless," he thought. He berated himself. What was he doing? Just because it had the word infant in it did not mean it was anything but meaningless. She was just being too polite to him. It was all just superstitious nonsense. Just because she had passed her stress on to him she was more relaxed and had become pregnant; or her husband had stopped wearing tight underwear, or loads of different explanations. Anyway, she might not be pregnant. The thoughts went racing through his mind.

"Now, miss you should not be here." Before them stood an official Gregory had not seen yet, dressed in a smart green uniform. There was a badge on his blazer which Gregory could not make out. "You must not pass the barrier. Seeing the mystic is limited to certain times each day and you have to pay to see him."

"Oh I'll happily give a donation." She turned on her charm. "I know I shouldn't have come but the mystic has been such help to me," she cooed.

Gregory returned to a recumbent position on his bed but he could not recall Wicher fen and he felt wound up and cross. He cursed himself for the stupidity of giving her a line from the black book and he took his anger out on it by kicking it around his cell.

Twenty-four hours later she was back at the front of the queue. Her face was alight, she glowed, she beamed, and she could not sit still. The excitement crackled in the air and such was her innocent joy that it took away her allure for Gregory and he thought her less sexy and much plainer. She gushed with joy and Gregory had to sit and listen to her go through blow by blow the opening of the envelope, the joy of her husband and most of the subsequent phone calls to near relatives. Eventually, she began to slow down. Gregory wondered why nobody came to replace her. She must have read his thoughts. "I paid for a triple session," she said, "I hope you don't mind." Gregory relaxed.

"And the verse?" he asked.

"Yeah, great," she said, "thank you." He knew that she could not even remember it.

[F2] The Urban Mystic is unafraid to touch, savour and study the artefacts of the urban landscape.

[K2] The weather plays an important part in the life of the Urban Mystic; it is that part of primary creation and nature that intrudes most successfully into the urban landscape and by so doing influences the mood of the community.

Chapter 12

For the rest of the night she tossed deliriously whilst the purple patch on her midriff spread like a cancer. He sprinkled sea water on her neck and wrists to keep her cool but try as he might he could not persuade her to drink any water. Time and time again he poured it onto her lips but it just ran uselessly away. Through that dark night the raft tossed on the heaving seas, throwing her about and making her moan with pain. With the morning came calmness, both of her spirits and the vast ocean. When he looked out from the raft he was amazed to see a coastline within a mile of them. He took the paddle and drove it as hard as he could, working the raft to the shore. Fortunately, there was not the coral reef that the normal romantic expectations of a desert island would suggest, rather the surf washed them straight onto the beach. Greg was not sure it was even an island: they had been carried into a shallow bay and he could not tell. After dragging the raft onto the broken shell beach he carefully lifted her and carried her up towards the trees. Free now from the cooling effect of the sea, the temperature seemed to climb with every footstep he took and the stark light reflected off her pallor. Greg reasoned that it would be cooler taking her into the wood.

A narrow path carried him forward until again, to his relief, he found some running fresh water. He put her down carefully on a grassy bank by the edge of the stream and bathed her face with the cool water. She awoke at his embrace and after a moment smiled up at him. Greg kissed her tenderly on the forehead. "It is going to be OK. We will get you some help." She nodded weakly. "Let me go and get the rations in the raft." But she got hold of his hand and clutched it feebly. He dare not disengage himself so he looked down into her eyes. "I really love you - you've captured my heart." A cloud appeared on her face. Greg was about to say he was sorry for being so strong when a voice spoke behind him.

"How quaint and old-fashioned." It was Mr Kertz. Greg turned to look at him sourly.

"They were private words. We need to get her help."
"I've brought some."
"You have some medicine?"
"The best."
"Show me." From behind his back the man brought a revolver. The girl looked startled.
"I really don't mind you stirring up these young bucks at all. In fact I find it entertaining - but your soul is mine. I have always expected one hundred percent loyalty and now I find you have cheated on me." She shook her head but remained mute. Mr Kertz coolly lifted his revolver and shot her in the heart. She twitched and lay still. Greg raised his hands in horror and incomprehension. The words would not come and neither for a moment would any reaction. Mr. Kertz, with a determined look on his face, stepped right up to Greg and putting the revolver to his chest shot him twice and at close range. The blood, fired out of his back by the percussion, sprayed over the corpse of the girl and, as Greg's knees began to crumple in death, the man gave him a push so that he twisted around and fell face down on the girl's body. The man took a handkerchief from his pocket, wiped the gun meticulously, then leant down and placed it between the fingers of Greg's right hand. He stood back to admired his handiwork and with an expressionless face walked away back to the beach.

Chapter 13

[P3] The first stirrings of Urban Mysticism begin when the individual is drawn through the beginning of things, by his natural sensitivity and fascination for nature, to fall down that slope into the handiwork of the created [What humans have made]. From there he must use the newly presented hand and footholds in the steep face to draw him back to that first testimony and thus the heart of the divine spirit.

Let us pray that one day we will all be able to say with confidence that spirit has walked there before us.

The Dean would often come and check on Gregory. Occasionally he was prepared to talk and he flagged this up by pausing for a moment and drawing nearer. On one occasion Gregory postulated, "So surely it must be possible for me to simply make it up. To pretend to be a mystic." The Dean looked at Gregory quizzically for a few moments.

"You don't really believe that is possible yourself or you would not say that and warn me in advance."

"Well it's all imagination anyway. Your whole great work here." Gregory cast his hand around. "The cathedral is just a work of imagination. You are selling a service to your clients - like any entertainment. Just because you hide behind the word spiritual doesn't really make it any different."

"Now I know that you don't believe it. If you think you can do it - try. Be a made up mystic - a pretend one. Create visions for us and lie when you tell us about them. But you can't can you?   And you know that. The thing is, Gregory, you are basically too honest. That's another reason to keep you here and to encourage you to become a mystic. Credit us with some intelligence." Gregory was itching to reply but the Dean continued without a pause. "We could have had half a dozen charlatans but we wanted something authentic."

"Oh, that's rich coming from you. You who have shown a blatant lack of integrity over the way you have dealt with me - now becoming all self-righteous about getting it right. Bah!"

The Dean ignored it and went on. He seemed to derive some satisfaction from having these spats with Gregory. "I am not saying that imagination does not have a part to play in the role of the mystic. The divine spirit must have some material to work from."

"Do you have an imaginative life then?" Gregory asked with a slight sarcastic edge to his voice. The Dean's eye twinkled as he replied: he was in an indulgent mood that day.

"Of course and a very rich one. I write poetry you know." He said it in a matter of fact way. "Just like you."

"Actually, I do not write poetry. I wrote one poem - an unfortunate decision it now turns out to be. For a competition - for a book and I made it up."

"You can't rile me over that. You only need to read the poem, as we did, to see that it does relate to something real, something other."

"If you write poetry," pursued Gregory quickly, "maybe you should be the one who is in here instead of me. If that is your criteria for choosing someone for your experiment." He pursed his lips as if tasting something acidic.

"It is not an experiment because we are confident of the outcome."

"Why are you always changing back and to from I and us. Who are us? You hide behind other people when you want to convey something unpalatable."

"Of course. But you interrupted. My poetry is philosophical and not religious."

"It cannot have any integrity to it as your basic character has none."

"I am not upset by your comment you know." The Dean did not say it to get an answer.

"Shame. Do you have a fantasy life then Dean?"

"Naturally - surely most people do."

"What's it about?"

"It's private," he replied calmly but his eyes darted around the presbytery.

"Is it sexual things?" Gregory could not help himself. He

wanted to goad the man.

"Well mine is," he retorted without a blush. "What is yours like? If we are being honest with each other today. Share some of yours with me."

"You would just use it against me to prove that your twisted theory that I am mystic is true." Gregory gave a cheeky smile.

"Inevitably! But that is why I'm here - to help you to see your own vocation. Tell me?" Gregory surprised himself and did. He had always been the sort of person to keep on risking part of himself in order to make contact. He had kept trying at his work even though he was rebuffed so often.

"I make up stories. More so now that time hangs so heavy on my hands. Thanks to you." The Dean nodded in acknowledgement. "I have always wanted to write a book. I tried once - but well - the images seemed strong in my head until I try and write them down - then my language does not seem up to it."

"Practise."

Wouldn't that make that me writer in residence and not your pet mystic?"

"You know that you do not have to be so pejorative about your role here. You are not our pet mystic but our actual mystic. What genre are you stories in?"

There was a long silence as Gregory debated whether to be more open but there were questions inside himself that needed to be answered and nobody else to answer them. "Love stories." He expected to be ridiculed. Yet the Dean remained un-perturbed and sat silently waiting for him to go on. "They are not romances - they have adventures in them."

"Are you the main character in them or perhaps I should say is the main character like you?"

"It has to be doesn't it?"

"You would do well to take a writing course to help you explore...." The Dean dried up as he became aware of how stupid his suggestion seemed. "So you stories are full of sex and lust and daring do?"

"Well yes. Is it wrong to have sex in books?"

"Arr! A moral question. You cannot expect me to answer that." Gregory was exasperated.

"If I cannot ask the Dean of this religious institution a moral question who can I?"

"The individual must decide. Men and women are very different," he said ambiguously. "Most women are very naive about the determination and sexual drive in a man's imagination. Not all and we fail them as well." Gregory shook his head in despair and began to regret embarking on this conversation. "What is your present book about?"

"Well it's not a book," Gregory now denied.

"Well story. What is in that?" Gregory did not want to tell him now. He sensed that, given half a chance, the Dean would be psychoanalysing him from the fruits of his imagination.

"It is about how easy it is to kill someone and how well."

"So it's about the lack of morality in some people. How they use others like pawns?"

"Yes."

"You will not doubt derive inspiration from the way you think I treat you," he commented. From anyone else this would seem like an excuse for a minor foible. The Dean just sat still, staring at Gregory, wanting to be believed but his skin was oily and his eyes small. There was something feral and disturbing in his features.

"Maybe. There is something missing in you isn't there?" Gregory asked intently.

"Not at all. You are missing the realisation of your vocation. I already have mine." Then, he brought the conversation back immediately. "I rework my poems though - revise them until I think they are right. You should write your stories down. How can you hold all that in your head?"

"It's easy because there is nothing else there," he said sarcastically. "Where does imagination come into this mystic business? You said it would be impossible to counterfeit a mystical experience but you also said that the divine spirit used our imagination." Gregory shook his head. "This really is a ridiculous conversation. How on earth would you know?"

"Even evil people may have some wisdom. So to answer your question: it seems that the contents of your head are a bit like an artist's pallet that the divine spirit, as artist, uses to construct his visions or dreams for you. And I suppose," he continued more slowly as he thought through what he was saying, "he can add extra colours if he wants. Unusual out of the world kind of experiences.

But he must value what he has made us or we must believe that." The Dean seemed to have some doubts now.

"So you think the divine spirit is like an artist?"

"Yes."

"So when I write things like you do.... In your poems I suppose you don't just write it and then it's done you correct it and change the first draft. Like a fine artist would paint over a sketch and change things as he went along."

"Yes. What are you getting at?"

"Well, so did the divine spirit revise things he had made? Does he try things out first and then make them better? Because if he is perfect how come he gets it wrong initially?"

"Well an artist does not get it wrong the first time."

"He might draw the line in the wrong place, get the perspective wrong."

"OK but the point about being an artist is that it's to do with the process first and the work of art second."

"The satisfaction is in trying to get ...it right?"

"No that's not it. Rather in trying to define your vision, in enjoying the process and the curiosity."

"How can the divine spirit have curiosity when he is all knowing?"

"These are bare theological popular characteristics of a god - that he is omniscient for instance - but they can never describe the fullness of what it is to know everything. I can know all there is to know about paint but still enjoy playing with it, mulling over how to use it, what picture to paint. You are making him a machine."

"The divine spirit plays?"

"Why not?"

"Like you play with me?"

"He is not a torturer."

"Good word. I agree."

"Well I must go, as entertaining as this is." He was back to being condescending.

"One more thing," persisted Gregory, "can our imagination, our artistic endeavour, be prophetic?"

"I think so but that is not mystical. You cannot catch me out there. You are still trying to kid me that you think you can make up being a mystic - but it won't do. Your stories may be prophetic whether you want them to be or not. When you are not looking the divine spirit may squeeze a bit of the future onto your pallet and you mix it in without thinking. You are too much of a control freak Gregory."

"God that's rich coming from you."

"And the sex," he volunteered, "all that sex in your mind - it doesn't bar you from being a mystic. The spirit understands." The Dean grinned and went away.

"Well I've made his day," Gregory said quietly to himself. Yet it was not a pleasurable notion because he felt very bleak inside. He began to think of a story about a man who killed without compassion in order to survive.

When Gregory's list was over for the morning he picked up the black book and sat with it on his knee. If he expected that the words in it would prove to be some sort of catalyst to change people's lives it had not been very promising so far. That is what holy books are for he pondered. Turning back the cover he began to examine the pages more closely. It had obviously been a much longer book once because he could see where great swathes of pages had been ripped out and where, following that butchery, somebody had gone through systematically censoring it. Had that been the Dean? No it all looked too old for that. The missing words had been lost for some time he decided. But why would anybody need to expurgate them? On a cursory examination it looked very boring and dull. However, he supposed that in its original form it may have been more galvanising. He counted the pages, there were exactly forty-nine left out of a possible fifteen hundred he guessed. There was no narrative in it. The sentences that were left were so separated from each other as to be devoid of any continuity. They all stood or fell on their own. Gregory began to read, skipping from page to page and missing some because the sheets adhered to each other. He gave up about half way and put it down. There were about three hundred sayings left to him. Gregory shrugged, his imagination provided him with more stimulation than what was written there.

Relaxing for a moment his mind fell into an imaginative free fall, he was tired after the pilgrims and his gaze idly followed the shafts of light and the swirling specks of dust in the Presbytery. When he was busy he became less aware of the noises and smells of the Cathedral but now as he concentrated he could hear them and smell the dry mustiness of the stone work. Then almost without any effort the thought came to him that he should study the book one more time. After all he had nothing else to do. Perhaps there was some creative mind behind the choice of thoughts left to him or, even if it was purely random, then maybe the divine spirit would help him make some sense to it. In his heart he knew that if he was ever to escape then he must become a scholar of mysticism. The frightening uncertainty of each day had been replaced with a dull acquiescence in which he made little effort to rescue himself. He picked up the book again, turned to near the middle, and read:

"For there is hope for a tree,
if it is cut down, that it will sprout again,
and that its shoots will not cease.
Though its root grows old in the earth,
and its stump dies in the ground,

The first response to the words provoked a deep sigh from which he fell into a reverie. There he was back at Wicher Fen in some remote part away from the main paths, and there was an old mouldering stump with delicate green shoots sprouting from the circumference. It was cold, damp and the background to his day dream was filled with an impenetrable mist. Gregory felt happy to be there cocooned in the damp fog and at peace.

He read the lines over and over again and drank them in. He felt strange emotions in his heart. "Was this the divine spirit?" he wondered. He looked around his cell nothing else had changed. The noises and the smells continued. Maybe it was just a kind of resonance to what the original writer had inscribed. Surely if he had the previous and following verse it would make more sense, or even less, simply robbing him of any significance he felt it had to his situation. He tried to push it from his conscious mind but the words so haunted him for the rest of the day that he could not even bear to read another word, so sated was he by this comforting image. The pericope had given him a smidgen of hope.

```
[Q3] The Urban Mystic finds himself drawn
to water. He finds it comforting and
reassuring. Water speaks eloquently for the
divine spirit.
```

[S3] It is a wonderful experience for the Urban Mystic when the urban and nature collude together to form something beautiful: she sees in the wonderful view that presents itself an image of comeliness and a feeling of redemption. By contrast, where there is no sympathy in the urban landscape between human organisation and nature, then such environments can become soulless and destructive, robbing the community of hope and a sense of the numinous.

[T3] Smell is a powerful stimulus. It is possible to smell health and beauty or to smell corruption. Many urban environments are cancerous in reality, because they cause real cancers and because they do not multiply cleanly or evenly. Rather than splitting into good cells to repair or recreate they produce monstrous things like sickness, hopelessness and spiritual disease among those who live there.

Chapter 14

Little came one evening and brought him a bag of sweets. He determined not to eat them all at once this time but to savour them.

He told her about his pregnant woman but she had already heard. It was the talk of the Cathedral she told him. "Everybody is really excited, they are congratulating my dad, as having done something special for the Cathedral."

"It was ever thus," said Gregory, "nobody ever gets the kudos for their work. Actually, I don't think it had anything to do with me."

"That doesn't matter," Little told him, "as long as they think it has, it will improve your chances."

"Don't any of the other staff think it wrong that I am kept a prisoner here?"

"Some do - but they are too afraid to say. Getting work is very difficult and, with the economic situation, people have enough suffering in their own lives to want to stick their necks out for somebody else."

"But they know it's wrong?"

"Well not exactly, dad has told them that you are an ex-mental patient with special powers. That is how he accounted for all the noise you made at first. He has told them that you are perfectly safe as long as you are in your cell but that if you were to escape you would be very dangerous."

"The best lies have some truth in them," observed Gregory. "Have you tried to tell the other staff the truth?"

She hung her head down a bit. "I have tried - but then I am already considered a bit odd - because in the past I have not been well myself. I was at university for a while before I had a breakdown and well - nothing can be kept secret in a community like this. So I am seen as a bit of a case anyway - they expect me to take your side and they treat everything I say with a pinch of salt."

"I am sorry. Are you better now?" He meant, "Are you quite well now?"

"It wasn't really an illness, it was a readjustment of my life. Unfortunately, I didn't have much confidence to return to my studies."

"Oh dear." She looked so small and vulnerable sitting there in front of him that he longed to take her in his arms and hold her. It was torture to think of her soft body and not to be able to touch it. In with those sexual feelings there was much more - something primitive, something that made him want to merge himself completely with her. In his blood a powerful convection current of heat created the magnetism of an attraction between them that none would be able to separate if they could only be together.

"Too late now."

"Surely not."

"In the light of today's news, probably."

"Why what has happened?"

"Your miracle only just topped the chart in gossip today. It's the referendum. The vote was, yes, by a slight margin - there are to be City States. Dad's over the moon about it. It is going to strengthen his hand completely and his plans for the Cathedral."

"What will it mean?"

"Well it means we will have no university within the boundary of our City State - which was why I said earlier - anyway - our local government will be based here in St. Arburn's and the regiment at Sylbent will become our militia. It is a light infantry one, which they say is a real bonus."

"Surely, as a nation, we will need our troops to work together?"

"You would think so and - still lots of details to be worked out. The old Corn exchange over the road will become the parliament building. Work has begun on that already. Some people were very confident."

"Will it make any difference to me in my little cell here?"

She reached in to his cell and he gave her his hand. It felt cool in the fever of his own. "I hope so for your sake."

"Do you feel sorry for me?"

"Not sorry as in, you are a pathetic specimen, for I believe you are a strong character, rather I hate seeing you in here."

"I hate seeing you out there," he said flippantly.

"What do you mean?"

"I mean it would be nice to have you in here with me." She blushed. "Sorry I've embarrassed you." He wanted to back-pedal. He was worried she would think he was declaring his undying love or that he only wanted her sexually.

"No, it's all right I know what you mean," and she raised her eyebrow which confused him completely and puzzled him for days as to what she had meant.

He changed the subject, "Did you know that your dad has given me the black book?"

"Well I sort of guessed - I noticed that it had gone from the glass case in the Cathedral library."

"Precious is it then?"

"The Cathedral holds it with a kind of sentimental value as something from a previous age."

"There is not much of it left." Gregory fetched the book and held it out to her. She took it gingerly and, putting it on her knee, flipped through some of the pages.

"I see what you mean. It's a wreck of a book. Anyway you may find some use in it."

"I wish I could have other books."

"Very forbidden I'm afraid. I dare not give you one lest you be punished. They want you to keep you mind clear for the communication with the divine spirit," She said it in a mock spooky voice. He laughed. She turned again to the book and was about to shut it when something caught her attention. Here is a bit for you. She began to read it out:

> *'For there is hope for a tree,*
> *if it is cut down, that it will sprout again,*
> *and that its shoots will not cease.'*

And he completed it for her,

> *'Though its root grows old in the earth,*
> *and its stump dies in the ground,'*

He felt the hairs stand up on the back of his neck. He must have looked strange because she stared at his face.

"Is something wrong?"

"It is quite bizarre - spooky even. I felt somebody walked over my grave then. You see I read that section this morning and it felt noteworthy - the words have been buzzing around my head ever since."

"I have read about that," she said. "There is a book on medieval mysticism in the library. It's what happens. Incredible."

"Is it the divine spirit then?"

"It could be. Wouldn't that really be great if she started to talk to you."

"Scary!" They continued to chat and ruminate on this strange occurrence.

In the morning the Dean came early and launched into a speech straight away. "Great news. Splendid about the miracle. A real fillip for everyone at the Cathedral and a confirmation of bringing you here." Gregory could not be bothered to contradict him.

"I heard that you have said that I am a dangerous lunatic." The Dean looked puzzled.

"It's true - you acted really mad when you first arrived."

"Well," spluttered Gregory, "and so would have you done so if the same had happened to you."

"I would not," the Dean said petulantly. "Anyway I cannot be bothered to get into that again. Little tells me that you have heard about the referendum. That is also great news for us, it will increase the influence of the Cathedral tenfold."

"You mean your influence." The Dean put his head to one side like a wise owl.

"It is going to make changes for us. It looks as though they are going to use part of the old monastery at first for the assembly. The old monk's dormitory. And I am going to be given a seat." If he expected Gregory to be pleased then he was disappointed. Gregory scoffed.

"They want a lying kidnapper to govern them and advise them on welfare policies. How bloody stupid! You stupid, stupid man!" He could easily have begun screaming if he had let himself go. "Why do you come and tell me such stuff?" The Dean began to colour and get angry.

"I try to be kind to you and involve you in these great matters and you continually act in childish ways. I am not going to debate it with you. Our new president is coming to see you and I demand that you treat him with respect or there will be consequences. Do you understand?" Gregory got up from his chair and turned to the other wall of his cell. After a few moments he turned back and the Dean was gone.

After pacing disconsolately around his cell for a few minutes he threw himself heavily on his bed. Gregory let his mind rove freely

and chuckled quietly at the bizarre images his mind through up; it was an absence of television and other stimulation that was bringing on these weird pictorial thoughts. Even the stories or 'thinks' as he had always called them since childhood were becoming more compulsive and detailed. Huge chunks of images continually broke from his subconscious and rose to the surface of his mind. His conscious was becoming lean and hungry for ideas. He picked up his book again and handled it gingerly. Gregory turned too that special verse he had noticed the day before and, as he read it again, another tingle went up his spine. He wasn't frightened by it. Some kindly spirit was affecting him. That was a good word he thought kindly. He certainly needed that where he was now in the cell. Was that the divine spirit? Was that the God he was being forced to seek? If so then maybe it was trying to get in touch with him. He let the verse rest in his mind, like you would some nice titbit of food that you wanted to savour. He thought through the picture in his mind. A tree being cut down, he let his mind wander onto how the trunk was used for wood, furniture or building a house - even this Cathedral. As in a newsreel he watched the stump ooze sap and go green with moss in the autumnal weather, then the seasons speeded up in his mind until it was spring again and finally bending down he saw the first green shoots appearing around the ragged edge of the stump. This was to be him, always wounded - even if one of these new shoots would survive it would always look distorted by its unnatural position on the side of the old trunk. And then he thought of the monstrous roots underground. As large as the old tree they had supported, drawing all of that nourishment from the earth, and like a restricted ejaculation straining to shoot that vitality once more into the air. There was wonderful fecundity about the images that he could not deny. He sighed with the thought of them. They were comforting and hopeful. Then a little doubt crept in and he remonstrated with himself for being so soft. Within seconds his mood had turned to anger and depression that he should be placing such reliance on a few physical manifestations and the words of an old mutilated book.
Notwithstanding his feelings the words would not go and he relaxed again as he let the image cheer him. Are there others he wondered? He flicked through the pages dipping in here and there. Some of the sayings were totally obscure and left him cold. He noticed that he was trying to gauge whether a verse made sense by the physical

effect it had on him like the first one had. Gregory was about to give it up as a fruitless exercise when he read:

> 'Listen to me, you who know righteousness,
>   you people who have my teaching in your hearts;
>   do not fear the reproach of others,
>   and do not be dismayed when they revile you.'

This produced a similar tingling affect. It was not that he knew what it meant. In fact he could not really relate to it at all accept the last clause. He felt reviled and if this gave him the hope that he craved to survive then that was to the good.

He went to his bathroom and, after his evening ablutions lay down on his pallet. The evenings were drawing in and he was going to bed earlier.

Chapter 15

On Tuesday evening, as he lay quietly fidgeting in his bed, in preparation for sleep, he made the decision to create a place of safety for himself. He resolved that if he could only absent himself from his present difficult life, that grated so much on him, by imagining a sanctuary he would cope better. Where would he go? In his mind he constructed a gate and walked through it. From there he strolled through a wildflower meadow and down to the coast. The sea was shushing in the distance. A path took him down the cliff face to and an enclosed estuary. In the distance, where the huge oceanic rollers crashed onto the shore, a golden beach stretched in either direction from the estuary mouth. A narrow spit constricted the mouth of the estuary and calmed the water that rushed into it. In front of him was another private beach of sharp sand and, nestling under the cliffs, a wooden bunk house. He sauntered slowly past it and beyond. Off to one side and, behind the cottage, was the entrance to a steep valley which had been hidden from the meadow field above. Water cascaded from it over a low waterfall and beside it a path led into the comparative gloom. He would explore that tomorrow. On returning to the cottage, he found an old cushioned swing chair on the balcony. He sat down and pushed himself to and fro. Gregory had not swung there long when a giraffe came around the corner of the hut and came right up to him, looking down to watch him over the guard rail at the front of the balcony. It looked old and it was breathing heavily as though after some exertion. He had never really been very fond of animals, never even owning a dog. This made him generally wary of any contact with any creature yet at that moment he felt uncharacteristically serene. There was something companionable about the giraffe. It looked dolefully at him for a while and then turned its head to look over its shoulder. There were sounds off, as though someone or something else was coming. It sounded large, but Gregory was filled with a new tranquillity and could not be bothered to stir to look. When it arrived, would be soon enough and there was no fear in him. He felt no surprise in himself when it turned out to be a rhinoceros. The giraffe had not turned from looking over its shoulder. "About time," the giraffe said to the rhinoceros. "I told you he had come. Go back and tell the others to hurry up." The giraffe rotated her long neck back to face Gregory. "Hello Gregory," it said to him. We are pleased you have come."

```
    [Y3] When a warm river goes through a
cold gorge it begins to steam in a most
amazing way. What a lovely sight to see the
river steaming gently as though it is boiling
and bubbling. Then the Urban Mystic turns on
the boardwalk and sees a cold stream running
out from a dark cleft and wonders what its
origin is?

    [Z3]. Will a tree that lives in a dark
cold damp gorge be any less happy that a tree
that lives a life in a sunlit valley?
    What of Self-pity and the Urban Mystic?
There will be times when the Urban Mystic
feels condemned by God to a miserable
existence when other of his fellow religious
spend their lives in the sunshine.
```

The next day the pilgrims were to be cancelled an aide came to tell Gregory. He felt disappointed at the news. "Why?" he asked. The aide shrugged. "Is it the President?" Gregory asked.

In losing control of his life in this way Gregory felt a new kind of freedom beckoned him. "The man who has no expectations - he cannot be disappointed," he told himself in a Chinese Confucius kind of voice.

It was indeed the President.

Gregory sensed his appearance before it happened; there was kind of hush in the Cathedral and then he was there in front of him. Gregory had half expected a fanfare or a round of applause - nothing - only that momentary stillness, almost as though the building itself had held its breath. Maybe the fabric was responding to the kind of man he was: perhaps it remembered other such men from its long history. The Dean was at the President's right shoulder.

"So this is your specimen," the President announced. "Come nearer - you need not be afraid." Gregory was not afraid, but he was mesmerised. In front of him stood a huge man in a small body. The Dean, who was only just above average height, came a head and foot above him, yet it was the Dean who was dwarfed.

The Dean was oily and ingratiating. "Yes your uhmmm. Yes, President - our very own mystic and proving already to be very successful. Maybe you read in the paper."

"Are you a mystic?" the President cut across the babble and addressed himself directly to Gregory.

"They say I am," he replied quietly.

"But you now believe you are too. Don't you," he noted perceptively. Gregory did not answer. Previously he would have felt intimated by such a man: full of arrogant confidence. But now he felt indifferent. What intrigued him more was the Dean's deference. He was finding it hard to grasp how the Dean could have been so cruel to him when, now in the face of a greater power, he seemed incompetent and weak. Maybe that is the nature of some evil, Gregory mused. By contrast the President was much more of a force. His features were sharp, like his mind Gregory suspected. He would be logical and merciless if he needed to be. And strangely for a politician, he would not lie - there would be no need. Perhaps he was an anti-mystic. "It is a shame you are locked in there. I could use someone like you."

"Get me out then," Gregory challenged him. "You know that I am held here against my will."

"Of course. All of us who have a part to play are as well." It would have sounded melodramatic and trite coming from another person but the President carried it off with suitable gravitas. "When you are free come and find me and I will reveal to you something better." He stepped forward and looked intently into Gregory's face. "You know better than to oppose me. Even the Dean will not be able to protect you if you try it." The Dean looked perturbed by this conversation Gregory could see that it had taken a completely unexpected turn to how he must have imagined it. There was not a pat on the back for him. A sinister and dark gloom hung in the air.

"*do not fear the reproach of others,*
and do not be dismayed when they revile you." said Gregory. The President listened and turned to the Dean.

"You know that these writings are forbidden?"

"Well yes - but uhmm he is not going anywhere."

"We may have to take them from him," the President said to himself.

"The kindly spirit will protect me," Gregory added. The words were as much as a surprise to him. A moment of madness and daring. He did not know exactly what it meant but he knew that if he did not counter the president's threat here in the moment, in the same air, within the walls of the Cathedral, the threat would eat away at him and cause endless anxiety. The President looked thoughtful, an expression of unease flitted past his eyes. He was discomfited by the words and clearly not used to anyone brooking his own.

"This is a dangerous man Dean and you are clearly stupid to have unleashed him on us. You were right to single him out - there is something about him - but keep him closely guarded."

"Should I get rid of him do you think," the Dean whined.

"Not yet. It will remind us both that the church and the state are duty bound to have an uneasy alliance and that we should expect at least one turbulent mystic in our midst. I am sure there will be no trouble, Dean, after all it is a personal favour of mine that we have secured a seat for you on the council." They were wandering away as they spoke. The Dean dipped deferentially to the President and said something that could not be heard. As they were moving away Gregory caught sight of a small colour party or something like, almost out of his vision. They were armed.

Gregory felt raw. It was as though he and the President had recognised each other on a deeper than visual level. They had made each other self-conscious and, despite Gregory's bravado at the time, he now felt very shaky. He wasn't alone long when Little sidled up. "What did he say? What did he say?" she asked.

"Well I don't know how to interpret it." So he told her what he could remember.

"How bizarre," she said. She was looking at him strangely.

"What does it mean?" he asked her.

"I think it means that the divine spirit is drawing near again. We may well need him," she observed.

"What is going on out there?"

"Things are moving fast. Central government has collapsed almost straight away and everything is just separating on geographical lines. I told you there was no university well - there is going to be one apparently."

"Don't tell me - here at the Cathedral! I will teach degrees in mysticism."

"Wrong this time. It is going to be at the old grammar school building on the other side of the city."

"Phew. Why is your dad in such awe of the President?"

"They were at school together." Gregory expected her to go on but she changed the subject and showed him her elbow which was covered in a big bruise. He offered to kiss it better and she let him. He took her hand in his then, drawing it carefully through the window and turning her arm gently, he kissed the bruise. She winced slightly but did not withdraw her hand and so he held it and stroked it gently. "That's nice," she said.

They were interrupted by the return of the Dean. He was bustling and fussy. Gregory could not help notice a kind of disintegration in him, a certain fall in confidence. In himself he felt stronger and he wondered how to capitalise on it. "Don't irritate the President again. He could have had you got rid of. And I mean got rid of," began the Dean.

"Don't talk like that dad," interjected Little.

"Go away," he commanded, "now."

"Don't talk to her like that," Gregory retorted.

"Go away." Little went but when the Dean turned back to Gregory she turned and winked at him. Gregory grinned. "As I was saying the President wanted me to get rid of you and that doesn't mean letting you go. He thinks you could be subversive."

"Well that's your fault if that's what I have become. You have subjected me to a level of adversity that has made me react like this. Don't threaten me. Don't threaten me! I heard the President tell you not to get rid of me. It sounded to me like he has become my protector and not my enemy as you would have it." The Dean was drawing near and going red in the face. "You were kow-towing to him like some lap dog. Where has the great master plan of the church running things gone? And it being at the centre of things again?" Gregory was not prepared for the blow. The Dean hit him square in his right eye and sent him sprawling back into the cell where he fell onto his blankets.

"Don't ever speak to me like that again," said the Dean and walked away. Gregory lay there feeling dizzy and sick but with a grim satisfaction: he had got to him.

[B4] The Urban Mystic realises that he is the final product in himself of his own search into Urban Mysticism.

Chapter 16

On the next Sunday Gregory noticed a change in the procession that came into the Presbytery. It now included a colour party carrying a flag he did not recognise but assumed was the colours of their new City State. They were laid reverently against the reredos and then collected at the end of the service. The service included a talk or sermon for the first time or that was what he assumed it was but he could not hear it distinctly enough from his cell to make any sense of it.

The following day he noticed that the male attendant, who ushered the pilgrims to see him was, wearing a new uniform. That evening he asked Little about these changes. She confirmed it was a military uniform. "Our new government," she rolled her eyes slightly, "has decreed that any former soldier can wear a uniform commensurate with their old final rank. It has immediately become a prestige thing - old soldiers never think they have been valued enough - so they are all rushing out to buy one. It has resurrected our ailing clothes industry," she said ironically. "And the funniest thing." She looked around before she spoke, "is Bailey. Apparently he was a sergeant or something and he is now wearing a uniform to work. Dad is furious and has told him to take it off. He wants people to wear the new Cathedral colours which he is organising. But Bailey is being stubborn and is implying that dad is jealous because he can't wear one. Dad was still at college during the disturbance before the Great Eclectic." Gregory shook his head he could not imagine Bailey saying anything. He was just pleased that the man was keeping out of his way. Whenever he saw him it still made him go cold.

Little and Gregory had fallen into a companionable pattern. She would generally pop and see him for five minutes at lunch time and, if her dad was away, she would come and bring food for them both to eat in the Presbytery together. Then she would call briefly after work and finally, come often for an hour in the evening. The most wonderful part was that if she were not able to come she would tell him what she was doing. Gregory found this comforting and he took it as a sign of the measure of their growing relationship.

Two days before he had asked her rather nervously if he

could kiss her good night and she had agreed. It was very dispassionate - a simple peck on the cheek that she presented to him - it would have to suffice for his lack of opportunity to walk her home. Occasionally, she would let him hold her hand. Nevertheless, he sensed that she was still holding back and he guessed that she thought that his interest was simply cupboard love. If he was not imprisoned maybe he would have no interest in her. "Maybe I wouldn't," he thought.

On the Tuesday Mercy came to see him during the late afternoon. He had not seen her for some time. She was smartly and modestly dressed. He noticed that she had a lovely figure and felt that she looked far sexier than when she had displayed herself more obviously. "I have been for an interview," she told him. She had brought a chair with her and plonked herself down right by his window. Her elbow rested on one of the cross beams. She had no fear of him at all which was pleasing.

"Oh what for?" She seemed quite dreamy and sleepy and that coincided with his mood. "With the new government - just a secretary." There was a pause before he spoke for there did not seem to be any rush.

"Did you get it?"

"I don't know - they were interviewing a lot of people. I think such a job would be like gold dust - they are paying more that other people. Even some of the Cathedral staff are applying. Dad is wrot." Gregory guessed at the meaning of the word.

"It doesn't seem as though this is going according to your dad's plans," he hazarded.

"No you are right. I think he is quite worried about it. He keeps wittering on about it at meal times. He seemed to think that when we got our local government, the Cathedral would be drawn back into the centre of things, like it was many centuries ago. But actually he thinks the government," she lowered her voice here, "is full of bully boys, the worst sort of people with no spirituality."

"Why did you lower your voice?" he asked.

"You don't know who is listening," she said casually.

"Are people becoming afraid?"

"There have been rumours of arrests," she answered.

"So soon," he muttered to himself.

"They can't arrest you," she said cruelly, there was an edge to her tongue. "You are banged up already." Gregory had been puzzled by this newly nice Mercy and was now partly relieved that it was only a veneer.

"So is it not a good thing what has happened?"

"I don't know much of history," she observed, "but won't the Cathedral just end up having to oppose the bad things in government like it always used to do in the past?" Gregory nodded more sagely that he felt.

"Is your dad up to that?" She laughed.

"No he's as soft as butter."

"He's cruel though."

"Oh you mean to you? No you are the best thing that has happened to this Cathedral." This truly was a complement. He would have asked for more but, aware she had been too warm, she concluded nastily, "You tosser."

"Did you come for a reason?" he asked sharply.

"No, I'm bored."

"Why do you behave like this? You are not a young teenager anymore."

"Hark who's talking. You're not the most emotionally stable person I know. I heard all that screaming when you first came." It was useless to point out to her that anyone of any degree of maturity would have made a fuss about being kidnapped.

"No I was thinking more about the other things."

"Yeah?"

"The sleeping around - if it was true."

"Of course it's true. I like sex why shouldn't I? Is this a come-on?"

No...errr, no this is me trying to be kind. I mean well errm." He blurted it out, "If you make it too easy - some men - not all - will take advantage of that and say they care when really all they want is you." She sat silently for a while. No screaming. No calling for Bailey and his cattle-prod this time.

"So what do I do?"

"Have more respect for yourself."

"I don't have any respect."

"Did something happen to you to make it go?"

"What do you mean?"

"An event when you were younger." He could not help

himself, he desperately wanted to find that her dad, the Dean, had abused her. He knew he was being simplistic and crude, and not really thinking of her, for he wanted to pay the Dean back.

"Did someone molest me - like a family friend or an uncle? No. I would remember surely."

"I read that sometimes people's minds blank out traumas." Gregory was finding it hard to say even though he wanted to press his point home. "Maybe your dad." She looked up sharply and stared at him. "I mean your dad - I saw him pat you on the bottom." He was struggling. She laughed.

"You really are a pervert aren't you? Trapped here in this little cage with all your sexual frustrations, thinking dirty thoughts about me and Little I expect." Gregory was shocked at her words. He did not want anyone to think about him in that way. "Well you are barking up the wrong tree you sad little man. Sicko," she tortured him. "Never, my dad has never touched me inappropriately. He likes his ladies though. I bet he had even had an affair. Which is more than you'll ever have. No you are not going to psychoanalyse me into child abuse. Try again." She was calming down.

"Maybe you are doing it to hurt someone?"

"Like who? No let me guess my dad!" She thought for a moment.

"Or the divine spirit for taking your mum."

"Leave my mum out of this." He moved his chair back.

"You are certainly hurting yourself." Gregory sat quiet, he had no more to say. The silence went on and on.

She sighed. "Whatever it is - I want to stop," she said plaintively.

"Yeah," he agreed.

"Will anyone help me?"

"I don't know - I will try if you want."

"But you are sad and dismal yourself."

"I know, but I bet I am the only one who has offered."

"True."

There was bustle behind her and Little appeared crying. Gregory stood up. "What's happened?" he asked urgently. Little went straight to Mercy who rose from her seat and put her arms around her. A pang went through Gregory's heart - it ought to be he who was comforting her. He grabbed his window frame and rattled it in frustration. Through the sobs she began to speak.

"It's Bailey he has been really horrible to me. It's cos he is wearing this uniform now, it has gone to his head. He said something obscene to me. I'm not going to repeat it because it was disgusting." She looked up towards Gregory. "He said that he would fuck me before you got the chance to and that he would make sure that you never have me." She cried again. Mercy made soothing noises and Gregory raged. He began to shout calling Bailey's name but Mercy and Little shushed him.

"Don't let him get to you," they pleaded, "it will only make it worse." When they had calmed down a little Mercy suggested that she take Little straight to her dad and report Bailey. As this seemed the best short term plan they departed. It sunk Gregory into a profound gloom. He did not see anybody until the next day after a sleepless night of worry. However, he reasoned with himself, that as he was part of a community that was lawless at its root, as shown by his own kidnap, then he could have small confidence that it would not condone other bad things. He felt sick to his heart.

Surprisingly it was Mercy who returned the next morning. She looked fairly riled. Positively, she reported that her dad had said that he would deal with it, but he had been quite off hand about it, putting it down as no more than talk or bravado, without any real substance to the threat. Little had gone to work. It was clear, as she spoke, that Mercy was outraged by what had happened and a steely glare came into her eye at further mention of Bailey. She observed that he had been becoming too powerful of late anyway and that her Dad had trouble controlling him. "But I will get him," she continued, "don't you worry."

"Please do not make it any worse," Gregory pleaded with her.

"Some things always get worse, however conciliatory you try to be," she observed with a wisdom Gregory had not previously seen in her.

Following closely on her heals was the Dean himself.

"I have dealt with Bailey," he began, "Little should not have any more trouble. However, you would be best not to pursue this thing with Little anyway."

"Let me get this right," said Gregory. "It is sorted but it is not sorted. You have reprimanded Bailey but we still need to be careful so as not to make him jealous. That does not sound as though you have dealt with it. If we now need to modify our behaviour - it becomes a loss of freedom. A bit like being banged up in here. But then you are good at that." The Dean ignored the jibe. "Is there any reason why Bailey should think that he had any chance with Little?" There was a long silence, the question had discomfited the Dean. He looked as though he had an unpleasant memory.

"Not at all," he murmured eventually, implausibly. He was looking at Gregory - he could see he was not believed. "So," he added, "when Little had her breakdown and came home from University, Bailey was very kind to her and attentive. He must expect some return on his investment."

"This is your daughter you are talking about," Gregory pursued.

"Yes, indeed - and she will be protected. If it happens again I will dismiss Bailey. I still have that power over him." Again he did not sound so sure.

"So no other reason why Bailey might think he had a claim on Little?"

"None," said the Dean quickly and firmly. Gregory was not convinced.

"Things going badly are they?" he tried another tack.

"What do you mean?"

"Well this City State business - the state is not going to be as amenable to interference from the Cathedral as you hope."

"You do speak nonsense. Maybe we should allow you some news instead of the snippets you pick up from Little. She does not have a full understanding of the situation. Everything is going according to plan. The council has started to meet here in the Cathedral. We have made some room in our office block for some of them until the Corn Exchange is ready. I am on the council and the President has been very attentive."

"It didn't look like it to me. The President seemed very forceful and a bit barmy." The word 'barmy' seemed to echo around the Presbytery before it escaped into the Choir. Although Gregory had not said it very loudly, by the effect it had on the Dean, it seemed to take on a life of its own. The Dean cringed and turned pale. He seemed to have trouble speaking for a moment. Gregory said it again quietly for effect, "Barmy!" and then he stepped back rather than be punched a second time.

"My dear boy you must be very careful about what you say of our new leader."

"What for?

"It could be considered seditious."

"I expect they would lock me up and throw away the key," noted Gregory flippantly, "or put me in the control of a religious madman and his evil rapist henchman." The Dean was having trouble breathing.

"No - no - no," he said. "You could be in real danger." There was the smallest glimpse that the Dean had some concerns for him - Gregory - and this calmed him down.

"So things are bad then?"

"Noo, noo just a period of settling in. Everybody is a bit stressed by the new order of things and feathers can be ruffled very easily." The Dean began to recompose himself. "Anyway I am not here to discuss politics with you but to tell you of some more great news for the Cathedral and for you as well. Actually this has come about because of you. The baby you made!"

"Don't be ridiculous, I didn't make a baby." Gregory shook his head in disbelief; his beard and hair were now long enough to shake. Behind the whiskers his face was sharper with stress and loss of weight but his eyes were more luminous. The Dean could not help being held by them and he refused to be locked in their gaze more and more.

"Well the miracle of restored fertility. It's in all the remaining national newspapers today and I think that the TV might be coming to see you even. Anyway, it has created an amazing amount of interest around the country and I have had calls from other colleagues - Deans in other cathedrals. The one from Persfeld, our neighbouring Diocese, wants to come and meet you. They are very keen. I have cancelled your pilgrims for tomorrow morning. There will be a bit of pomp but you must not worry about that. Our President wants to show you off apparently."

"So they are going to get me out of my box?"

"Of course not, that would destroy your mystery."

"You do know that I am not a mystic yet don't you?"

"Well you are getting there. That is the main thing."

"You do not seem afraid that I will say the wrong thing."

"No I detect you have changed and submitted to your role in

life." Gregory said nothing. There was some truth in it.

"I want to preach a sermon soon," he said. "I have things to say."

"What sort of things?" Perspiration came to the forehead of the Dean. "Mystical things." The Dean relaxed. "Prophetic things." The Dean twitched. "Maybe even political things."

"Impossible!" the Dean ejaculated. "You must show me what you are going to say first." Gregory scowled. "It happens to us all. You will have to have it passed by me and even maybe the censor."

"You are joking surely?"

"No!"

"Does anybody check your sermons or talks?" Of course not. He was lying. They were gagging him. "I will speak only what the divine spirit tells me to," said Gregory grandly. "Or you will let me go." The Dean sighed. Bailey appeared behind him. Before the Dean turned to look at his officer Bailey made an obscene gesture that only Gregory could see. As Gregory's lip turned to a snarl the Dean spun around.

"Bailey away with you." He shooed him away and Bailey went meekly with the Dean trailing behind him.

That evening Little told Gregory that she felt frightened. She had trouble putting it into words. He held her hand for about an hour as she tried to make sense of the nameless dread that she felt. It was a mixture of Bailey's threats, all the changes that the City State was bringing but also a new sense of the frailty of her father, whom she had both hated and relied upon. Gregory listened stoically. Her fears hooked up his own: his own perception of security, given by virtue of his imprisonment, had been threatened by the Dean's warnings that he might not be safe even in his cell.

After pouring her heart out Little realised that she had upset Gregory and so to calm him asked "What sort of childhood did you have?" She would have preferred him to ask about her own but it would have been against her nature to be so pushy. Even so, she longed for him to take such an interest. However, his eyes gleamed at her question and he looked pleased. She derived pleasure from knowing that she was doing a good thing for him. They were sitting as close as they could, save actually touching the barrier between them and its cold stone touch.

"I had a happy childhood - but a lonely one. I have a sister, yet by the time I began to pay her any attention she had married and moved away. My parents were not great travellers so we didn't seem to visit often or I don't remember so. They were old compared to most people's parents. I must have been an afterthought or a mistake." Little kept a steady eye contact on him as he spoke but Gregory's eyes flitted here and there seeming to lose focus as he thought and spoke.

"What about you?"

"No, not the same - mum and dad has us young and close together. Mercy and I were always great friends - inseparable always playing together."

"I had nobody to play with," Gregory interrupted her. I was very solitary not that that seemed to matter. Good preparation eh?" She smiled. he put his hand on the sill of the aperture but she did not take it immediately.

"Where you a spiritual little boy?"

"Was I mystical? Still don't know what that means. I certainly had a love for nature. We had a big garden and I had lots of dens in it. It used to drive my dad crazy when he had to find me to call me in for a meal. I am not aware of anything other out there but I wasn't lonely. Whether I was comfortable with my own company, or whether there was a presence with me that made it OK I couldn't say. I wrote some prayers once for school and got an A. Most people would consider that I had a very uneventful life. I had one best friend at school - but it was only at school - we never saw each other in the week. Well, not until we were teenagers but he got married young and we drifted apart. Then my mum became ill and dad didn't cope and I got stuck at home. I wanted to go to university. Got the grades." Now she took his hand from its resting place and gave it a squeeze.

"You were very kind."

"It did not feel like kindness. When I look back on it now it looks like cowardice. I should have been tougher. My parents urged me to go but I didn't and they were grateful. I feel stupid." He sighed. She stroked the back of his hand with her free one.

"You have been a good son, a better son than I have been a daughter. You are a sensitive person. It's not an illness. The world needs people like you - priests, prophets. I wouldn't like you if you were a warrior. You know what I mean - you are a warrior... in your own field. Those other people, the ones you feel have it altogether, would not have survived in there. You have internal resources, an ability to nurture yourself. You mustn't be hard on yourself.

"No spirituality though, none to enable me to deliver what your dad wants to get me out of here."

"Not yet. You are willing to reach out to the spirit. I know you are. If he is there - and wants to - he will respond - you cannot make him. It is not possible for you to wish yourself to be a mystic."

"And you," Gregory turned and returned the compliment.

"I was sent to the cathedral after-school club for kids."

"Good?"

"Hated it." As she spoke she looked down and Gregory's eyes came to rest on hers. He still found it hard to meet her gaze.

"Did you get to write prayers?"

"Not formal ones, we had times of communication though. Silent sitting, waiting, meditating. Anything nothing."

"Is your dad the only one who actually believes in the spirit?"

"No. Do you?" He hesitated.

"Yes, can't say why, but yes."

"Me too."

"That will have to be enough then, for now. I'm still anxious. It goes around in my mind. There ought to be something there from my past. It cannot just be a gift for the now. If the divine spirit were to use me for mysticism he would have been preparing me all this time. Surely?"

"There was your innocence."

"Oh yeah." He did not dare tell her how his mind oscillated from shame to pleasure over the sewer like nature of his own indulgent thoughts.

"Yes. The best preparation. But hush now! Put it down for the moment. You don't need to concentrate on it all the time. But HUSH!" When she said it for the second time her hand went to his lips to stop him saying anything more. He caught her hand and kept it pressed to his lips for a few moments before sliding it around to his cheek where he nestled it for a while. She put her other hand on to his head and stroked his hair. He fell silent and still.

When it was time for Little to go they had a stony hug through the bars of his cage and a lingering kiss.

As he lay down on his mattress he went immediately to his safe place. He walked down to the cove across the meadow and to his log hut. Although the outside of his hut was primitive the inside was now quite different. A huge built-in wardrobe had appeared and even as he spun around to examine the contents new things continually presented themselves to his sight. A bathroom materialised.

Going into the bathroom he found all he needed for a shave inside a small cupboard . Everything was new and he judged to be expensive. He calmly ran the hot water and shaved leisurely. When he had finished patting his skin with an oily lotion, he turned and ran the bath. It was all very peaceful and the unguent he had found to perfume the water filled the space with wonderful scents and tones of colour. After drying himself he went to explore the wardrobe. The comparatively small doors belied its size for when he opened them he discovered he could walk in. It was more of a room than a cupboard and he selected a woollen suite, shirt and tie with matching black shoes. He dressed slowly savouring the feelings of the new and expensive clothes. Later he went outside and sat under the porch on the veranda at a large wooden table. The air was warm and balmy with the sweet scent of the neighbouring pine wood fighting with the residue of his bath scent. There was a cool beer on the table and he took a sip automatically. Then he reached in his jacket pocket pulled out a gold cigarette case and lighter and undertook the ritual of smoking. He felt entirely content and began to wonder where the animals had disappeared to. As he looked down the creek he could see the disturbance from the large waves as they were caught and subdued by the narrow entrance to his private harbour. In the far distance there were black clouds and distinct ocean breakers but he knew that it was not going to rain where he was.

The rhinoceros came first and put its head on the coral fence around the veranda. It breathed heavily but said nothing. He had heard the crashing noises and its heavy breathing for some time before it appeared. Then other noises followed and the zebra arrived. "You should tell us when you are coming," it said "and we would wait for you." Gregory could not be bothered to ask how he should communicate that. The rhinoceros sniffed at the curling cigarette smoke. Finally other creatures appeared including what appeared to be a jackal, it was quite smelly and when it came and put its muzzle on his knee it dribbled onto his trousers. He patted it absently on the head and like all canine creatures it immediately tried to shove its damp nose into the palm of his hand. The animals stared expectantly at him waiting for a reply of some sort.

"I am really pleased you have all come," he said at last to this. They reacted very positively making both animal and human noises before they, apart from the zebra which remained to stare and teach, dispersed around the lagoon edge into the growing gloom. Gregory felt so relaxed, almost dozing off, that he let the zebra talk on. It told him of the geography of this strange land and most importantly suggested he might like to sail round to the next cove and enjoy the beach there. Gregory thanked him kindly and retired to bed.

When he woke the next day there was an assortment of small animals quietly contemplating him. When he got out of bed they parted to let him past. He tried to put them at their ease and he spoke very positively about how nice it was to wake and see them all there. This speech seemed to thaw them out, they began to move around and talk to him, across him and to each other. Some of the rabbits kept nuzzling against his legs and impeded his progress across the room. When he stooped down and picked one up there was a sort of corporate sigh which confirmed that he had done the right thing. From then on he always made sure that he took one of the creatures with him wherever he went. The smaller ones were very like little children and prattled on about food or things they had seen or what their friend had said. And Gregory found he did not have to listen too attentively. They seemed content with his company and any interest he showed.

After breakfast he wandered out to the creek edge and noticed a boat that had appeared overnight. When he got in the animals came up and wished him bon voyage. Then as he rowed away the jackal jumped in and dove past him to stand in the bow. He rowed on up the creek to the continuous greeting of well wishes from the increasing number of animals that seemed to be gathering there.

Chapter 17

[F4] When listening in the Urban Landscape, situations may be spoilt by other people who get in the way - they occupy that spot where you wanted to stand in to hear. There are times when the Urban Mystic, because he is in conversation with the unseen Spirit in a public place, just wants to be left alone.

Gregory awoke refreshed in his cell the next day and reached for the black book. But as soon as he touched it was as though a great gloom overcame him. It felt hot and heavy in his hand and all his own fears came flooding back. He felt caught in a completely intractable situation and he did not know how to resolve it or even how to move forward. Like a pair of cast bronze wrestlers, caught in an eternal embrace to best each other, there was now no movement for him - only pain and strain. He was crushed by the impossibility of escape. He opened the black book, it was just a sea of words. Although he shut it immediately he dare not put it down, something compelled him to hang on to it. His lips were dry and his heart beating fast. Should he shouldn't he? He prepared to take a step of faith, vacillating on the edge both terrified but enervated. The words would not come immediately, they followed after the thoughts like some echo. "Kindly spirit fall on me in your mercy." Was he merciful? Who knows? "Take my heart and mind," then as an afterthought, "my soul and use it as you wish. Forgive my failings. Show yourself to me." He waited holding his breath. There were only the usual Cathedral noises in the distance. He interrogated himself. Did he feel any different? No. The gloom was dispersing possibly. The black book felt lighter. He opened it again and scanned the pages. All the words were familiar he had read them all through several times now. His eye stopped on a verse, he read it slowly. As if in response to the words he felt a surge of prickly electricity up his spine. It was not that his hair stood on end but he definitely was having some sort of response. The verse said:
    'I will rise now and go about the city,

> *in the streets and in the squares;*
> *I will seek him whom my soul loves.*
> *I sought him, but found him not.'*

What did it mean? Was it a command? His life seemed to be full of endless questions: he was either interrogating the Dean or Little and now the spirit. He rolled the words around his mind, shrugged and read on. Then he turned back and re-read them, there was a similar physical reaction but more muted. Selection by electricity he thought. Further on another verse seemed to jump out at him:

> *Who among you will give heed to this,*
> *who will attend and listen for the time to come?*

Yet one more:

> *Stand by the road and watch,*
> *you inhabitant of ---------!*
> *Ask the man fleeing and the woman escaping;*
> *say, "What has happened?"*

And a final one:

> *Look at the heavens and see;*
> *observe the clouds, which are higher than you.*

Gregory fetched a sheet of paper and carefully transcribed them so they were now adjacent to each other. It was very puzzling, notwithstanding, he felt excited as though he had received something concrete for the first time.

He was so absorbed that he did not hear his first visitor of the day.

"Busy I see, you little fuck." It was Bailey. When Gregory heard the words he had not known who it was, never having heard his voice before. Gregory was so astonished that he did not respond but waited for what might happen next. Bailey threw his breakfast bag at him. This was also unusual as Bailey did not do such menial tasks. He looked very agitated. He was wearing his uniform still, obviously the Dean had not been able to extricate him from it. "You are to be on your best behaviour - the Dean has sent me to see you. There is a delegation coming today. But I am telling you that if I see any excuse to get you I will. Leave Susan alone. I am warning you." Gregory stood up and rested his right hand on the sill of the orifice. It was his injured hand. With the speed of a viper Bailey had it in his own grip and gave it one crushing squeeze. The tears started to

Gregory's eyes even though he tried to stop them. With a heave he pulled the freshly hurt hand away. Bailey continued to eye-ball him but said no more. Gregory waited until he turned away.

"I suppose evil always follows closely on the footsteps of the divine," he observed more to himself. But if Bailey heard he made no indication. However, the man left behind him a black hole of pestilence. It was not really a smell but a sense of corruption. Gregory sat down again and hugged the black book to his chest and sobbed quietly for a while.

It was some time before he could bring himself to return to his sheet of paper. He berated himself. "What a wimp!" he addressed himself. He felt very conscious of his own weakness and angry about it. If only he could have a fair fight, he thought. He made himself read the verses again. They were all about looking for or searching for something. There seemed to be three themes: looking out for what was going to happen in the future, making sense of the world events and then searching for the spirit himself. Maybe this was to be his calling. Perhaps the divine spirit was going to use him as a spokesperson for himself. But the verses did not imply it would be easy. Gregory needed to make some effort to discover these things for himself. Yet how could he do it in his cell? He certainly could not see the clouds and he had no freedom to wander around the city. I need a map, he thought naively.

As he pondered he became conscious that the noise was building up in the Cathedral. Somewhere some military music was playing. The more he listened the more convinced he became that it was a band, a brass one. At one point a trumpet played a solitary solo. Then as if in response the Cathedral organ struck up with a melody of religious music. "It will be my delegation," Gregory said to himself. But nothing happened for about an hour although there seemed to be lots of bustle and noise. Finally the party appeared in his line of view. There was the Dean dressed in a fine black suit, looking very smart. He had some sort of chain around his neck. There were three other men with him and a tall middle aged lady in a rather bizarre ball gown type of dress. It seemed most unsuitable for the occasion. In attendance was Bailey. Then as Gregory watched, mesmerised by this novelty, a small party of army officers appeared in full regalia complete with scabbards and swords. Following behind them were two armed men in fatigues. They could have been army or police men, it was not clear but they carried machine pistols and their eyes darted here and there. Then finally, a small woman, again in battle fatigues, appeared with a large Alsatian which strained away from her in an attempt to escape. "My, my," observed Gregory.

The Dean stepped forward and said with a flourish, "this is our mystic brother Gregory." Gregory spluttered a bit at this new address. The Dean looked a little nonplussed. "He is helping us with....." and then dried up. He may as well have said with our inquiries, reflected Gregory. Gregory turned to the delegation for a response. He expected one of the men to step forward, as they had been leading, but they actually took a step back and let the lady come forward. And a lady she was, a Grande Dame in every sense of the word. She looked completely eccentric. "I am the Dean of Persfeld," she said in a very cultured voice. Gregory was taken aback this time. "You look as surprised as most people do young man when they first meet me. But I can assure you that I am. This is my subdean," One of the other men stepped forward and gave a curt nod. "and two of my canons." They also greeted Gregory. They were nondescript compared to this vision in front of him. She looked quite older close up but it could just be that she had the dry wizened skin of a heavy smoker. Her hair was finely coiffured but brittle with hair spray. Although she looked fierce close up she was not unkindly.

"Your Dean tells me that you are here against your will."

"I must protest madam," the Dean spluttered, "I implied no such thing." A clever woman and direct. Gregory would enjoy this.

"Oh come on John it's common knowledge that you kidnapped this man. Don't be coy about it." And turning again to Gregory. "So you are held against your will?" Gregory lent forward a few centimetres and nodded in the affirmative. "Interesting but a risk. The papers seem to think you are mystic. What do you say?" She looked directly into his eyes and there was an immense power there. He was going to find it difficult not to answer her.

"I don't know whether I am or not," he replied blandly.

"Do you feel like a mystic?" she pursued the question. He hesitated. The silence went on for a time. He did not want to admit anything before his Dean. She turned to the Dean of St. Arburn's. "Look John, now that I am here, I wouldn't mind spending a few moments alone with brother Gregory - as a pilgrim." She gave him her effort at a sweet smile. The Dean was still hurt by her previous directness.

"Well it is rather irregular." He looked at his watch. "Your itinerary is very tight. Maybe another time on a private visit," he finally suggested.

"Hmm. I don't think so John. With the present situation I couldn't tell when I might be able to travel freely to come here on a private visit. A few minutes would not harm - after all I am not going to seduce him," she said with a laugh. And everyone else was forced to join in. The Dean looked doubtful. "I am not going to spring him free either." She smoothed her frock. "No jemmy or master keys hidden here." The Dean sighed.

"Very well." Gregory was pleased: he had warmed to her, this dry stick, and he got immense pleasure every time the Dean was discomfited.

The party withdrew out of sight and the woman stood before him. "Would you like to be free?" she asked him. "Maybe we could help you." Then before he could answer. "Would you come and be our mystic?" And again she continued. "You probably don't realise, being stuck in here from whenever it was." She named the date. Her information was impeccable. "But there have been immense changes out there. And the opening up of wonderful opportunities. Politics has changed completely, maybe not for the best." She did not lower her voice but showed a careless fear. "And people are turning again to institutions like ours. But they want a spiritual reality that we have lost. You are breaking new ground here and therefore have an opportunity to better yourself."

"Isn't being a mystic the antithesis of bettering yourself? Surely it implies giving up material considerations."

"It need not," she replied. "If you came to us we would pay you."

"Mmm," said Gregory thoughtfully. It seemed to run counter to his own emerging thoughts about his vocation. "I would certainly like to be free to begin to pursue what I have started in here, during my imprisonment. Can you free me?"

"Well, as I said, new opportunities are emerging all the time. At my Cathedral we have far greater historic resources."

"You mean you would buy my freedom?"

"We could possibly secure your freedom so that you could

come and work at my Cathedral."

"Does that mean you would free me so that I could be free - because you see I am suffering an injustice here, or would it be more in the nature of a transfer?" Throughout this the woman had continued to stare at him in an unblinking fashion.

"I think you are being rather naive. Nobody has that much freedom of choice."

"In the past I had a darn sight more than I do now," he retorted. Then more calmly, "You said you wanted to speak to me as a pilgrim?"

"Did I? Well maybe not today." The kindness was wearing off. "Say the word and I will be your advocate." She passed him a card which magically appeared in her hand.

"I certainly need an advocate," Gregory said, "but I need one to think of my good."

"We must all serve the common good at the moment," she said.

"As you say," he replied. He had heard that before. She reached our her hand, he suspected that he was supposed to kiss it but he took it and gave it a squeeze.

"I hope to see you soon," she said and turned to one side. He could not read the tone or the meaning of her last simple statement. But his Dean, obviously seeing her take a step away, had come scurrying back.

As she walked away Gregory called after her,
"Look at the heavens and see;
    observe the clouds, which are higher than you.
She looked back with a grimace but did not reply.

```
[G4} How does the divine spirit make
something holy? Can he not will them to be
holy, to be separate, to be set apart for his
special purpose alone. He need not consult
anybody else but himself if he chooses.
```

Gregory was relieved that he had no pilgrims that morning. It was not that their naive attention was not pleasing to him - it was - and some of them had become such regular customers that he looked forward to their visits especially. But now he had other things on his mind. He grappled for a while as to what he was feeling and in the end described it to himself as a sense of destiny. Something was moving out there, he moved his hand around the invisible city beyond his cell walls and also in here. He put his hand on his heart. Maybe, maybe, he was going to be used for some great purpose. He just hoped that it did not involve too much more suffering. A new resolve began to harden in his breast and he turned once more to his sentences. Gregory had discovered that it made more sense to study them carefully and individually. The huge gaps between them made absurd any sense of narrative or connection. Their only affinity was as they came to mean something in his mind as directed by the kindly spirit. He picked up his sheet of paper and looked first at the one that had moved him most and even then, as he read it again, another tingle came up his spine. Whoever wrote this had a real sense of loss, towards the object of her affection - the mislaid person she cannot find. A lover or the divine spirit? "In my context," he spoke to himself, "I must assume it is the divine spirit and I suppose, if he wants me to pay particular attention to this verse, and the others, then I must take them to be commands to apply to myself." So he reasoned. Re-reading each of his chosen and divinely nominated verses in turn. "Mmm. Conclusion. I am to look for him in the city." A gloom filled him. "Yeah right stuck in this cell. I don't even know what the city looks like." He sat forlorn for a while then a new idea came to him. He stood up and went to the grill. "Bailey, Bailey," he shouted. The man appeared almost immediately.

"What now?" he did not seem to speak without some menace in his tone.

"I need a map of the city now - either you get it or get the Dean and explain to him why you have not done as I want." Surprisingly Bailey went. "It was my voice of authority," Gregory mused. Within five minutes Bailey was back, and even more stunning - he had a copy of a map in his hand.

"There you are you little shit," he said and threw it at him. It bounced off one of the window dividers and fluttered to the ground just out of reach on the Presbytery floor. Bailey smirked and walked away. Gregory tried to reach down but it was too far away for him to get it. Of course he could have shouted and blasphemed but what was the point. He had a calling to patience after all he reminded himself. Gregory stood and looked down it. He could see the cover, it was quite old by the look of it and well used. At last after staring at if for some time he said quietly, "I need that map divine spirit to do what you asked me." Nothing. Defeated he was about to sit down when one of the deaf carpenters walked up picked up the map and handed it to him with a grin.

Gregory fell back into his chair with wonder and then chuckled to himself.

"What are you laughing about?" It was Little. She had come in her lunch hour.

"It's amazing. I'll tell you," and he did.

"That's an old map," she observed when he showed her.

"Never mind it is enough to get going with. Will you help me?"

"I'll bring you a better one."

"Yes please - but now will you get me started."

"What is it you want me to do?"

"Can you describe some of these roads around the Cathedral so that I can get an idea in my mind what it is like." Gregory had been looking at her as they spoke, drinking in her appearance. Little tended to dress fairly casually even for work but whatever she wore he was always delighted. He loved to look at her face and hair. Her skin was smooth and he couldn't stop himself imagining what the rest would be like. As his mind ran on he fantasised about stroking her belly and kissing her belly-button, smoothing away the flush of goose-pimples as he uncovered her slim torso.

She sat and grinned, "I know what you will like." Fortunately she stood up and disappeared immediately or she would have caught the blush that her naive response to his thoughts had caused. She was gone ages and he began to fret. After about ten minutes she returned. "Sorry big queues." She was holding in her hand an illustrated guide to St. Arburn's. "I picked it up in the book shop the other day to look at."

"Brilliant that is so kind." He felt quite overcome and a little tearful. "But I still need your help - your impressions. Look have you got time?" She looked at her watch. "Take me on a walk from here."

"OK." She took the book back and turned to a plan of the Cathedral. "This is where you are." When he looked with her it was a revelation, he had not known that he had no concrete map in his mind even to the layout of the Cathedral. It was bigger than he thought and the ruins of the old Abbey were also quite extensive. Then she took the map from his hand and opened it up. "Let me take you on my favourite walk." Gregory was lost immediately in her voice, her delightful description of the imaginary saunter and all that drew her attention. It made him both fulfilled to listen but infinitely sad at all he had lost with his physical freedom.

"That was lovely." But what had been the best was that she had taken his index finger and used that to trace the route as she talked. "You are so lovely," he said naturally at the end. She blushed and cleared her throat.

"So you were not listening then?"

"Of course I was."

"You were paying too much attention to me and not the map."

"No I was following the map." She gave him a playful punch. "Missed opportunity there to pay me one more complement."

"Errm I was looking at both at the same time," he countered.

"Oh I don't go out with cross-eyed men," she giggled.

"You're lucky, I don't go out at all!"

After she had returned to work he took the map and lay down on his pallet and went for the same walk all over again. "Divine spirit reveal yourself," he whispered.

This imaginative walking seemed to come naturally to him, after all it was what he used to do when he was free; both in his imagination and in reality, he had always been a dreamer and it had been his pleasure to wander and explore his own neighbourhood and surrounding towns. Gregory had always enjoyed going off the beaten path. By the end of his detailed scrutiny he was not left with any strong feelings other than it had been worth doing and that he had found it comforting. Next he took the book Little had given him and painstakingly compared the pictures with his map. Trying to work out what direction they had been taken in. St. Arburn's, by the book's account, was an ancient medieval city with character and atmosphere. It looked lovely in the bright sunshine of the glossy photographs. But where was the divine spirit he wondered. Then with another chill he knew he was in the cell with him. "Next time," he said, "go with me."

After his lunch he felt tired and unwell for no specific reason so he lay down on his bed and fell into and uneasy sleep. He began to dream he was alone on a flat windswept beach bordering some fenland. However as he spun around on the beach he had a sense that there was someone there with him just beyond the periphery of his vision. The wind had a keen edge to it and he imagined himself with some warm clothes on which he then rearranged and pulled up more tightly under his chin. He tugged a thick hat down to his eyebrows and right into the nape of his neck. The sun was thin and wintry, the surf to his left a reasonable tinnitus. He set off south, marching with his head down to the wind. He had not gone far when a huge anger swept over him and there in the illusion of his dream he began to contend with his hated enemies. First the Dean - he shouted at him above the wind in a new found eloquence. He ranted and cried against him and the suffering that he had caused. Within seconds he was experiencing a full gestalt moment and was uttering primal screams against the Dean and punching the air as he walked. Then came Bailey, more substantial than the Dean, but almost unrecognisable for his face was overlapped by previous bullies from Gregory's history: a bad teacher and a hectoring boss. They too were hooked up and dragged into this new released diatribe against all the evil ones who had afflicted him. A huge hot wave of injustice scoured over him crashing like the surf on the beach beside which he walked and then as the back swash began the tears also came, slowly at first, then in a flow of caustic saline. He veered off from his forward course towards some low sand dunes and threw himself into the lea of them. He snuggled up face down in an embryonic position and broke his heart. The presence watched him and very gently rested a hand on his back. Just the slightest, merest touch, like gossamer, like a feather briefly touching his skin. It was immensely comforting.

When he woke up his pillow was wet with tears and one of his dumb friends was peering in at him. When their eyes met the young man gave a rather shy thumbs up as much as to say, 'Are you all right?' Gregory nodded and smiled at him. He disappeared immediately.

That night he sat calmly with Little. They did not speak much, they were both reading books and held hands through the bars. She was reading a novel and she had given Gregory an old pamphlet by one of the great preachers of the past. It was a published sermon on grace. He found it heavy going because of the antiquated language and phraseology but he took in the way it was organised. Soon, he decided, he would write his first sermon.

"Dear kindly spirit may we get to know you better. So be it.
Pilgrims, My text for today is a sentence from this black book. It goes like this:
> *O you who dwell in the gardens,*
>> *my companions are listening for your voice;*
>> *let me hear it.*

Now I am no scholar but I believe my time here, in this imposed exile in my cell, has given me a head start. I know from your visits that you are beginning to trust me. Yet I also know that human curiosity and intellectual discipline will not let any statement go unchallenged. We all seem to have a huge appetite for facts as though if we could only get it all straight in our own heads then we would believe it. But sometimes, too intrusive questioning or even outright dissection can destroy the very thing, because of its frailty, that we want to understand.

You will want to argue first of all that the black book is too old and out of date to take seriously: that it was of no help to those before the Great Eclectic, that old scholarship proved this or that about it to its detriment, and probably that the divine spirit did not and could not have inspired it, and finally that he does not exist.

But I believe that those of you who have come here today want him to exist, or her, and want some proof to base your longings on. I may not be able to satisfy that need in you but if I can simply encourage you be more determined pilgrims then I will be well pleased. We must start somewhere and if that starting point is that we want it to be true, and we need it to be true, then that is good enough. Even if we join a story somewhere in the middle it does not invalidate the way it ends up.

I can be no help to the cynical. And yes, we may discover it is some big plot of our primitive imagination or the result of our chemical-driven emotional needs, but if it works for us then whether it really is true is immaterial. And if it is genuine, then we have a bonus. Living the disciplined life of a pilgrim may be self-delusory nevertheless if it brings peace to our minds and health to our bodies we have nothing to complain about.

So what does our sentence tell us? If we look at it logically it is addressed to an unknown person who lives in a garden and it explains to us that a group of friends of the author are wanting some communication from this unknown person. Does that not explain clearly our business here today? You true pilgrims are my companions and I am yours. Friends I hope - and in our hearts we have this longing to hear the voice of the kindly spirit. It is a commission we must take upon ourselves together. Let us pledge ourselves to listen corporately for the voice of that unknown spirit that lives in the garden of his nature. So be it."

The next time the Dean came Gregory told him that his sermon was ready to preach and that he wanted to deliver it this next Sunday. The Dean tried to prevaricate. "Are you afraid what I might say?" Gregory asked him.

The Dean met his gaze and replied, "Yes."

"Would you like to read my sermon?"

"Will you let me?"

"I will this time." Gregory did not really know why he had agreed. The Dean took it away and must have read it immediately as he brought it back within minutes.

"Yes I would be happy for you to preach that," he said. He scrutinised Gregory carefully for a few moments and then went away without saying any more.

```
     [I4]31. The Urban Mystic has keen
searching eyes that dart hither and thither
noticing things that more unobservant people
would miss. She sees the moth fall in the
stream, the nodding rock, the large lump of
granite that has fallen from the rock
formation. She notices the wry look on
people's faces and other things like that.
Things that others would not spot[or value]
she holds with intense scrutiny.

     [T4] Will not the divine spirit walk in
the cities?
```

Chapter 18

My girlfriend was not pleased to see me. I had found this before when she had been with her parents. Their frostiness towards me rubbed off on her. That's why I never went for more than a few hours and certainly did not stay overnight. They had some very old fashioned ideas. After the perfunctory kiss from all of them and a slow, boring and unfriendly meal I was itching to get off. My girlfriend had asked what the matter was. She had observed that I seemed very jumpy. I passed it off as best I could. I just wanted to get home then.

After the meal, when she was packing up and I was sitting with her in her bedroom watching, she said, "You have to make allowances - my younger sister has not turned up and they are cross with her."

"Err, the wild one." I commented. "I wish she was here, so I could meet her, it might liven things up." I was shushed. "Where was she coming from?"

"We don't no. She moves around a lot." I shrugged.

The leave taking was painful. They were into the emotional blackmail kind of, come and visit us again soon. It was good to be away. I had not been driving more than a minute when I had a premonition that my girlfriend was going to dump me but that she would wait until we got home first. "Canny girl, she needs the lift home," I thought.

We drove most of the remains of that day in silence and as the miles passed I began to calm down. After all, I reasoned, it wasn't my fault. It was just a pure accident that nobody could have foretold. And even if I was driving faster than normal then, even at my usual speed, she would still have been killed. We stopped at a hotel for the evening and although we shared a bed I did not feel like sex and my girlfriend did not offer it.

The next day dawned bright and after a good breakfast, in the fusty dining room, we were on our way. My girlfriend seemed more relaxed now that the influence of her parents was wearing off. However, I was still sure I would get the boot very soon. On the whole she was good company. "Tell me a story?" she asked. The one good thing about her was that she would indulge my predilection for storytelling. I began to tell her about the latest offering. By some strange osmosis and against my will I had included the elements told me by the other girl.

Nevertheless, I had not gone very far when the girlfriend piped up with, "I know this story."

Well I flipped, I went mental and began to shout, to which she responded with tears. If she was not going to ditch me she would now. "Look," she said to placate me, "who knows where your influences come from. Maybe subconsciously you picked up a plot from the telly. Anyway you should write them down and try and sell them." This was to placate me, reminding me of one of my long cherished dreams. "It was that bit about the twin," she continued, "I have heard that bit before."

"Impossible!" I snapped back. "I only thought of it yesterday on the way up. You're the one who is picking up bits from the telly." I began muttering to myself and then as if inspired said, "I suppose you have heard the one about the alien who falls to earth and steals - an invincible alien by the way - who steal some blokes virginal wench." I turned to my girlfriend who had put her head on one side and was looking contemplatively but did not respond. So I related all the clever stuff I had made up about purple men on the journey to collect her, with the other woman, and ended by saying, "So by the time of the story there are quite a few of them on earth - about seven."

"That's not a lot."

"Well more than one - and about twenty years has gone by so everyone's used to them - and because they keep to themselves nobody thinks much about them. However, what most people don't know is that they are a bit like a new born chick: they adopt the first person they see. Anyway the hero of the story is minding his own business one day when the latest one falls out of the sky by his feet. The alien is glowing hot from re-entry and follows him home. It takes a bit for him to become house trained. It doesn't crap or anything. Just eats but never excretes. Clever Eh? After a while it settles down. But this man is courting a young woman with religious scruples and they are going to get married and so on. Before they - you know what - but unexpectedly, the purple man takes her as his wife and beds her. Never happened before. None of the others has shown the slightest interest in sex."

"Actually it's possible I heard that.... Somewhere." She shook her head as if to drive the memory away or further in. "I hope you are going to have some proper romance in your story," she said at last. I sniggered.

"It's a man's book."

"Don't you want women to read it?"

"If they want but I am not changing it for them."

After a few moments I tried to mollify her. "What do you suggest." She thought for a moment.

"You need to explore his fiancée's mind." I have always hated the word, fiancée. "You could try something unusual for you - write it from the woman's point of view."

"You're joking. I can't do that."

"If you don't it will be all about - well - rape. That's what you are saying - the purple man rapes her. There should be more to it than that. You see in her mind she has to justify what has happened to her - because he is irresistible - she has to fit it into her religious view and so she takes the alien as her real husband."

"Who would want to read about all that psychobabble?"

"Your stuff isn't sensitive. People are interested in such things - how the mind works. Your stories....they are just action, and although you have what you call love in them it is not at all. There is nothing sacrificial about it. All your men are controllers and the romance is getting sex with someone gorgeous. There is no meeting of the minds. You need to read more books."

"I read a lot."

"I've seen what you read."

We drove on. Unconsciously I had reverted to my original up route which in time would take us back past the accident. I dared myself to drive past and see what was happening.

"I need a pee," the girlfriend said. I stopped at the next lay-by. "Have you any tissues?" I shrugged.

"Use your hand." She raised her eyes.

"Why do you put on that coarse act? You're not like that really. You can be better than that!"

"No, I can't," I replied. With those words came a new dawning of self-awareness. A new sense of inevitability in my life choices. I was setting like concrete. I hadn't always been like this. Maybe it wasn't a bad thing - a new determination. What was wrong with always getting my own way? In believing that I knew best?

Then she twisted around in the car and suddenly put her hand behind my seat.

"Arr ha! What is this?" I turned pale when I saw what she had retrieved. It was that girl's bag. She looked expectantly at me. My mind raced. "Some guilty secret?"

"No way. I found it at a lay-by yesterday and I was going to take it to the police."

"Have you looked in it?"

"No, I don't need to scrounge any tissues."

"Not curious at all?" she was teasing me.

"No." She unzipped it, pulled out a purse and when she opened it and looked at a student card inside she inhaled sharply. She looked visibly shocked. "What is it?"

"My sister's bag. Where did you find this? Her hands were trembling.

"About fifty kilometres south of your parent's town." I needed some good answers fast. My words stumbled out at first, however, the by-product of having a good imagination and practising its use continually is the ability to lie. "I actually found it in a lay-by." I mentioned the name of a village nearby. "It was just propped up against the dustbin there. I was curious and I looked inside."

"So you did open it?" she interrogated me.

"Well, yes - only to establish whether it had some value to it. I saw the purse, and the other things, and decide that someone had lost it and that rather than leave it there I better take it to a police station. So I tossed it in the back and what with the excitement of being with you forgot all about it. And of course I didn't know where the nearest police station was." She was looking sceptical. I scratched my head but there was nothing I could do to make it any better at that moment. I decided the more I added the worst it might seem. She rifled through the bag and found one of those small wallets of tissues that women carry and got out of the car without a word. She was gone some time during which I took the student-card and looked at it more closely. It was definitely her sister: the address given was where I had just picked up my girlfriend but nothing about her present or, should I say, former address. I was feeling very stressed again and took another two of my Idelmadol. It was the beginning of taking them much more regularly. In some strange way they never really had an effect on me. At any rate not like other people: I have seen other punters rave on them.

    She got back in the car and we drove off. I tried to engage her in general conversation about what the week ahead held for us but gaining only monosyllabic answers I gave up and drove carefully. We were now committed to drive past the spot where the accident had happened.

    As I entered the wooded area, that contained the fatal bend, I could see blue flashing lights ahead through the thin trees and as we turned into the final straight I could see the road was partly blocked by emergency vehicles. I stiffened immediately. As we approached it became clear that the traffic was being stopped. I pulled up behind a car, where the driver was talking to a policemen. When he had finished the officer walked back to me. I beat him to it. "What has happened?" I enquired.

    "A road accident."

    "Is someone hurt?"

    "Killed, I am afraid," he said genuinely. I nodded sagely. "Are you local sir?" I shook my head. "Is this road a part of any journey you make?"

    "No, I'm returning from the North to the City with my girlfriend. I don't believe I have ever driven this way before."

    "Not the most direct route sir."

    "No, but I enjoy the drive."

"Not surprising - a lovely car. I like it." It felt good to be told that, even by a policeman. We pulled off again. The journey continued as strained as ever.

At one point I declared, "You should have got me to give your sister's bag to the policeman."

"Not the right sort. I will take it to a police station." She picked the bag up and hugged it for the rest of the journey.

That evening at home was very sombre, therefore, after a couple of hours of her moodiness, I went out to the pub to see my friends. Fortunately, I did not have too much to drink because when I got home she was in a high old state. She was crying and re-packing her bag. "What's up?"

"Mum and dad have rung, my sister has been killed. I must catch a train up there straight away. They need me."

"It's late darling." I tried to reason with her but she was not having it. "Look I'll drive you back."

"No, you're drunk and you've only just driven all that way home."

"I love driving. It's OK. Perhaps we both better be there." She looked at me puzzled. This was such a novel response from me that it stopped her in her tracks, yet she said nothing. It took some time for me to persuade her that I was up to it and that I was prepared to make such a sacrifice. In the end, when it sunk in, she was really very grateful and there was a return for a few moments to the warmth of our earlier relationship.

We packed the car and set off. After a petrol fill-up at a garage we set off for real. This time I took the motorway. When we had got into the car for this return journey I had to help her shut the passenger door and she commented on it. She had not noticed that it was damaged before: it had worked for a few times. Now the act of my having to help drew her attention. It seemed to need an explanation, so I told her that I had stopped on a busy road and stupidly got out leaving the door open for a moment. Then the back draft of a large lorry had blown the door back on itself. This satisfied her for a moment but then she wanted to know how that could be when the door is not on the road side.

"Oh," I said quickly, "the lay-by was on the other side of

the road. I was resting in the passenger seat and when I got out an overtaking lorry, on the wrong side of the road, rushed by and the tail wind caught the door." I was getting good at this. Lying seemed to have a momentum all of its own and I had taken another two tablets before we set off.

I really think everyone should take Idelmadol. It doesn't make you drowsy or have any anaesthetic effect. What it does is to make things much clearer. It helps you to focus down on the important issues without any of the peripheral factors influencing you. You could say that it makes you clear-minded, purposeful with a real desire to make everything work out for yourself. Let's face nobody else has a more convincing duty than you to yourself.

After an hour she fell asleep and I drove on fast; my beautiful car crashed through the night with all the inside comfort of the twinkling dials.

I tried to drive as long as possible, swallowing a further two tablets, but in the end I needed the loo and so I pulled into some services. The girlfriend woke up slowly and I helped her out of the car. We both had a coffee. While we were sitting in the restaurant she said, "I know where they found her." She mentioned the name of a road.

"Oh." I responded noncommittally.

"Do you know where that is?" she asked directly.

"Not without looking at a map."

"Caught you out then. You are usually hot on such things."

"Can't know everything," I said weakly. But she wasn't finished and when we got back in the car she insisted that I get out a map to show her. The only map I had was the one I had planned my route on for the previous journey. As she watched me, I studied it carefully, as though I was discovering the road for the first time. "Here. It's in --------shire," waving my finger vaguely around where it was. But she wasn't satisfied and further insisted that I showed her particularly. This time she made me actually point out the road number. As I drove off she held it up to the comfort light and studied it more carefully.

"You could have waited," she said irritably. "How can

you drive with the light on?"

"It's OK," I muttered but it wasn't. Slowly inexorably her mind was working it out. I felt in a state of real tension and could conceive that I would be relieved when she got there. Part of my brain was telling me to have a plan ready but nothing would come. I had never taken four Idelmadol so close together and I felt strange. I surreptitiously took another two to punish myself. Then it came.

"Your line goes through this road."

"That was our route home," I said quietly. Out of the corner of my eye I could see her following it up to the top of the map.

"Why have you written the date of your journey to my parent's on it? Where is your journey up?" I did not answer - it would now be too painful to lie anymore. Suddenly and urgently. "That road accident we passed yesterday, it was my sister."

"Well done. I'd worked that out but I did not want to upset you." She nodded as if grateful. There was a long pause. I heard her tapping her foot and became aware that her eyes were on me.

"You have her handbag. You went that way on Saturday. Your car is damaged. The story! I knew I had heard it before - it was hers from school, she read it to me once" I wound the window down and slowed a bit. I reached across with my left hand and took the map from her knee and hurled it out of the window. In the rear view mirror I could see it swirled out behind us. The electric motor shut the window. "Did you kill her? Did you hit her with this car? You must tell the police." I did not know what to say. "If it was an accident you must tell them." That sounded very plausible on the outside but on my inside I did not feel very logical. She was going to dump me anyway I reasoned to myself. I let the speed drop a bit more.

Sometimes you can be influenced by the forces outside yourself; it's like acquiescing to an imperative from the other side. Some of my best stories are horror ones. A mile ahead I could see a motorway bridge. The only sadness was for my beautiful car. The girlfriend was continuing to question me in a whining voice but I was not listening. She began to pummel my arm and asked me to let her out. I let the big car take its last journey in one marvellous swoop towards the stanchion of the bridge, aiming it so it would catch the nearside and leave me free to survive or not. I was surprised how loud the crash was. Then the jolt and the suffocating air bag knocked me clean out.

[U4] The Urban Mystic is like an umbilical cord, swollen and strangely transparent, sometimes varicose in appearance, carrying the nourishment derived from the womb of God to his unborn but growing children in the spirit.

Chapter 19

A couple of days passed and then the cancelling of Gregory's daily pilgrims notified him of another change. The Cathedral staff had not told him and neither was it that an inner sense of missing something made him look at his watch and realise that they were late. He called out a few times but nobody came and he did not feel bothered enough to pursue it. Then he heard a change in the pattern of noises in the Cathedral and he could tell someone or something was on its way. Then it all went quiet before the President appeared on his own. He was carrying a chair and he sat down in front of Gregory.

"I am sorry to change your plans," he said with genuinely apologetic voice, "but I needed to see you about something." Gregory was intrigued. "I understand that you know nothing about politics - that is probably all to the good - I don't need lessons in diplomacy, rather I need spiritual help."

"Go on," said Gregory. The president was dressed as a professional business man but his small stature gave the impression of a small child sitting before Gregory. His physical nature was lively and his face animated; these were signs of a huge internal energy. Gregory felt worn and scruffy by comparison.

"I am sure that you would agree that we are not all equal. If it were true then anybody could do any work. We would all be interchangeable. I imagine the craftsman who built this Cathedral," he swept his had around the space around him, "were specialists. They had a natural artistic skill which became honed with practice and with maturity. Not everyone has the eye or the manual dexterity to be a stone mason." He paused he was waiting for Gregory to agree.

"Yes I accept that," said Gregory as if prompted. He could not see where it was leading.

"So consequently some people are more fitted for a job than others." Gregory nodded as he was expected to. "It's common sense really," continued the President. There was a fake sickly smile on his face. Gregory did not trust him. "Of course some people are not intellectually competent enough to understand subtle arguments or be able to teach or lead others. There is a natural hierarchy in society that means the strongest and the brightest will rise to the top and be called to give themselves in the service of others."

"True," said Gregory but he thought, "I don't know how altruistic the strong and intellectual really are." The President may not have been an imposing physical specimen but he did radiate a psychological strength.

"You would agree then that the weakest and least intelligent in society need to be cared for, inspired and led by those who show greater capabilities."

"That is how it happens generally," replied Gregory. He was going to say that it was not always a good thing. His was a case in point; he had been imprisoned by those who were stronger and, for a moment, cleverer than him. The President leant forward confidentially.

"There is an opportunity to do more good and you can help me and advise me." He sat back again. "I gather from the Dean that you are kept in some ignorance as to what is happening in the outside world. For the purpose, I understand, to give you a chance for peace and contemplation on your primary task." Gregory shrugged. He was wondering when he would be allowed to say something. "You are becoming very popular and much appreciated." This gave Gregory some goose bumps. He knew that he was about to be exploited. "I understand you are to preach a sermon. Did you know that it is advertised in the newspapers today? Very frequently there is something written about you. There is a great deal of speculation. The Dean has done a good job in protecting you from too much intrusion, he has forbidden journalists to contact you. But I have told him that that may need to change. You are a wonderful resource for our City State and, as I said, there is now the opportunity to do much good. I believe the pilgrims who come here trust you and given the opportunity you could reach a much wider audience."

"Well that's very flattering," said Gregory, "but....." The President interrupted him.

"And I need your advice as well because I have many opportunities to do good. I am not dissimilar to you - I also feel that I have a vocation, for me it is to lead our City State. Unfortunately there are many frustrations to my work, our constitution is very limiting and continually hampers me from doing the good I can see clearly. It has occurred to me that I should strengthen my position - so that I may serve more effectively - to grant myself more authority to do the work. Therefore, I want you to tell me whether the omens are auspicious."

"Omens?"

"The divine spirit is he with me - will he help me?"

"What do you think? Have you asked him?

"I have no time for such leisure that is why I have come to you. You must realise that I have to delegate continually and now I am delegating this to you. I want you to intercede on my behalf and make sure things go smoothly."

"I don't think it works like that," Gregory protested. "The whole point of the pilgrim thing is to follow your own destiny with the divine spirit. To go to him without preconceived ideas of what he wants from you and then to submit to his calling." Gregory was becoming rattled and, as on previous occasions, the stress manifested itself in his demeanour. He began to jerk slightly and he screwed up his eyes to concentrate more.

"I have explained this already." The President was becoming exasperated and treating Gregory like an imbecile. "I already believe that this is my vocation from him."

"How?" Now the man was becoming irritated. It was clear that he had not expected any opposition from Gregory.

"The people voted me in."

"So?"

"Well the divine spirit organises everything. The election was prayed over so it must have come under the divine will otherwise I would not have been elected." Gregory sighed.

"That is like saying that everything that happens is ...." He suddenly stopped because he knew that it was no good arguing. There was a silence. Gregory said coolly, "I believe it is wrong for any one man to have too much power." There was a glint in the President's eye.

"Damn you - you have thrown away an opportunity and you will suffer for it." Gregory began to tremble. "I am not a man to trifle with or to make an enemy of. I will be speaking to the Dean about you. I have changed my mind - I don't think that anything profitable can come out of your having a wider audience." He got up and stormed away. Gregory began to shake from head to foot. He hated himself for being such a coward. He felt as though he had received a death threat. He withdrew to the corner of his cell and cried. He was cold and ill. He looked upwards. "Why? Why? I'm not fit for this job. You've trapped me into it. Let me go."

"Nobody is going to let you go." It was the Dean, he had obviously heard the last thing Gregory said. "You stupid, stupid man do you realise what you have done?" the Dean was livid. "You have probably jeopardised all that I have worked for over the years. Here am I trying to bring the Cathedral back into the centre of community life and you can't even help. You have wrecked everything. I have a good mind to get rid of you myself. The President is pressing for you to be disposed of. I don't know what you said to him but he is not a man to mess with."

"Quite," said Gregory he was feeling angry now. When he pulled himself up he had to use his hands because his knees felt so weak. "And neither is the divine spirit. If this is anybody's fault it is yours, you're the stupid man. You brought me here. You insisted I devote my time to finding the divine spirit and finding out what he wants to say and now when I begin to say it you hate it. You pathetic egotistical slug. You never wanted to find out about the divine spirit in the first place you only brought me here for your own glory. Well now I can't be turned off. And if you had any guts you would support me. You spineless little creep. Can't you comprehend - the only way this Cathedral will be the centre of the community again is when it stops compromising itself and sucking up to the politicians but rather concentrates on giving the people a sight of the spirit. The President is using you to get his own way, in the same way as you have been using me. Well as long as I am locked up in here I am not going to be silenced or be deflected from my destiny. If you want me to stop let me go and I will disappear. Or are you going to have me killed like the President wants?" The Dean's mouth was moving like a fish and he was clenching his fists. "You're going to have to take a big gamble now and you are going to have to decide between the President and me."

"Well that is very simple," said the Dean scathingly. "I voted for the President and I will support him."

"Piss off!" said Gregory. When he had gone Gregory collapsed on his pallet. The storm was over and he felt drained and poorly. He even retched a few times but nothing came up.

    He lay down on his bed to rest but tossed about anxiously. He tried to force himself to think of something different. Even so he could not focus for about half an hour and then slowly he began to calm down. In his mind he forced himself to imagine that he was walking on a beach. He did not know whether it was the beach near the chalet with the animals or a beach from his real past. It did not matter. As he made himself look around he could see that it was not a very good beach. He was sitting on a rampart of shingle overlooking a calm sea. The weather was cool and he pulled his clothes tighter. A cold dampness began to seep into his buttocks. When he cast his eye around further, new detail swung into view and he knew that he was quite alone. His mind told him that he was on a shingle bar caused by some great storm in the past. There was not a bird in the sky and the beach stretched on forever, featureless in both directions. When he turned to the sea again it was nearer. Either he had moved without awareness, or the tide had come in supernaturally fast. As he looked at the surface of the sea directly in front of him, a bulge began to rise and the water ran from it greasy and slick into the less turbid water each side. Then, as the surface tension broke, a colour was born from its watery womb. It was dark maroon and menacing. He watched frozen to the spot and fearful as it glided towards him. There was no definite edge to it, no charcoal marks to define it and neither was it a mist but truly substantial. Like a block of colour escaped from a canvas it oozed towards him and brought with it the stench of menstrual blood. He was terrified and his chest constricted and his breath refused to come. Gregory believed it had come to murder him. With a fluid motion it was moving closer, blocking out the daylight, running over his feet and dragging itself onto his legs. It was inescapable. Ruby red, bursting with danger, slowly drawing itself up as if to pounce. Then a new noise began above him; a paving slab crashed to the shingle beside him and broke in two. Gregory jerked away from the splattered remnants but another fell close to his other side. He brought his arms up to cover his head - a useless gesture as now it began to pour great lumps in earnest. The sky was dark and noisy with the sound of falling building rubble. Huge junks of masonry, single bricks and concrete slabs whistled down around him. They began to fall onto and bounce off the colour but missed him entirely. Each successive hit crushed it a bit more. Sounds of deflation came from it like a human gasping from a blow to the diaphragm. He looked up cautiously, the storm of baked clay and set lime continued for as far as the eye could see. They swirled down towards him like flakes of snow and - then he saw they were not missing him but passing through him. The colour was withdrawing back to the safety of the gentle waves from which it had come. The hail lessened and the sun gleamed weakly and a voice called him, "Gregory, Gregory wake up." It was Little.

    He got up immediately and pushing himself through his bars placed as much of himself into her arms as he could manage and began to sob. She stroked his hair.

    "I am so frightened," he said, his breath hunting with the effort of his tears. "Now, now," she said.

    "I think the President and your father are going to kill me."

    She kissed his forehead. "Tell me."

    When he had finished he was calmer and she drew back and let him go. Her face was pale and now her eyes were red rimmed, although she had not cried. "Yes you have made a real enemy. Things are getting bad out here. I haven't wanted to tell you but there are curfews in some part of the city and the police are all being armed. It's safer out in the country but the news from the other city states is that similar things are happening. Some of our new leaders are showing their true colours."

    "Our President?" he asked. She put her fingers to her lips. "What can I do? It is bad enough being trapped here but at least I had been allowed to keep my integrity and say what I feel. But now. If I am not allowed to say what I think is the truth I will shrivel up." Gregory began to sob again.

    "Don't upset yourself. You must just refuse to be involved in the politics."

    "How can I be when I am asked to endorse a political point of view. It is true, I am not a political person and I don't understand what is going on, but, if when faced with telling the truth and I speak it out, that then becomes political, what can I do? She tried to comfort him but she had no answers.

    "We must assume it is just a threat and no more," she said trying to be as soothing as possible.

For the rest of the week nothing untoward happened and that Sunday he preached his sermon. He had half expected that the privilege would be withdrawn in the light of his rebuke by the President. As the day had approached he began to calm down and cheer up. On the Sunday morning a microphone was passed to him and a verger stood near with a walkie-talkie. It was impossible for Gregory to hear the service properly from his cell: with the main focus of it being in the distance at the far end of the Cathedral. He was puzzled as to why the technology to bring him a microphone could not bring him a speaker to hear what was going on. Nevertheless, on a nod from the verger he began the sermon and he could hear his voice booming in the distance. It all seemed very bizarre and he felt very detached from it all.

It was only later when Little came and told him in detail how it had been received that he began to get some idea of what had happened. Apparently, in the light of the public notice in the newspaper, the congregation had swollen to twice its normal size. There had been journalists there and photographers. The latter had tried unsuccessfully to get the Dean to give them access to Gregory but had been thwarted. After the service there had been a real buzz and people had stood around for much longer than normal and discussed it all. People were very pleased and proud and there had been a sense that this was a good day for the Cathedral. Her dad had a permanent grin on his face and the President, who uncharacteristically had attended, also seemed in a good humour. Gregory felt very relieved. One journalist, realising that Little was the Dean's daughter, had tried to pump her for details, which she had not given, but she had discovered that the sermon was to be printed in the national newspaper the next day. Gregory began to grin as she related this and they spent a good humoured half hour together before she had to go away and cook the Dean's lunch.

`[H4.1] At a concert the Urban Mystic finds himself observing the people who are watching the band or enjoying the music.`

Chapter 20

Early that evening a cold mournful wind began to blow through the Cathedral. It was as though somebody had left a door open somewhere. Gregory took it to be a sign of a severe change of weather outside but nobody came to be consulted. He found it difficult to get warm and the wind made him restless as if he were a small child. He took to his bed early and wrapped himself in all the spare blankets they had given him. After some restless tossing, until he became warm and snug, he fell into a deep sleep.

At about 2am he was woken by noises and light. In the distance he could hear the whoop of fireworks or of a shell exploding. He could not tell which but nearer at hand, in the depths of the Cathedral, there was shouting and the crack of pistols. Lights were coming his way. Gregory's heart began to pound. He knew that they were coming for him. There was an unholy stress in the air. Next he heard scratching at his door and a distorted voice shouting, "cover your ears." With a reflex action he did and just in time because there was suddenly an enormous noise which rocked the cell and filled it with smoke and dust. He took his hands from his ears but could not hear as his ears were ringing. His hands fell to protect his mouth from the fumes. Now there were people in his cell standing over him with torches shining down. They were just sooty shadows to him. "Have you come to kill me?" he asked. Several of them laughed - they were men.

"No we have come to rescue you." They had southern accents. He saw a hand outstretched towards him and when he took it he was pulled quickly to his feet.

"We must go," a voice said, "now."

Without thinking Gregory told them, "my book," and pointed to the black book. One of the men picked it up. He could see now that they were soldiers, but not from his city state, their uniforms were green. Their torches played around revealing how well armed they were and their blackened faces. He was full of questions but still very afraid. A soldier pulled him around to face the smouldering doorway and as he did so somebody else behind him, gripped his head tightly and forced his mouth shut. Some gaffer tape was stretched across his lips and his hands were secured behind his back. Somebody knelt into the back of his knees and in a second he was face down. Before he even had time to struggle his ankles were also bound. They were competent rough men and it was terrifying. Gregory felt his bladder go. One of them cursed. Gregory could smell his own urine. They put a pole between his arms and legs, hoisted him up and then they were off at a double. There was still the noise of small arms firing and the crump of larger guns seemed nearer. With their torches turned off they sped through the Cathedral with him. Every so often they dumped him unceremoniously on the ground or dragged his head banging on the floor. Gregory felt shocked by the violence of it. The vibes were glaringly wrong for a rescue. They stopped for what seemed like ages by the double doors.

An engine began near his head - a motor cycle. The driver kept over-revving it. They picked him up in one smooth movement, cut his bound ankles and put him as pillion rider on the motorcycle. Then he was efficiently roped on to it with his feet and waist tied to the seat and foot pegs and his torso to the driver. One of the solders with a malicious grin put a bag over his head and they were off with a jerk. The bike must have shot over the steps because it landed with a bone crunching jolt. Gregory had no way to prepare himself for the next crises. The gag on his mouth began to panic him, his nose was running with mucus and tears and he could barely breathe. He needed to take big gulps of air. And worse was to come, it was freezing cold and wet, he suspected it could even have been snowing. The rider offered scant protection and the bike bucked and squirmed beneath them. For ten minutes they alternately accelerated hard and braked in long skids whilst Gregory began to freeze. Then with a heart breaking lurch they took off up a ramp and landed, by the noise of the echo, inside some metal container. Gregory slumped in pain. Strong hands un-strapped him and bound him again as previously.

When they tried to make him stand he crumpled to the right. "Damn," someone said. They were cutting at his trousers. "Only a flesh wound," the voice said. For a while they left him shaking and shivering on the metal floor. It was vibrating, he guessed he was now in a lorry. There were dim lights. He gathered his shattered nerves and made some grunting noises and strained at his bonds. The bag was pulled from his head and he found himself looking into the face of a young woman. She had cool steely eyes and there was no compassion there. Gregory continued to groan. Slowly she took a pistol from a waist holster and held it to his temple.

"You must be very quiet." She sounded foreign. "You understand." She ripped the tape from his mouth and Gregory was promptly sick. A soldier standing near kicked him in the back.

"Piss and sick," he ejaculated. "We've lost good men for this worthless shit. It would have been easier to kill him." The woman still had the pistol to his head he felt her hand relax and she took it away. She stood up bent down and dragged him from his vomit; she was very strong. She manhandled him into a sitting position and one of the soldiers threw a blanket over the mess. Gregory continued to shake with occasional violent spasms. Behind him, there was sort of bulkhead with a door in it. The woman disappeared and came back with a cup of coffee. He took it in his hands and took a tentative sip. One of the soldiers stood on the blanket, twisted it under his foot and then kicked it onto Gregory's legs. The women scowled at him but said nothing. Gregory sipped away at the coffee. He looked very small and wounded - like a broken animal.

There were half a dozen soldiers in his section of the van and apart from one they were all smoking. The motorcycle was lying on its side but its driver had disappeared behind the bulkhead. The lorry was moving quite slowly and the swaying motion was soothing. The soldiers were talking very quietly and kept staring at Gregory. They were strung up from the action and moaning about the results. He could guess what they were thinking: he had not been worth it. After his coffee he pulled the blanket around him not caring that it was covered in his own vomit. There was blood all over his leg and he felt very sad and ill. He hunkered down and drifted off into sleep.

The journey seemed interminable. At one point he had made to ask a question but there was a gun pointed at him in a second. It did not make sense if they were rescuing him: why did they not let him go? He discerned that there were deeper purposes going on here. He started to worry about Little and experienced a rush of panic when he thought that she may have been hurt or killed in the action. He was desperate to ask but the soldiers continued to look grim faced whenever he stirred.

Gregory did not know whether he had slept or passed out, when he came to the van had stopped and he was on his own. His leg throbbed painfully and it hurt terribly to flex it. The pain was more than he imagined a flesh wound to hurt and he feared it was worse. The only thing that comforted him was that the wound looked to have stopped bleeding. His reflections were interrupted by the end door of the truck being thrown open and a fearsome snow storm boiling into the entrance. There was a light wind and the large thick flakes whirled down from a lightening sky. It was dawn. Some soldiers emerged from this cold furnace and swore as they shook snow from their fatigues. "Time to go," one of them said as they advanced on him. He cowered away from them but their strong hands grabbed him and lifted him up. No pole this time but he was carried as a log resting on his side. The snowflakes covered him in seconds and he had to blow them away from his face. There was only pain and dread. Immediately they stepped up some stairs and entered a building. It was very dark and gloomy and it sounded large, echoing just like a cathedral. Then he knew where he was. They carried him down the great length of the Nave over the stone flags into another ecclesiastical prison. Past the sanctuary they trudged and into the Choir behind the high altar then they turned right into a small room. The soldiers dropped him onto the floor without comment and obviously in a fit of pique: they had not enjoyed the challenge of capturing him. They left the door open as they withdrew, however Gregory had no heart or strength to move. He groaned and succumbed to the evil he was encountering.

Somebody coughing drew his attention. It was a large burly man in a uniform. "My name is Jinks sir I am to be your valet. What can I do for you?"

"My leg and my freedom." The man squatted down beside Gregory and looked at the blood matted trousers. "I am afraid that your new room is not quite ready yet sir but I am to make you as comfortable as I can until it is." He turned away and spoke as he retreated, "I will go and fetch some appropriate help." Once more the door was left open but Gregory did not care.

He had a bad headache developing and he was close to nausea. A woman arrived with a doctor's Gladstone bag and Jinks returned with a flask and a cup. The woman did not say anything but knelt down by Gregory's leg. Taking surgical scissors from her bag she cut up his trouser leg until she reached the wound. "We will need some hot water now," she said turning to Jinks. Gregory put his hand on her arm.

"Will you help me escape?"

"I don't need to," she said, "I have been told that you are free." She set to work again using some warm water poured from the flask into the cup, for this is what it contained. Slowly she ungummed the material adhering the wound. It hurt Gregory like hell but he tried to keep the noise down. When the material was free they both looked at the leg. There was a dark scar like a shallow runnel across his thigh. "You're OK. There is nothing in it, just a flesh wound."

"So the soldiers said," Gregory retorted sarcastically. She applied antiseptic and wound a bandage around it. Whilst she worked Jinks had disappeared again and brought back food. "I need some clean clothes," Gregory told him. Without a word he disappeared a second time. The doctor finished her work and stood up. "Thank you," Gregory told her. She fetched some tablets out of her bag.

"Painkillers and antibiotics. Just to be safe." She handed them over and smiled. "Good luck," she said and walked away.

"Free at last," he murmured and began to eat.

By degrees Jinks brought him fresh clothes and helped him to dress, then a mattress and sleeping bag. He pointed out the portable toilet he had not noticed under a canvas cover and, showing him the light switch, wished him good night, even though it was clearly dawn.

After a couple of hours Jinks came back to wake him up. Gregory felt weak and exhausted. "Madam Dean is coming to see you and would like to meet you in your new room."

"Why do I need a new room?"

"I believe she has an offer to make you and she wants you to see what we can provide for you. You will be able to shower and shave there - and have some breakfast." Jinks helped Gregory to his feet and together they staggered out into the corridor. Jinks was much about Gregory's height but stronger and broader. Nevertheless they were an odd looking couple as they lurched along.

There was not far to go, it was a substantial chapel, behind the Choir, with a high ceiling. It must have been a military chapel because the entrance was blocked with fancy iron work. When he came into it Gregory could see that the chapel had been divided into two because there was now a false wall with a door in it. Jinks manhandled him through the door beyond which he found a study bedroom, shower and small kitchen. It was tastefully decorated and there were books on shelves. However, this was not what Gregory noticed first, his eye was drawn to a book on the bed, it was his black book. His spirits lifted immediately. Jinks helped him to the edge of the bed and let him go. "I will come and check on you later sir, I understand the Dean wants to see you in one hour." As he left the door clicked behind him. Gregory lay back on the bed with the black book clutched in his arms.

After a few moments Gregory dragged himself into the shower room. He discovered that it also had a bath and gallons of hot water. Gregory rinsed himself down taking care not to wet his bandage and finally, exploring the wardrobe, he found a selection of clothes. He dressed himself warmly, although the room was quite hot already, but he was responding to a hunger for luxury and to a need for consolation. He made up his mind that he would continue to grow his beard and so eschewed a shave, not even bothering to look for razors. After a second of reflection he decided to explore the rest of the chapel and the Cathedral. He went to the door and found that there was no handle. He pushed it but it would not move. It looked heavy and solid. "Fuck!" he cried out and slammed his hand against the door. There was a buzz, a metallic click and the door sprung open. It had been released electronically from somewhere else. He was suddenly on the defensive and his earlier joy evaporated. A new suspicion was born. Gregory marched straight for the entrance to the chapel, the iron gate was shut and he guessed it was locked. As he arrived the Dean appeared before him, walking from the Nave side. She was closely followed by four other men, one in the uniform of a high ranking officer and one his adjutant. She was, in appearance, as he remembered, but now dressed in an elegant suit with a dog collar.

"Good to see you on your feet," she said with a forced smile.

"What the hell is this locking me in my room ," he said petulantly.

"Now, now, be calm, it is for your own good. You are not safe yet - they may try to take you back and we must protect your freedom. We're only being kind and watching over you." Gregory responded immediately to her clipped tones - they were irritating. "We have a complete surveillance system in the Cathedral to protect ourselves and you. I don't know about St. Arburn's - well I do actually!" She turned to the officer and they laughed callously. "Clearly their Cathedral and the militia do not have such a close relationship as we do." Gregory felt cross but too weak to really give vent to his emotions.

"So I am going to be free soon am I?"

"Of course," she said soothingly, "if that is what you want. But you have a clear choice. There are no pictures of you so far in the newspaper so you could change your name and return to anonymity, however if you did that you would have to give up your calling."

"How so?"

"You would have no public platform for your words."

"That was never my intention; it has come about as a by-product."

"Well I think you are being a bit naive. If as you say the divine spirit it giving you things for our generation then they must be published and heard. If you are an urban mystic, as opposed to a hermit, then you must ply your trade in the market place, so to speak. If you choose that way then obviously you cannot have a private free life - you will be like any other celebrity - you will need to be protected. That is simply what we are providing you with - the opportunity afforded here - should you choose. However I must say that we cannot be messed around. If you decide to walk away then that is it." She smacked her lips as though finishing a mouthful. Her jaw was set sternly towards him.

"You will wash your hands of me?"

"Yes!"

"Sounds good to me."

"Well it probably does after what you have suffered by your imprisonment. However, the Dean of St. Arburn's has proved to be right in his discernment of your gift. You must concede that."

"Yes I suppose."

"That really is a material change from when you began this work isn't it?"

"Yes. You're right."

"So if you are to continue your work, then it may as well be here where we can give you the support and protection you need in these difficult times."

"I am to free to speak my mind then?"

"Of course." She put as much warmth into this last statement as she was able. It all sounded logical and appeared to make sense, however his spirit was filled with unease. "Now," she continued, "you must listen to my colleague." She stressed the last word as if to make a point but there was a glint in the officer's eye that belied his agreement with the statement.

"Politics," Gregory thought to himself, "I will stick to the spiritual."

The officer, in a very flat voice, explained the security arrangements in the Cathedral. Gregory was to have an armed guard on hand to call. There was the fear that St. Arburn's might try to get him back. Two panic buttons were pointed out to him, that he had not noticed, and the officer explained about the doors. They were self-shutting but he could gain access at any time by speaking into one of the two camouflaged microphones, one situated above the door [he had not noticed it] and one to the left of the gate. Gregory protested at this intrusion and the officer tried to reassure him. During this conversation the Dean had been talking to her two cohorts but when Gregory balked at the arrangements she turned back to him. "Perhaps we are being too careful," she confessed, "but try it - if there is no risk, and we have been too thorough, then we will step it all down."

"I will agree if the intercom is not on all the time. Perhaps it could be an electronic switch where I press the button when I want to be released." The Dean and the soldier's eyes met and they nodded to each other a secret sort of nod.

The Dean turned back to Gregory, "Agreed."

"And I would like to look around the Cathedral."

"That is OK," said the officer, "if the guard comes with you. Please don't go outside yet."

"Why - because it is not safe," he answered his own question.

"See we are in agreement," continued the Dean. "Of course once you start to work and see pilgrims, or as soon as you are recognised, we must ask you to stay in your cell during public hours or..."

"Or what?"

"It will create the wrong impression. Part of your charm, part of the interest in you is that you are shut in, dedicatedly trying to contact the divine spirit. Your mysticism will be lost if you are - if you just wander about."

"I don't quite follow that."

"OK, just leave!" the Dean flared up suddenly. "Just walk away be Joe Public again but I cannot guarantee your safety out there."

He was tempted and he could tell the Dean was staking all to bring him into line. "I want to send and receive letters. I want to write to my girlfriend." The word sounded good.

"Fine," the Dean said in a hoity-toity way and turned to go. Looking back, "Make your choice, Gregory, stay and submit to our rules or just go." She was gone. The officer shrugged and went also. The other two men and the subaltern stepped aside and talked quietly amongst themselves but kept looking at Gregory. He tried the gate to the chapel it was locked.

"Open sesame," he shouted. There was the tell-tale hum and click and it stood a few inches ajar. Pushing it open ahead of him he walked unsteadily out. Immediately Jinks was there and another soldier dressed in fatigues, carrying a sub-machine gun. It was one of the soldiers who had rescued him. He had a malevolent look in his eye. "I am going for a walk," said Gregory grandly and then looking at Jinks, "and you can come with me if you want," and to the soldier, "and you may stay here." The soldier gave a low snarl.

"How's the leg?"

"Now soldier," said Jinks turning to him," you will be disciplined for that." The look faded fast and he said, "beg your pardon, Sir."

"You are not to speak when you are on duty."

"Yes. Sir."

"Are you an officer?" Gregory asked Jinks

"No, I am simply your valet." Gregory shook his head to himself, he was too tired, and it was too confusing. Gregory walked slowly and painfully towards the main door. When he got to the transepts he turned into the main aisle and continued down the centre of the Cathedral. When he was half way down he turned and looked up at the banners hanging from the Cathedral organ above the main cross trees. It said:

'Look at the heavens and see;
    observe the clouds, which are higher than you.'

Gregory gasped. He recognised them as his parting words to the Dean when she had come to visit him. Perhaps he really was famous he thought. Jinks saw him start. "Yes, they are your words, sir."

"From the black book," Gregory corrected him.

"Quite so. We have all derived a lot of inspiration from them."

"But they were supposed to be personal for the Dean," he protested.

"Well now we can all enjoy them can't we?"

"They are not meant to be enjoyed. They are to capture the heart and change it." It occurred to him that the Dean had escaped their impact, by giving them as a gift to the Cathedral and had not let them change her own heart. "You bloody clever woman," he said half aloud.

"What sir?"

"Nothing." The soldier was a couple of metres away with an impassive look on his face. "Do these words mean anything to you soldier?" The man looked at Jinks who nodded his head.

"No, sir," the man answered. His reply had been completely honest, the man was indifferent to the words.

"I am very tired. I must go back."

"Would you like a chair, sir? We have some close by." Gregory collapsed down onto a pew seat. This was his answer. Jinks walked away and returned promptly with a wheelchair and Gregory was trundled back to his chapel cell. On his bed were the day's papers.

Chapter 21

[U4.2] I love you, creator of that small part of the universe that ended up as me.

A numbing tiredness came over Gregory and the thought of reading was too much. He put himself straight to bed requesting Jinks that he not be disturbed until he emerged. After some hours of sleep he stirred and sleepily picked up the papers that were on his bedside table. He felt the real luxury of having extra furniture and a proper bed with pillows. Gregory made himself comfortable and began to read. The wounded leg was painful and had become more and more so as he regained full consciousness. He took the pills the doctor had left him with some water.

There were two national newspapers and a local one. The latter was obviously the new voice of Persfeld. The first national, which was a tabloid, had a banner headline that said, 'Brother Gregory does a bunk' and went on to describe how Gregory, having being given a better offer by Persfeld had changed his allegiance. Little's father was quoted as being very saddened by Gregory's change of fealty, especially after all St. Arburn's had done for him. The other national included a similar article as part of the other news on its front-page. This did not say very much more about Gregory's transfer but included more speculation as to what Persfeld could offer him in terms of a wider ministry. The article ended by drawing attention to a press release from the Dean of Persfeld who had promised much greater access to the journalists in view of her certainty that Gregory's ministry deserved a wider audience.

Finally, the local City State newspaper took a very jubilant line and bragged at how its Cathedral and government was clearly superior to any other to offer refuge to such a great talent.

What staggered Gregory most was how well known he seemed to have become. Although Little had told him as much, now he could see it with his own eyes. He felt that he had become a ecclesiastical icon and felt good and smug about it. It also made sense of the care that Persfeld's Dean was taking of him. The effects of his painkillers began to take effect and he dozed for a while longer. When he finally surfaced Jinks was waiting for him in the chapel with a broad grin on his face.

"Did you like the newspapers?" he asked.

"Yes great, but why no mention of what really happened?"

"Arrh, that's politics sir and I don't feel qualified to answer." Gregory felt Jinks was hiding something - there had been that fear of the soldier towards him - but decided to let it pass. "What would you like to eat sir?"

"Can't I go to your canteen and choose for myself?"

"Certainly not, sir, mixing with the hoi polloi. No sir, the Dean made it clear that you must retain your mystery."

"But I have no mystery."

"Oh you do sir," Jinks said flatteringly.

"No really, if I have real mystery it won't rub off by mixing with others and if I haven't then I cannot feel it right to pretend."

"Sir you have real mystery." There was something oily in this and Gregory was beginning to feel an antipathy towards the man. Still, when he was free, he could sort himself out. Jinks presented him with a menu. "Better to do it this way. Whatever you want, and even what you can't see here, is possible," said his servant knowingly. He sounded like a pimp for a moment. There was a steely twinkle in the man's eyes. Gregory decided to be on his guard against him. After making his choice Jinks disappeared but was soon replaced by two workmen in overalls.

"We have come to change the doors so you can let yourself out." They showed him two boxed switch units. He nodded for them to get on with it. It took them three hours to sort it out but it made Gregory feel good.

The meal when it came was excellent, later, when he tried to go for another walk, he was told firmly that there were a lot of visitors in the Cathedral that day and it would be inappropriate until the evening. In addition, he was informed that the press were coming to meet him in two hours' time. Opposite the chapel entrance a soldier stood on guard with an automatic machine gun. Gregory still felt too tired and wounded to make much protest: he had learnt from his previous experiences at St. Arburn's to bide his time.

Exactly at the time stated the Dean arrived and Gregory was asked to come out from his bedroom, to which he had retired to watch the electricians at work. They had been uncommunicative and neither had he wanted to talk much.

Whilst he had been lying down the chapel had been set out with a table and chairs. There were ten journalists seated ready for him and the Dean, sitting behind the main table, beckoned him over. A few cameras flashed. "Please," began the Dean, "if you wait there will be a good opportunity later to take pictures." The questions came like machine gun bullets.

"Madam you must be pleased to have secured such a famous spiritual resource for your Cathedral?"

"Of course. We were over the moon when Gregory responded so positively about coming here."

"Did you have to offer compensation to St. Arburn's?"

"Not as such, but there were some delicate discussions before the matter was resolved. However, at the end of the day Gregory is a free agent and made up his own mind." Gregory felt uncomfortable at the Dean's assumption that he would go along with these fabrication and felt bad that they had not had taken the time previously to plan what he wanted to say. He even had a suspicious thought that the electricians had been sent on purpose to distract him.

"And you sir are you happy to be here?"

"Of course the facilities are so much better here." Gregory felt stupid saying that. He started to correct himself, "of course my work is to open myself to....."

Then in the infinitesimal pause between words the Dean said strongly, "to all of the influences that this great building has to offer in terms of tradition and history. We have a magnificent library here and a full team of academics. Gregory will receive every support he needs."

"Will he find the solitude he needs to pray?" asked a female journalist. Once again the Dean again jumped in before Gregory could formulate his ideas.

"Of course this building has been soaked in prayer for generations."

"Was your journey here easy," this was directed to Gregory yet again the Dean jumped in.

"I am sorry but that is privileged information and is not really germane to today's session. Travel is not easy for anyone at the moment as our new City States organise their borders. But suffice to say it was uneventful."

"But you were limping when you came in?" Gregory opened his mouth but had no expectation that he would be allowed to speak, the Dean was a manic firebrand beside him and was twitching and speaking too fast to be interrupted. The journalists tried their hardest to engage with Gregory even so the Dean was too strong and Gregory felt too low at that moment to bother.

"Have you got a message for us from the divine spirit?" a journalist finally asked. Gregory looked expectantly at the Dean who ungraciously conceded that she could not dare to answer this one. Gregory let the silence continue for a moment and calmed his own heart with a deep breath.

"I haven't at the moment," he replied," but the Dean has promised that I may preach this Sunday at the main Cathedral service and I hope to have something to say by then. That is right?" he said turning to her. She grimaced and fixed a sharp smile on her face.

"Of course all the arrangements are in hand. Now photographs - Gregory's still tired after his journey and if you want to know more then you must take your turn with the other pilgrims."

The journalists made a number of apparently gratuitous friendly photographs of Gregory being welcomed by the Dean and then she shooed them away. When they had gone the Dean turned to Gregory. "I can see we are going to have some fun," she said to him, "but remember I am the Dean and I can ask you to leave at any time."

"Please do," thought Gregory.

"Is there anything else you require?" she asked acidly.

"I need some privacy in this area for the pilgrims and myself. Is this a right of way for the general visitors?" He pointed through the chapel gate.

"Not anymore! We have diverted the traffic another way to protect you."

"Nevertheless it is very open and when pilgrims come - I assume you will allow pilgrims to come?"

"Naturally that is part of your function."

"Some screens then and comfortable chairs over here perhaps," he pointed to a space in the chapel."

"It will be done tomorrow. In the meantime you had better

get on with your sermon."

The next day proved busy. Gregory tried to be quiet but his medication and the workmen kept disturbing him. In addition, he felt intimidated by the sensation that he was being watched. He did look carefully all over his living quarters but could not find any camera. And now he had the electronic switch system he simply had to buzz for the door to spring open. By the end of the day his private screened area was tastefully begun with low walls constructed and carpet laid. He could not complain that his wishes were not carried out quickly or efficiently. After another night's sleep he was feeling stronger and fitter. His leg pain was subsiding and because he had awoken early he determined to go for a walk around the Cathedral, but although he could get the door to his private quarters open the outer gate would not respond to the button. Even the soldier had gone so there was nobody to call. Gregory's heart was full of a continuing antipathy to being shut in because of his treatment at St. Arburn's. Later, when Jinks came with his breakfast, he confirmed it was too late again to go out because of the Cathedral visitors.

Gregory could see from the newspapers, which were plastered with his face, his privacy had gone. It made him wonder if anybody would recognise him from his previous life. Thus he acquiesced to Jinks' refusal to let him out but accepted his unusual servant's promise that he would arrange for him to go for an early walk the next day or later that evening.

Within the hour some temporary screens arrived to complete his interview area. Gregory was once more favourably impressed at the generosity with which his general requests were met. This bode well for the future he acknowledged to himself. A further half hour later and his first pilgrim arrived. It was strange to sit down in a more casual situation with her and not have any bars between them. He was not sure he liked it particularly.

She was a pleasant-looking middle-aged woman. She had some light tears in her eyes as though suffering some emotion. This was not uncommon. "I am sorry," she said. Gregory looked puzzled.

"Do I know you?" She pointed.

"Your leg. I am the doctor."

"Oh yes it is much better - you did a good job and it is healing well. No infection."

"No I am not sorry about your leg." Gregory frowned. "Of course I am sorry you were wounded." She leant forward so as to lowered her voice. "I am sorry that I did not help you to escape. I am a believer like you." She smiled warmly. "I have been reading about you with interest. I was thrilled when we were told that you were coming here and, reading between the lines, we all knew that you were being held against your will at St. Arburn's. It was so frustrating that nobody could help you. And your sermon!" Then she took his hand which Gregory found slightly intimidating although not unpleasant. "But I should have helped you escape then before all this was in place."

"It's OK, I have been assured that this is for my protection - and that because of the danger of recapture and media interest I must submit to the curtailment of my freedom for a bit longer."

"Why?" she looked puzzled. Gregory could not answer this. He was silent for a while.

"Have I been duped again and too trusting?"

She still had his hand and began reassuringly, "I am sure not. No it sounds genuine. But you must press to be free, they will not give it easily, you are a focus for true religion that the Cathedral has lacked for decades. You will make them money and give them kudos. But you don't need to be protected. People out there would want you to be more available to them. They are going to make it difficult for people to see you."

"How so?"

"I guess it is because your unavailability gives you a greater mystique." She leant even nearer. "They are frightened of you. They feel your spiritual energy or transparency cannot be controlled by them."

"I can't control it." She nodded.

"I must go, I was told to be brief or someone will come and rescue you."

"Come again - please - I need a friend." He had not said this before. There was something genuine about her.

"Yes I will need to come and check your wound."

"Thank you." She left. The rest of the hour was fairly standard in his experience, although not for the pilgrims, he was humbled by their trust in him. Only his last client proved troublesome when she asked him to curse her husband. He told her politely that this was not his function but she would not take no for an answer. She began to shout and abuse him. In the end he had to walk away but she followed him to the wall of the chapel. He was thinking that he might have to defend himself when Jinks arrived propitiously and escorted her off, swearing. Gregory had to rest after that: his health was still not as good as it had been.

    Later in the day there was another frustration: Jinks' continued refusal to allow him out for walk. This time it was because a review of security was in progress. Jinks promised that after his sermon on Sunday he would be allowed out of the Cathedral for a walk but that until then he must be patient for the next three days. Gregory accepted this news with some ill grace yet there was nothing he could do except to be patient and marshal his strength. In the afternoon he found some peace within himself to open the black book and lost himself in its words for a good hour.

    The next day, as he waited pensively for his second pilgrim, he looked up and saw Little standing in front of him. "Don't react," she mouthed as she faced him with her back to the steward who had brought her. The expression froze on Gregory's face.

    "Come and sit down," and he ushered her behind the screen. They fell into each other's arms and wept. "Thank God you are safe," he whispered. I was so fearful that you may have been hurt in the kidnap." She felt thin to his hands: her shoulder blades were angular and bony under her jacket. Even so a heat flowed from her trunk and inspired his pulse.

    "Are you free now?" she asked breathlessly: Gregory had been holding her too hard.

    "Supposedly but not in reality. I am beginning to think not."

    "That is so cruel. You deserve to be free. I hate the Dean of Persfeld."

    In a control room 100 meters away a man was listening intently on headphones and watching the expression on Little's face as she spoke. A bank of video recorders whirred behind him. He pressed the red button and within seconds Jinks came in. He immediately picked up the a spare set of headphones and began to listen to Little. "We were worried also, but the newspapers put our minds at rest and yesterday we saw your picture."

    "How has you dad taken it?"

"He is livid and tried to complain to the President about lack of security but the government has been left with egg on its face and doesn't want to be reminded of its failings, dad has felt he had better shut up. But the pilgrims have taken it worse, they will be trying to travel here to see you."

"How come you got here?"

"It was very difficult." Jinks rang the Dean and invited her to come to the control room. "The border controls have been strengthened and identity cards cum passports are to be issued soon, which will inevitably mean curtailment of travel. I came as soon as I could before the new regulations came into force. When I got here there was such a large crowd waiting to see you that I despaired. So I prayed to the divine spirit. There was a lottery of tickets. You had to take one from a bag and I got a winner," she beamed, "and here I am."

"I miss you," he said, "and I want you."

"I miss you too." They cried a bit more.

"They are not going to give you long." The Dean came in to the control room and looked at the video.

"It's the Dean's pathetic little daughter," she said scornfully. "His so-called girlfriend. It was inevitable. Make sure she does not pass him anything. Shall we deal with her?" she asked Jinks.

"No I will have her followed, as you said it was inevitable and once the new controls are tighter it will not happen again."

"So are you free or not?" pursued Little. Jinks left the control room.

"They say I am but I haven't seen much of it. They are treating me better than your dad though. I am to be allowed to send letters. I will write to you. How can we be together?"

"I do not know but I will come to you." A steward coughed by the chapel gateway.

"There are others wishing for your council," he announced.

"OK," Gregory acknowledged him, "a few seconds more." Turning back to Little, "Will your dad try to get me back?"

"He can't but I cannot speak for the government, as I told you, its pride has been injured." The Dean had taken up the spare headphones when Jinks left and now nodded at this remark.

"We are best forewarned," she muttered to herself.

When Little left the chapel she was trembling and felt very

self-conscious when she walked past the armed guard. It had been a long and difficult journey for her, without her father's knowledge, and now she must face his wrath on her return and her own lonely feelings away from Gregory. A large unkempt-looking woman, cramming a burger into her mouth, detached herself from the milling crowds in the foyer of the Cathedral and sauntered after Little.

    After his last pilgrims of the session the Dean visited him, she looked bright and purposeful. I am afraid there is a bit of bad news. Intelligence has suggested............"

    "What intelligence?"

    "Military intelligence has suggested," she continued patiently," that there is a real danger of St. Arburn's mounting a counter-offensive to reclaim you. We are going to have to double the guard on you and we may need to take extra precautions." Gregory was beginning to look stern himself at this. "However we will do everything in our power to make sure you can get out after the service on Sunday. We don't want you to feel like a pet bird in a cage do we? Certainly not."

    "Is that all?"

    "For now." As she turned to go the doctor appeared around the end of the chapel. "Arrh the doctor," said the Dean, "to check your wound I expect. How is it?"

    "So, so!"

    "Good, good bye for now."

    The doctor was not so smiley today she looked a bit jittery. "May we go in your private quarters," she nodded with her head as to indicate what she meant.

    "Of course." They walked towards the inner door.

    "Please lie on the bed when we get there." They passed through the doorway. Once in there she seemed to calm down. She opened her black bag and took out a blood pressure test kit. After this she asked him to pull his trousers down so she could examine the wound. Then it was blood she wanted, a syringe full to run tests to check his general health was good. "Now your ears and throat," she said loudly. A spatula was produced and put in his mouth. "Hmm a bit sore here. Do you feel it hurts?"

    "No," said Gregory as best as he could with the spatula on his tongue. Slowly she assembled her audioscope for looking in his ears.

    "Turn your head." She bent down and put her eye to the eye

piece and began to look in his ears. She seemed very close. "There are microphones and cameras in all your rooms," she said very quietly as she withdrew the earpiece. "Yes, I think you may have minor infection there. I am surprised that the antibiotics have not cleared it up. You might experience a bit of deafness. Do you understand what I am saying to you?" she said slowly.

"Yes thank you." Gregory's blood was running cold and he felt very shaky. "I will certainly bear in mind what you say and I will let you know if I experience any soreness and loss of hearing." She came to the other side of the bed and checked his other ear.

"You must be very careful, the hearing is very precious." She packed up ready to go. "I will need to come again to check how you're doing."

"Please. You are a good friend," he said, "thank you." And she was gone.

Gregory lay frozen on his bed, this had become his worst nightmare. When would it ever end? A fresh sense of self-pity rolled over him and he turned to the wall to cry a bit. He was careful to make no noise.

```
[V4] The Urban Mystic needs to become an
expert at recognising idolatry. He notices
that when an object, or an image, is embraced
with more or less respect than it deserves for
its intrinsic value [Measured absolutely in
how the divine spirit sees it.] then it may
become an idol.
     When we give an idol too much respect we
are giving the divine spirit too little.
```

Chapter 22

This time he would go inland, the animals were much more used to him now and there was a happy chatter among them that he was on the move. They seemed to like his unpredictability. Gregory followed the well-worn path, that the animals always appeared from, and treading in the soft indents of their paw and hoof prints he walked into the forest at the bottom of the ridge. At first it followed parallel to the bottom and he only made ground slowly, but it was all so beautiful that he did not rush. Here in the forest the animal sounds were natural rather than human and he felt a peace begin to descend on him. His journey began to take on the image of the pied piper as more and more creatures joined in behind him. Everybody seemed to be enjoying it as much as him.

After about a quarter of an hour along the main path, there had been many tributaries joining it along the way, there came a sudden right handed bend and when he followed it through he found a steep ascent ahead of him. Gregory pulled himself up with the help of overhanging branches and protruding roots. He wondered how the larger animals following him would manage but when he breasted the rise he found them waiting for him. "There was a short cut," he said aloud, to none of them in particular, nevertheless he was met with the equivalent of animal's guffaws and hoots. He smiled at their simple merriment.

When he had recovered his breath, it had been steeper than he anticipated, he looked around. Immediately behind the larger animals was a wonderful sunlit pool fed by a short waterfall. Only now did he become aware, by the contrast, how the trees had filtered out a lot of the sunlight on his journey there. Not that he had found it oppressive. But this new vista was glorious and awoke in him a boyish delight. He pushed past the larger animals and drew the smaller ones behind him. When he got to the edge of the pool there was a hush as they all watched what he would do next. He pondered for a moment and then crouched to feel the water - it was pleasantly warm.

He began to strip off his clothes and the animals watched in amazement. He felt a little shy in front of them but gritted his teeth and pressed on. When he was left standing in his boxers, he did not know whether to remove them. "Oh what the hell," he thought and taking off his fig leaf he dived into the clear water. As he hit the surface he heard an animal cheer go off but the impression of the noise was short-lived as he continued to swim down and down to the bottom of the pool some five metres below. He drifted for a moment before propelling himself lazily to the surface. As his head broke the plane of the water there was another cheer and he grinned affectionately at his new family. Within a matter of seconds many of the animals rushed into the water. A huge bow wave swatted him away as a hippopotamus, that he had not seen before, pushed him away towards the waterfall. There was lively play and chatter for several minutes as the most unexpected animals took to the water. Even the lion was rolling its great mane in the shallows and now looked up with it all flattened against its head. It looked as though it had changed sex. Gregory dived several times and found otters, and small shrew-like animals, plus a penguin joining in with their underwater frolics.

On rising for the third time he found that all had gone still and silent, many of the animals were scrambling out of the water. He was puzzled for a moment until he followed their eyes. Treading water and turning around he found himself facing a huge crocodile which stood contemplatively on the bank. As a panic arose in Gregory the huge creature shot into the water and surfed towards him. Paradise had suddenly become spoilt for him and the reaction of the other animals seemed to endorse this. Fortunately he did not end up in its jaws, it came within an inch of his face and opening its large mouth grunted melodically at him, "Nothing is at it seems." After this utterance the crocodile did a smooth barrel roll and it disappeared out of sight. Gregory cautiously began to swim to the bank fearing to make a dash for it. But an otter barred his way.

"He is our king," the water mammal told Gregory, "and we are not afraid of him but we are quiet and leave the water out of respect."

"Oh I understand," said a relieved Gregory. Another otter appeared

"He is very old and very wise," it said. A duck floating near nodded agreement but only quacked several times. Gregory began to relax and swam away from the shore towards the waterfall instead.

As he was doing so the crocodile came up under him and lifted him clean from the water on its scaly back. Shooting him into the air. The animals screamed with delight. Gregory swam down behind it and grabbed its tail. With immense power, but surprisingly gently, the crocodile dragged Gregory behind him. They had a lot of fun and Gregory went back to his cabin tired but relaxed. The crocodile had not spoken to him except at the end when it had asked if it might come and see him tomorrow.

"Of course," replied Gregory and as he walked home he wondered who was the king now.

Gregory got up from his bed and sat at his desk. With the black book open before him he began to write his sermon. He took as his text:
> *Do horses run on rocks?*
> *Does one plough the sea with oxen?*
> *But you have turned justice into poison*
> *and the fruit of righteousness into wormwood--*

'The divine spirit is not hampered, as we are, by any boundaries. She does not recognise City States or our ownership of property. She does not pay head to the distance we put between each other or even from our own internal errors. By her nature she assumes free access to all our prohibited areas, listens to every private conversation and remembers our each fleeting thought. She knows each one of us better than we know ourselves and she knows us each equally.

Fortunately, the divine spirit has good will towards us and shows calmness and forgiveness in the face of our crassness towards her. She seeks intimacy and friendship with her creation but she is no pushover and expects that in turn, with help, we also will have good will towards each other.

She wants us to begin by taking stock of ourselves - an audit - and to be honest with her and ourselves about our true motivations. For only when we are honest can we move into a deeper relationship with her. As the black book says:
> *'your heart knows that many times you have yourself cursed others.'*

But of course the question remains, is it wrong to curse? I am no philosopher or theologian and I have no sense of the origin of right or wrong save in my own conscience which becomes the more particular the nearer that I let the divine spirit draw to me.' Gregory told them of his former experiences of the divine spirit speaking through other of the sentences directly into his mind and gave some examples.

Then resumed, 'What then have I discovered of the divine spirit I can share with you? I have no religious volume, apart from a few remnants which have been expurgated by some unknown historical hand of most of its sense. I only have nature and then only what I can remember - I have spent so long in a cell secluded even from that - it has become only a reminiscence. Finally, I have my own desire to know the divine spirit and open myself to him. Yet even the paucity of these three experiences has to my mind become magnified by my concentration on them.

The relics of these old texts resonate the more by their repetition and my own cry to her, the only one who can make me understand. Equally, the sunlight and the wind, that alone permeate my cell added to my own human physicality speaks volumes of the care of their creator. Of course I have the time, without the same distractions as do many of you, to put my mind in gear to the possibility of the divine existence. All these have become the greater as I said for their paucity. So when I bring my particular text to you this morning then please believe me that I have studied it long and hard.

> *Do horses run on rocks?*
> *Does one plough the sea with oxen?*
> *But you have turned justice into poison*
> *and the fruit of righteousness into wormwood--*

I find that it speaks to me of a rage in God against the bad in us. Not everyone would recognise justice and righteousness, as even good, some will side with poison and wormwood, but to those who will listen, hear the anger of the divine spirit against the things that he finds wrong in us and be sorry.

My lonely residual verses in my black book do not make much sense, my mind tries constantly to group them together. Here is another that seems to fit with my text:

> *How the gold has grown dim,*
> *how the pure gold is changed!*

> *The sacred stones lie scattered*
> *at the head of every street.*

Is the divine spirit speaking to us here at Persfeld or to my former pilgrims at St. Arburn's. You must judge ultimately. The divine spirit cannot condone those things which do not resonate with her own nature and so when we are at odds with her intention she must act. Her kindness seems to me to be that she only acts against those who resist her and not in opposition to those who acquiesce but cannot change. In the divine spirit's eyes, to want to be forgiven and to receive acquittal are the same as being changed. Let it be so for us.' Turning to a fresh sheet of paper.

'Then with fear yet in trying to be true to my calling as an urban mystic, I say to you citizens of Persfeld beware lest there comes a time when these sacred stones of your precious Cathedral lie scattered at the head of every street. Turn from your negligence and seek the will of the divine spirit otherwise your most precious things will be lost. As the writer of the black book says:

> *My eyes cause me grief*
> *at the fate of all the young women in my city.*

All who suffer in tribulation become pilgrims with me. Amen.

Gregory got up from his seat and, taking the final page of his sermon, went to lie on his bed to rethink the ending. There was a knock on his inner door it was the Dean. She stood looking down at him, she was not smiling today. She turned at last and looked at his desk. "Your sermon." Gregory nodded. "I need to check it with the Cathedral solicitors." Gregory shook his head in disbelief. "Is it finished?" Gregory did not feel very communicative so he simply nodded. She picked it up and walked away and out of the door. He held out the last piece of paper to the door but she did not turn back. "Have a nice day," he said quietly and the man in the television booth grinned to himself. Gregory turned once more to his paper and with concentrated absorption rewrote and expanded his conclusion.

There was nothing to break up his day and he missed Little dreadfully. He had written to her but no reply had come. A deeper cynicism began to take root and Gregory suspected that with the continuous surveillance there was no way he would be allowed a private correspondence or in fact any correspondence at all. He made up his mind that he must try to escape again. It was clear that they would never let him go. At least it was a change from St. Arburn's, he consoled himself with.

He spent his time quietly waiting for his sermon to return and talking to the few pilgrims that got through the perimeter to see him. They were all rather uncomplicated and he guessed that there must now be some ferocious vetting system in force. At least at St. Arburn's they had allowed everyone in without fear or favour. This was unsatisfyingly sanitised and becoming boring as none of them shared in any great depth, even when pressed, seemingly preferring to ask him endless questions.

At an interval in the session the Dean returned his manuscript. Gregory put it back on his desk, joining it together with the last page. Within minutes a secretary arrived and the document was removed again to be typed.

Gregory's attention focused once more onto the pilgrims. After one particularly gruelling session, when he only managed to extract a few bare facts from half a dozen people, it dawned on him that he was simply the object of a very subtle interrogation. Did the pilgrims have to report back to somebody afterwards or record it on a return form?

In between times he sat quietly and read - they had given him a few classical novels and he studied the black book and rested.

On the Saturday there were no newspapers and Jinks seemed particularly attentive. He was still promising that after Gregory's sermon he could be let out and there were some special extra delicacies and treats with his food that day.

Towards the end of the afternoon a young girl appeared - another secretary it transpired - with his sermon. She was quite apologetic about the difficulty she had found reading some of his handwriting. In fact she seemed quite afraid of him. He put her mind at rest and sat down to check it through. The original seemed to have disappeared. He expected it to have been changed but he was wrong.

That night he took himself off to his cabin, hoping the crocodile would call. He was not disappointed. Gregory could never tell how long he had been there because time did not seem important but it had been a bright dawn on arrival and he was sitting eating a small loaf of bread with some cheese. It tasted the best he had ever had. He was constantly surprised how the simple things there always exceeded his expectations. There were several small animals dozing or preening themselves in the corners of his cabin but they ignored him when he finally stood up and went outside.

Some of the larger animals were dozing on their feet or cropping the grass delicately and steaming in the cold morning air. The distant boom of the breakers, beyond the estuary, and the tangy air filled his ears and lungs. He stood contemplating the scene for some time. A horse drifted by nuzzling his arm as it went. His reverie was disturbed by a cough. He looked around to find its source. It was the crocodile who had been lying, off to his left, like the proverbial log, but now with its eyes open. "I did not want to disturb your morning thoughts," it stated. Gregory walked over and looked down at it.

"You are the king of the animals they tell me." He felt uncomfortable standing so tall over someone that the other animals treated with such gravitas.

"They call me king and treat me as king so king I am to them, from earliest time. But I am not a king compared to you."

"How so?"

"I am only the king of the animals you are the king of far more."

"Do you see me as your king?"

"Should you wish it."

"No I will be your friend only."

"That is good." The voice rich and melodic came from within the crocodile, it was certainly not articulating its lips, although they were parted. It was like a ventriloquist. Gregory did not know what to say next. There seemed to be no rush to continue unless there was something important to divulge. After quite a long pause it was the crocodile who spoke next. "I have a real desire to be a crocodile. It is overwhelmingly strong within me. I could not conceive of being anything else."

"Good!"

"Each of us animals has such a strong yearning to be the thing that we are. Is that true of you?"

"I don't know. You mean instinct. Are all your instincts intact in this place?" he thought of the traditional image of the carrion crocodile.

"I have no desire to eat anymore. I have done enough of that formerly. I am full."

"Really!"

"To eat now would be a disservice to my brothers who could not eat me."

"Are any of you carnivores anymore?"

"Not in this place, in your presence."

"Right," thought Gregory. He wasn't really sure where he was.

"It is right," said the crocodile.

"Are you telepathic," Gregory questioned in his mind.

"Yes."

"Blast," thought Gregory.

"What I really came for today was to tell you about the glory of creation. I am so pleased to be a crocodile and I am so pleased that all my subjects are just as they are and you as well. You humans - how wonderful you are - the divine spirit has made you perfectly." Gregory did not feel perfect.

"Tut, tut," said the crocodile, "do not think unworthy thoughts about yourself or where you are. Find the ...." and here the crocodile did not speak but thought a picture into Gregory's head. It overwhelmed him and he staggered back. It was a concept that had no true explanation even though he could have used thousands of words and failed to explain it - this was beyond language. Yet it was not so great to be the divine spirit himself but rather the image of his essence in creation, his powerful force that had made it all begin.

The crocodile stood up and swaggered off swishing its tail behind it. "Until next time," it said. Gregory shook his head to clear it, not of the image, but of all the other stuff that seemed sour in comparison.

    The next day was Sunday and Gregory woke expectantly. But it was a slow start: his breakfast came late and then he was left on his own for a long time. Even after the service appeared to begin and all the distant noises of people filing in had stopped he waited in isolation. Then, without warning, two richly dressed vergers appeared with ceremonial staves and he was led bewildered into the Nave of the Cathedral. It was absolutely packed. A huge crowd stood down the sides. Gregory's heart began to pound. He couldn't do it he thought. I am terrified. The Dean was in her stall and she smiled sickly at him. "The bitch," he thought. She has done this on purpose to throw him. With trembling legs he climbed into the pulpit. He forced himself to say, "Good Morning." There was a murmured response from the crowd. "My first sermon here," he announced and began.

    At first he was very faltering and he noticed that the person controlling the PA system turned it up twice to catch his low voice. But as he proceeded confidence grew and he pressed on. It was clear that he had to speak much slower than was usual and he made himself consciously decrease the pace. Little's father once told him that in public speaking he must listen for the echo of his own voice and this seemed the only good bit of advice he had ever had from him.

    When he reached the end of the penultimate paragraph, he paused and he was gratified to see the Dean stand up, but at the point she reached her feet he continued onto his unchecked conclusion. The Dean sat down and looked nervously around, she calmed herself and appeared to be listening thoughtfully. But her colour began to rise. She turned to whisper to one of her canons but he remained sitting solidly where he was. Next she got up regally and turned to speak to another minor official who again did not respond as quickly as she wanted. She tried a sign language which Gregory could see out of the corner of his eye. Her hand was making a cutting throat sign and shooing the official away to attend to it. But it was too late, Gregory had finished and an ominous silence descended on the Cathedral. "Scandalous," said a voice in the front and a woman got up and walked out. Others began to shuffle with their coats. The Dean stepped forward and announced a song and the choir struggled to its feet, thrown by the unexpected turn of events.

    "Well done Gregory," shouted a voice from the back and there was a ripple of applause punctuated by some booing. Gregory walked down the steps to his escort. The Dean was glaring at him malevolently. He walked despondently back to his cell. It did not even cross his mind to take the opportunity to escape: he was like a caged bird frightened to do anything but return to the safety of its cage.

    Later, when the Dean visited him, she was incandescent with

rage. "Do not ever do that again. That sermon was not what we agreed. You do not realise the damage you may have done to the Cathedral and your tenure here. Nobody wants to be preached at in that way." She could not see the contradiction in the word.

"Just hang on," said Gregory," I preached the sermon that was typed for me. "Here," he held it out to her. She took it in trembling hands. A brief look confirmed that Gregory was right, she screwed it up and threw it on the ground.

"You tricked me."

"I think you tricked me - what happened was a pure accident - but I'm glad it has happened because it shows me that being here at Persfeld is no different that imprisonment at St. Arburn's.

"Of course it is not you silly boy. Wherever you come under ecclesiastical authority you will need to submit to it."

"Who do you submit to? The divine spirit I think not. If you did then you would be glad that I said what I said. You cannot expect to live vicariously through my relationship with the divine spirit and then reject all I have found out when it becomes uncomfortable. Find him for yourself and let me go."

"Yes we are going to let you go all right." She meant it like a firm letting an employee go. "I have no more to say on the matter," she said imperiously, "but you will never preach again. Every word you utter for public consumption must come by me and I will decide whether it is from the divine spirit or not."

"How?" Gregory asked calmly. There was no answer but her eyes glistened sickly with her rage. She stalked away.

Within seconds she was replaced by Jinks. "I expect you are hungry," he said cheerfully.

"No please leave me."

Later in the surveillance room Jinks and the Dean watched the screens alone.

"I am sorry sir," the Dean said to him. Her face was pink with the effort of her humility.

Jinks responded to her repentance with a curt nod and replied, "This is not going well. You assured me that he would be pliant. We needed an up building spiritual sermon from him not this rebuke."

"I know I reacted badly to it at the time," she said, "but on reflection my recoil was more to something I had not heard before than the content. What he said was not that strong."

"Strong enough for someone to leave and many to boo. The papers will lambaste us. We have no President like St. Arburn's and the ruling junta is not popular. I return to my original point, it was intended that he was to come and be seen to be an asset and thus to increase the prestige of this establishment. Now your position is in danger now."

"Surely not?"

"Why not - you decided to throw your lot in with the military and become the institutionalised religious promoter of our City State. Now if we rise or fall so do you. It is too late to withdraw and pretend to be the voice of the people against us. They will be laughing their heads off at St. Arburn's. The military council will not be pleased - you were to be our cloak of popularity. Sinuse in particular opposed the idea all along."

"But you also are in military intelligence, which is why you were made his valet." Jinks laughed.

"Remember Sinuse never laughs." The Dean felt clammy under her arms. The advent of the City State had not only brought a resurgence of an old politics but also an old method of ruling. "Let us hope that he does not want a martyr."

"Surely he would not have Gregory killed?"

"I was thinking of you," said Jinks.

The Dean changed the subject, "are you still to let him have his walk?".

"Why not, we will see what balls he really has - and you must limit the damage. You must become him."

"I understand - no more pilgrims - you were right, from his recent spiritual direction he is becoming too political, even on a personal basis. If I am to be his mouthpiece then maybe we do not need him after all."

"We cannot let him go."

"Maybe we should let St. Arburn's have him back now, or one of the other cathedrals." Jinks nodded.

"And maybe their rescue attempt proved to be a failure in some way!" They continued to debate the issue and make plans for some time. All the while they kept an eye on the monitors. "He never speaks aloud, when he is on his own anymore," observed Jinks finally. And answering himself, "somebody must have warned him about our eavesdropping."

"Perhaps he is intuitive," interjected the Dean. They both laughed.

```
[W4] Let us not be too triumphalist about
nature: it is messy.

[X4] The urban is an expression of nature
because it grows out of human creativity and
organisation. In the same way that plants
battle for light and nutrients so does the
results of human creativity. The divine spirit
calls part of all new growth and creativity to
holiness.
```

Chapter 23

    [Y4] The Urban Mystic stands by God in
the market place and listens intently to what
he says about what he sees.

When Jinks brought Gregory his tea later in the afternoon he was still on edge but Jinks kept up his usual bonhomie. When the table was laid Gregory said curtly, "My walk."

"Naturally. Immediately after your meal. Of course I will have to come with you and the soldier."

"Definitely!" said Gregory sarcastically. Within half an hour Jinks returned with an overcoat and a guard. It was a soldier that Gregory had not seen before. He carried a machine pistol. Jinks was smiling. Gregory felt very uncomfortable and the thought crossed his mind that this would be his last walk ever. He reasoned that he had displeased them and so it was not going to work out. It was impossible that he would ever be given the freedom to speak as he felt led by the divine spirit. Yet he know in his bones that they could not let him go for fear of him finding an open platform elsewhere. A great wave of weariness overtook him and he sunk low in his spirits.

"I thought you might want to go outside," said Jinks proffering the overcoat.

"Thank you." Gregory slipped it on unbuttoned and walked through the open chapel gate turning right away for the Nave and walking towards the cusp of the Chancel. There were other chapels lining the outer wall and then there was a barricade with a soldier. This was to guard his chapel presumably. He would case the joint, Gregory thought, in the eventuality he survived the next half hour. Gregory continued around the curved cusp until, walking down the side aisles past the Choir, he came once more into the Nave. He looked up behind him and was disappointed to find his words from the black book to the Dean had been removed. He looked warily behind him, it was as though he were dragging a heavy anchor astern in the shape of his two retainers. There were a few workmen busy in the Nave moving chairs and two women who were arranging flowers. There was nobody to help him and none of them paid him any attention.

"People are used to you now," said Jinks.

"No real pilgrims come here anymore then?" asked Gregory turning to Jinks. He just smiled and ignored the question. The main door was approaching and he wondered where the deed would be done.

Within seconds he was through and staring at the dark night outside. There was a moon and a brisk cold wind that cut into his flesh. In response he did up the buttons of his coat. He turned to his followers. "How much further?" He meant how much further will you allow me to go?

"As far as you feel comfortable walking."

"What happens if I want to catch a bus?"

"That would not be possible."

"Why?"

"It would not be appropriate for your armed guard to go on a bus with you. It would draw to much attention. I suggest you confine yourself to the local streets."

"Shops?"

"If you wish." Gregory took a few paces and then stopped; he did not have the strength for this charade, he had to bring it to a head for good or ill.

"Actually I wish to go on alone now." Jinks looked quizzically. "I know you have tried to do the best for me and protect me and all that." Gregory did not know why he was sucking up to them. "But I am ready to take my chances. I cannot say I have a belief in the divine spirit if I don't show my trust in him to protect me beyond the walls of the Cathedral." Jinks said nothing. Gregory turned and walked away. The sweat was running down his back despite the chill air.

"Wait," said Jinks. Gregory turned slowly, he expected the machine pistol to be levelled at him but the soldier stood impassively. "Won't you need some money?" Jinks was playing with him but Gregory had to dare to trust.

"Yes if you can give me some I will repay it."

"That will not be necessary. Where do you intend to go? If you go back to St. Arburn's they will imprison you again. Oh, of course you need to go back for your girlfriend." Gregory began to shiver with the cold. "Did she ever write to you?"

"Not yet."

"But she came to visit you."

"You know that already," said Gregory. There was no point trying to hide anything now.

"It's true, we know a lot about you and we know that you cannot survive out there on your own. You are actually a loser whose only meaning in life has to be part of all this." Jinks gestured to the Cathedral behind him. "You are a puny no hoper." The tears started to Gregory's eyes. He was raw and vulnerable, he just wanted to run away. "If I let you go - I let you go to your death probably. You made enemies today."

"Why should you care?"

"I have grown to be fond of you."

"Oh Yeah! Look, " his voice was desperate, "you turn around and walk back in there and leave me here. Go back and tell the Dean I have gone and not to come after me." With his newly frozen hands he swept his long hair back in the breeze.

"That would deprive us of saying good bye to you properly," there was a sinister tone in Jinks' voice.

"If you're going to shoot me - shoot me now."

"Oh dear God no," said Jinks, "what here in this public place. You underestimate us. There are thousands of more subtle ways of getting rid of you. But you are misunderstanding - we simply want you to serve Persfeld. You are innocent in the way of politics, we could teach you, you're bright. We would give you a mentor. "I have a mentor already."

"Really," Jinks seemed surprised and then realising returned, "Of course the divine spirit. That may only be the way of madness you know," he said dismissively. "Do you not believe in him?" asked Gregory wanting to know the answer.

"The Dean at least believes - ha - then we pay her to."

"I am going now," Gregory turned and walked away as confidently as his now shaking knees would allow him too. He heard Jinks say something to the soldier. He increased his pace. Then there were boot steps on the gravel. He turned and saw the soldier running after him but with no great exertion. Jinks was holding his gun. Gregory made himself run but his legs would not work. He kept turning around but the soldier was keeping pace with him easily, waiting until he tired. Gregory cut across the grass towards a lamp-lit path, it was downhill. It was only a matter of moments before the soldier rugby-tackled him to the ground and deftly, putting him in an arm lock, roughly hauled Gregory to his feet. It was humiliating more than anything to be paraded like this back through the Cathedral. As they walked down the Nave he saw the Dean look up from something she was doing and look away quickly. The soldier pushed him hard back through the chapel gate and clicked it shut. He disappeared briefly and came back with his gun then, taking up position against the opposite wall, he stood guard.

Gregory honestly could not tell what sort of emotion he was feeling but his whole body jittered and danced with the force of it. His body was flooded with some sort of natural chemical that played his nervous system like a cacophony of noise. First he went into his private quarters but he could not sit still or even stand still so he returned to the chapel proper and paced around it mumbling to himself. It did not really matter at that moment if the cameras picked up what he was saying or doing. He felt the bitter gall of the knowledge that his secret observers would find his behaviour amusing. Eventually he went to the gate and shook it defiantly at the silent guard. It was a different soldier now, one of the men who had wrought his original capture from St. Arburn's.

"Was it worth it," Gregory said menacingly to him. "Look what I have been reduced to - a prisoner. Is that fair? Did you know what you were bringing me to when you came to rescue me? Rescue - huh - it was just another kidnap like the first one. It's just more guard duty for you isn't it? I haven't done anything to improve your life, only made it worse. You would have been safer never coming to get me, your sacrifice and all that stress has just been a waste of time." He was rambling. He wanted some reaction from the man. He wanted to throw the responsibility on to someone else. He felt very upset with the divine spirit but could not express it to her. This man must do. "Don't you have any conscience?" The merest smile played across the man's lips. He had his hat pulled down and he was dipping his head slightly more and more now to hide his eyes: so that he would not have to engage with Gregory. "You know that you are going to have to answer for this. The divine spirit I serve will hold you accountable for all the misery that you've caused me." Gregory did not believe this but he was overwhelmed with a need to be cruel back to someone and there was only this man. "He is going to dry you up like a piece of old leather. You will become old before your time." Then with demonic insight, "Women will laugh at you - they will say he is not a man and why - because he has dried up." Gregory paused, the man was colouring slowly and his head was beginning to lift. "When you are in the changing rooms with the other men you will be ashamed to show yourself in public for fear of humiliation. Other soldiers will point you out and make crude jokes about you. You will never get a girlfriend again. You will never be able to satisfy your wife and your semen will run clear and dry." Gregory was getting some thrill of satisfaction from his words. It felt good to be this crude and vile. The man was raising his automatic woodenly. Now Gregory could see his face, it was florid and there were some tears in his eyes. Gregory was shocked, he had wanted a reaction but not this one. The man levelled the weapon to his eye and looked down the sight at Gregory. Was he bluffing? Gregory had no idea. He was transfixed, paralysed like an animal in car headlights. The soldier removed the safety catch. The moment seemed like eternity but could only have been a few seconds at the most.

Then a voice said calmly, "That will be all corporal." It was Jinks' voice but it did not look like Jinks, this new man was in the uniform of a colonel. The soldier cracked to attention and marched off. Jinks came and stood in front of Gregory. "Quite a performance from our meek man of the spirit. No more kindly spirit now. So this is you with your gloves off. Pathetic." Jinks took his service revolver out of his holster and levelled it at Gregory.

"It looks as though we are both showing our true colours." Gregory felt very calm and the flood of chemicals that had motivated him seemed to have miraculously disappeared. "How demeaning for a colonel to act as the valet of such a miserable specimen as me."

"We didn't know you would be so miserable when we bought you."

"You bought me!"

"What else. It's always possible to buy information. How do you think it was so easy for us to know the routines of that other establishment." He spoke with some humour. "You have not been a good deal."

"I have not proved to be as pliable as you wanted, that's quite different."

"On the contrary you have proved to be exactly what I

wanted. Things could not have turned out better." Jinks cocked his revolver.

"Time to dispose of me then?" Gregory felt preternaturally calm. Some anaesthetic ran in his blood now.

"Soon."

"Shall I say all I said to that soldier to you."

"You can try but you would pick on the wrong man. You weren't to know that that particular soldier is one of the few that actually believes in the divine spirit and that he has some delicate medical problems anyway." Gregory felt deflated and silently cursed himself. "You feel bad don't you?" Gregory nodded. Jinks laughed, "You see you are too easily read. I was lying about him."

"You bastard. What is truth?" Jinks laughed even more.

"I have the gun."

Gregory mustered himself, "Apart from what I said to the soldier, and I admit I overstepped the mark, I have to say that my understanding of the divine spirit is that he will protect me from you and eventually he will frustrate your plans."

With a terrible compression the gun went off and a bullet passed through the skin of Gregory's left arm. He was nicked by the bullet and it stung like hell. Gregory collapsed to the floor with shock. Jinks stood over him peering down through the bars of his cage. "So where was your divine spirit now?" Gregory was too shocked to answer, but the building seemed to tremble a bit and give a strange sigh and a few seconds after there was a distinct crump. Jinks looked around speculatively. "No way," he said smiling. "Does the nancy boy want a doctor now? You are the worst hypocrite I have ever encountered. This whole mystic thing is just an illness, an anxiety protection response to what has happened to you. You have duped those gullible pilgrims by offering them a fantasy of your own sick mind." There were tears in Gregory's eyes.

"I cannot understand," he began, he was talking to himself more than Jinks, "why it is that I am the object of so much hatred. I did not choose any of this. I do not harbour grudges or really hate anyone. I have tried to do my best in the task set before me." Gregory was whining like a petulant child. "So why do I keep coming up against people like you," he spat it out up towards Jinks who towered above him. He stood up shakily and felt the wounded arm oozing blood between his fingers. He felt faint and hot.

"Well life is not like you want it to be," explained Jinks. "I suggest you get over your self-pity and grow up. It could be a lot worse. Bend to the system and you will not have anything further happen to you." Jinks shook his gun menacingly.

Later the doctor came and dressed his new wound. She was silent and grim-faced. "Who shot you this time," she asked eventually.

"A devil," spat Gregory.

"Are they to keep you locked in here?" she asked nervously. He squeezed her hand.

"I really don't know. At this present time I suspect that I have become surplus to requirements." It was a wry comment.

"The pilgrims will be sorry that you cannot speak to them."

"That's comforting."

After she had gone he took some pain killers and fell asleep.

When he woke late the next morning somebody had thrown the newspapers through into the chapel. He had to collect them up and sort them out. There was no breakfast.

The national newspaper he started on had printed his sermon in full, apart from the last paragraph, which was a precis of what he had preached. Clearly they had been given the first bit as a press handout. Strangely there was no comment at all. When he turned to the local paper he found his sermon printed in full up to and including the penultimate page. The rest of what he had said was missing. The reporter spoke warmly of how well received his first sermon had been and made the point of how both pilgrims and government would be looking forward to his next.

For the next few days he was left alone, save for the daily papers and a reduced diet of snack meals, which were brought to him by a stony-faced soldier and passed or, if he was in his private quarters, thrown through the bars of the chapel. Gregory made no fuss but began so sink and withdraw in his spirits. He felt listless and ill at ease and could not concentrate on anything. Even taking his pain killers regularly to dull all the pain did not help. He hoped that some plan would present itself to him, yet the fact that he was dealing with such desperate people seemed to completely overwhelm him so that he could not function properly.

The days dragged on, Sunday came and went and although he could hear the service in the distance he could make nothing of it out. On the Monday he slept in late and when he passed through into the chapel he found the newspapers stacked neatly and a proper breakfast laid out for him. He was immediately suspicious and picked up the papers immediately. Both the nationals and the local paper carried the text of his latest sermon, read obligingly for him by the Dean due to his indisposition apparently due to a sore throat.

Because of his lack of self-worth Gregory had struggled with his fame and importance. Although he could conceive that appearing in a newspaper was a mark of something quite extraordinary and could acknowledge that for a sermon to be printed in full in a national newspaper meant something quite significant, the reality had not really impinged on him until that moment. This turning point was that someone else had pretended to be him. With a sense of foreboding he began to read, 'Brothers and sisters in the divine spirit, greetings in his Holy name and presence. It has been exercising my mind as to what I should say in this my second sermon to you and it is appropriate at the beginning to acknowledge the debt I feel to the staff of Persfeld for the new freedoms I experienced here after my long imprisonment at St. Arburn's. The spirit being free himself, works for the freedom of those who serve him.

Of course the great divines of the past have interpreted freedom in purely spiritual terms and they often endured long periods of opposition and hardship during which they could only rely on the inner freedom of their own human spirit. Yet this is not ultimately the divine spirit's plan - he wants his pilgrims to experience emotional and physical freedom itself. I have therefore spent long hours in communication with the divine spirit and he has shown to me, through the precious sentences of the black book, a way forward which I would share with you.

As it says in the black book,
'Why is light given to one who cannot see the way, whom God has fenced in?'

Gregory dropped the paper as though it was hot and ran for his black book. It was still there and as far as he could tell the mutilated pages were also all present. They must have copied it at some point he reasoned. "That is OK," he affirmed himself, "maybe it needs to be published." He leafed through the sheets and found the quotation. It was certainly there, he could have easily believed that they would have made something up. Gregory returned to the newspaper and continued to read.

'By this, the divine spirit means that we cannot enjoy full understanding of his words to us unless we have the personal freedom to hear what is being said by him. I tremble at the task given to me and I have become more aware of how much value you place on my words so it is important for me to take that responsibility seriously. As it also says in the black book,

'I must speak, so that I may find relief;
I must open my lips and answer.
I will not show partiality to any person
or use flattery toward anyone.'

There will be times therefore when I have to take my courage in my hands and speak out about important issues that those in authority would wish me to hold my peace about. I take this calling seriously and I will be unable to do it without your prayers or support. Pray for me that I have the courage to be fearless. At St Arburn's I had no real platform to speak out about the regime there. I was never allowed to preach. My access to pilgrims was limited. At times I was beaten and cruelly treated. I still bear some of the scars on my body. There was a kind of secret police that monitored what I said all the time and censored it. Thankfully the same is not true here at Persfeld and I have felt a new lightness in my spirit and sensitivity to the will of the divine spirit because of the freedom I enjoy here. It seems important to me that I devote even more of my time on this work, even if it means I have less time to support some of you. If the divine spirit has called me to a national ministry then I would be disobedient not to accept it humbly.

I have a sense that the divine spirit is calling us all to strengthen the relationship between this Cathedral and our national and state government, to return to the period of history when the spiritual and the secular were companions in a way that is lost in our contemporary society. To this end I want to encourage you to support our fledgling City State and its public servants. The divine spirit in his omnipotence has allowed them to rise to such prominence at the moment and we trust his judgement and power at this time. I can see great benefits from the partnership between spiritual significance and secular wisdom.'

Gregory threw the paper down with disgust but picked it up again immediately. He could not bear to read any more of his so-called sermon so he turned now to the comment. He felt a mixture of emotions. He was bewildered and he experienced the heartbreak of robbery and violation. This ministry that he had been so disdainful of at the beginning had, by its theft, given him an insight into the importance he held it in.

The comment in the local paper was laudatory and without substance: any journalistic freedom had disappeared from that establishment he noted. In the nationals he found a more gentle but wary criticism. One commentator pointed out the factual inaccuracy relating to the lack of opportunity at St. Arburn's. The journalist told his readers that he had the text of a sermon dating from that period in his hand. Others spoke of the obvious maturing and sharpening in this latest offering: Gregory's previous one had obviously been naively immature and somebody had therefore forced him to get his act together, whether it was the divine spirit or the politicians of Persfeld was not clear. It was noted that many would be relieved that he intended to keep his integrity and freedom to speak the hard word. Some political nous had come into his vision. Yet other commentators lamented a change from a more devotional style of rhetoric. On the whole the offering had been well received and there was no hint of suspicion that he had not written it: the liberal sprinkling of the mention of the divine spirit had put paid to that. Gregory put down the papers finally, left his breakfast uneaten, and returned to his quarters carrying the black book. Something momentous had happened. There was in him a deep sadness about it all, not a grief of his own making, it was more as though a deep disappointment had come into his bones from some source outside himself. He wept briefly but did not feel relieved by it.

After sitting in contemplation for a while he stood up with a new determination. An unfamiliar thought was driving him. If his days were numbered then they did not really need him anymore. For the first time he hunted carefully around his rooms and wherever he found the smallest speck of a hole he chewed up some paper and forced it in with his pencil. One by one the monitors went blank in the observation room. The technician looked questioningly at Jinks who shrugged and walked away.

Gregory plumped up his pillows and settling back into them

took the black book into his hands. He flipped through the pages and found the quotes used in his perjured sermon and he read them again pondering and thinking about each one. It was amazing how easy it was to interpret them in different ways. Within the context of what the Dean - he assumed it was the Dean - had said they made sense, they endorsed the false premises that she had based her talk on. These verses did apply to the uncomfortableness of his own ministry. As he continued to think and read the book he lighted upon another verse which seemed to sum it all up for him. "You should have used this one too," he spoke aloud and read it out:

Truly the thing that I fear comes upon me,
and what I dread befalls me.
I am not at ease, nor am I quiet;
I have no rest; but trouble comes."

With the familiarity of an old friend the buzz came as he spoke and he felt both comforted and challenged by the sense that it was meant specially for him. It also brought an ease to him. He knew that the moment had come, that moment he had been anxious about all these weeks - his probable death. But now instead of him feeling terrified by it, it was a real relief. It seemed to him the better option between that and going on as he was a prisoner. He spent some moments in grateful contemplation of the divine spirit.

There was a knock on his internal door and before he could respond the Dean and Jinks, the latter still in his colonel's uniform, came in. They had obviously been laughing about something as they came to his door because the vestiges of humour were on their faces. However, like two naughty school children, caught in some private joke at an inappropriate time, they wiped off the mirth in the face of his stern look. The Dean composed herself. "So how do you think I did?" she enquired arrogantly. Her repellent figure was sheathed in the ball-gown that Gregory had seen her wearing on their introduction at St. Arburn's. She looked like some geriatric debutante on the way to her coming-out-ball: her pretentiousness replacing what should have been the normal smug self-awareness of her own beauty on such an occasion. Now the glamour had gone and with the departing glory all was as mean as the deep lines on her face.

Gregory nodded sagely. "I imagine the words will all come true in time," he said enigmatically. The Dean coughed with embarrassment. She did not understand what he meant but decided not to pursue it or her initiative would be weakened.

"As you can see," she continued, "it is possible for us to take over your public ministry quite satisfactorily without anyone noticing. In fact on the whole the papers were more positive about my offering that your own."

"However. We don't want to do that," interjected Jinks hastily. Now he seemed impatient with the Dean.

"Obviously," she took the speech back, "it would be much better for us if you co-operated. We are not asking you to give up your principles but simply to operate them in the context of certain parameters. Which we will describe for you. Nobody really expects you to comment on political matters except in a supportive way."

"Indeed, it was great the way the army here, by rescuing me, have brought me all kinds of new freedoms that I did not have at St. Arburn's. Great."

"Look," said Jinks squatting down companionably by Gregory's bed, "this is nobody's fault - but it is a wonderful opportunity. What we said in the beginning is still true, once you have established yourself."

"And you can trust me," added Gregory.

"True - once we can trust you - you will prove to be a wonderful asset to our state and then who knows what rewards that will bring you. Your girlfriend, for instance, can start to visit. You would have real freedom and you could move into your own establishment out of here. Just try and trust us. You are politically naive and don't really understand what unguarded words can do. Let us help you and tutor you. You could learn so much. You could even become Dean one day." The Dean laughed hollowly at Jinks' words.

"Or some other Cathedral perhaps," she countered.

"No I'm committed to this City State," he said sharply and Jinks grinned.

"That's better, develop a sense of humour."

There was a long pause as they both contemplated each other. Gregory took an audible breath and said, "Go on then - enlighten me. Share your insights with me. Tell me what the Great Eclectic was all about?" Jinks looked steely eyed and licked his lips. His eyes flicked to the Dean.

"Surely you don't want a history lesson?"

"No, I know my history, as you say, I need a lesson in

politics."

"Are you serious?" For once Gregory had wrong-footed the man. Then Jinks, quickly recovering, answered himself. "Of course you are not - but I will tell you anyway, so that you can understand how you are about to eschew your place in this great saga - by your own stupidity. The Great Eclectic was about boredom and obsession."

"Boredom?" Gregory was scornful but curious.

"Human history is like a major current in the ocean, for the most part it fluctuates little, save for seasonal changes, but every so often there is a cataclysm. Minor factors that influence its flow, come together in such a way to precipitate a critical change of direction. The consequences, in this analogy, are that the coast of some continent suddenly finds itself bereft of this huge saline engine and faces a sudden change of climate. The Great Eclectic was one such change of ambience in the course of western history. Our culture had become invidiously more greedy for new experience, obsessed, driven by is unusual response to the hyper growth of technology. We had become so addicted to change that there came a point when we all just became bored. When there was nothing new that would titillate us again, it all collapsed. It went off its head for a few moments. But whereas an individual can go of her head for a while because the bits can be picked up by family, friends or health care - when all of society become irrational at once there is no hope for it no one to rescue it. As you know," he paused to stare hard at Gregory for any hint of a mocking expression, "there wasn't a world war this time or even a civil war but a personal war when society broke down for the loss of heart of its individuals to assert themselves as a community." He looked pleased with himself. Gregory would have liked to have staged a yawn to deflate him but he remained steadfastly listening to this monologue as Jinks got into his stride. "We were lucky, for against all odds we were rescued: the rest of the world, which had not reason to show us any benevolence, after the heartless way we have pursued our imperialist policies in the past, now showed us - and you will like this word - an act of grace. Order was re-established and a government began to govern again but the personal crisis had done for the institutions and most went to the wall. Only the vestiges remained, like this cathedral and a much slimmer judiciary and no local government and limited emancipation and so on - the facts you know well. And now it has all begun again, that steady creep to ennui but this time we will learn from history. Our new enthusiasm has brought us these city states - yet the stimulus must be managed this time - we cannot let society get so hyper that it breaks down as before. We must take on the challenge to engineer a change to a new society and those who have a vision for it are called to forsake the mistakes of the past and get it right this time." As he had spoken Jinks had swollen up and now his eyes looked past Gregory to some achievable utopian future. He nodded sagely to himself; he was now very pleased with what he had said and he had inspired himself further. He looked significantly back into Gregory's eyes. "You could be part of this Gregory." he underlined the words by pointing his finger at the same time.

"Perhaps I think that your memory is not long enough," was Gregory's first cautious reply. "You may avoid the mistakes that caused the Great Eclectic but I perceive that you are being blind to the lessons of history before that."

"Such as," Jinks spat at him.

"You believing that you know what is best on your own."

"Don't be stupid there is more than just me and I am offering you the chance to part of it."

"Yes but you are not offering me to be the part that is me. You are not prepared to include what I am in disagreement with you."

"As I said you are politically naive."

"Or perhaps you are?" The other man's eyes showed yellow. "Well I am very flattered," continued Gregory, "and I am the last one to deny that I am politically naive as you say. However, I do not believe that the divine spirit is politically inept. I think, because I believe he can see into our hearts, that he knows better than anyone the political process." Jinks stood up. "And I believe that he has called me to be his spokesperson."

"Is that your final answer."

"Yes," Gregory said quietly but firmly. He was throwing the dice to agree with their consequences for him of his refusal to join them.

"I am not surprised," confirmed Jinks. "I suspect there is nothing we can give you that would persuade you. No threat we could make?"

"None."

"Shame."

"So when will it be I would rather know."

"He doesn't realise we are not going to kill him," observed the Dean maliciously.

"No we are not going to dispose of you in that way. We have become concerned about your mental health." Gregory gasped, he had not expected this. "You might well react. You are a tragic case really but not without precedent. You have some sort of religious mania. Your treatment at St. Arburn's heated your brain rather. They filled your head with all sorts of grandiose ideas that are unattainable and quite frankly not real. We are to send you for psychiatric tests." The Dean was edging towards the door. Gregory was getting up slowly and Jinks reached for his service revolver. "Do not let us have to restrain you before it is necessary," Jinks continued.

"They won't believe it," Gregory said.

"Oh yes they will. The Dean can act out your deterioration and then the public will be able to watch your disintegration." The provocation was now immense on Gregory and he just did not know what to do. That old shake that had disappeared, he had thought forever a few moments before, had come back.

"You are trembling my dear. Perhaps some sort of sedation is required."

"Go to Hell," shouted Gregory.

"Maybe I will but I will not bother about it like the Dean." She scooted out through the door and made no reply. The handgun was now out and aimed at Gregory. "So tragic," said Jinks shaking his head. "What a waste, what a waste."

"I want to see the doctor about my arm." But he was gone and later when Gregory looked into the chapel he saw that he now had two guards.

Chapter 24

He was surprised when the Doctor came an hour later, accompanied by two soldiers who followed her in. She turned to them and told them to leave her with her patient. They were reluctant to go and one of them talked into his radio telephone for instructions. "Five minutes," he commanded imperiously. She turned to Gregory when they had gone.

"Is your arm bad?"

"It's all bad. I need someone calm to be with me for a moment. They say I am mad now." She looked around nervously. As if in response to her unspoken enquiry he said, "They used to listen to everything I said, and watch everything I did, but I've fixed it I think. Not totally sure. Anyway please look at my arm," he said, "it is quite itchy." He took off his shirt and she removed the bandage.

"It just needs some air now. Leave the bandage off. It is only a 'little' wound," she said significantly looking into his eyes, but he missed the point at first.

"It didn't seem little to me."

"No let me assure you it is quite small as wounds go, rather 'little' actually." He was about to react because he thought she was putting him down when he looked into her eyes more deeply."

"Yeah Little."

"That's a 'mercy'," she said, "could have been worse. So is this better than St. Arburn's?"

"No, they are different but as I said my time has run out here. I thought I already was institutionalised but now they tell me it will happen properly."

"I have relatives in St. Arburn's."

"Was it your city before all this?"

"No. My cousin used to live near the Cathedral, sadly she died a number of years ago and her children were brought up by their dad."

"Really."

"Look," she took his hand, "you must continue to trust. The divine spirit has allowed all this to happen to you for a purpose. You must continue to believe that."

"It's hard. My confidence is continually shaken by events."

"That is part of your ministry - to show forth that trust in the public arena."

"You would make a better mystic than me."

"I don't think so. You have quite a following among ordinary people out here. I am sure not everybody believes what they read in the papers." The soldier knocked on the door.

"Time up!" She got up to go.

"If I were you I would be prepared for anything to happen." He nodded despondently. "Really, I mean it," she said looking significantly at him again. He stared back at her, she was not as old as she appeared, and he decided her formal clothes made her look older, but now he could see that she had a pretty face.

"Thank you doctor. Little by little!" he said.

"And be thankful for small mercies."

"Absolutely." She turned and went.

It was a great fear of Gregory's to be thought mentally ill, he had seen the consequences in his own family and therefore had a real terror of it all. At about 3am in the morning, when he had fallen from his troubled slumbers into a more settled sleep they came for him. He was unaware of their approach until they turned the light on and then it was too late. Six squaddies pinned him mercilessly to his bed whilst an officer prepared a syringe. His pyjama sleeve was roughly pulled up and the needle went straight in. Gregory expected to pass out but his faculties remained quite alert, instead his body felt paralysed. It was like waking up during an operation; he could not move at all. It filled him with a deep panic. Nobody said anything and although he could not move his mouth either they still stuck gaffer tape over his mouth. He was then manhandled into a strait-jacket, roped to a stretcher and carried off into the darkened Cathedral. "O dear spirit, kindly spirit," Gregory spoke into his mind, "I honestly cannot bear this - please believe me. I will go mad. Please don't let me go through any more." But there was no relief and the soldiers ran him out of the Cathedral into an awaiting military ambulance. He began to gag on the foul tape across his mouth and it was only the keen eyed male nurse, that came with the ambulance, that spotting his distress whipped the tape of and pushed him, and the stretcher to which he was tied, onto its side. The acidic bile ran from the corners of his slack mouth and stank out the ambulance. Some of the soldiers that were accompanying him swore but the officer hushed them. Disturbing images came to his mind and mercifully he blacked out.

He came around temporarily on a number of occasions and then felt the ambulance stop and the cold night air on his face as he was taken into another building. Finally, he was thrust into a small dark room without furniture and left. It was a black night and he determined during the long hours of solitude that he would kill himself whenever he got the opportunity. His slender resources of endurance had been exhausted by recent months and all the confidence that he was on some great triumphant crusade had now left him. He tried to pray, as the feeling came back into his body, but he found himself retching instead. Eventually, a feeble light began to filter under the door, even so he could not get near it as his body would not yet respond normally and the straight jacket continued to restrain him. A deep loathing filled his mind. In a cursing self-pity he blasphemed continually and cried for help. He was wrecked. The hours seemed interminable and he began to wonder whether they did not want him to die there.

After another hour he became aware of noises, doors banging, sharp cracks and then muffled explosions. There was a lot of shouting. As the noises got nearer it seemed as though a major battle was going on outside. It had sounded like the normal waking noises of a big establishment at first simply because he had assumed he was now in a mental hospital. But the vibrations of the blasts, coming to him through floor, convinced his troubled mind that a war had begun.

Finally, the door crashed open and a short man stood there dressed in battle fatigues and blacked up. "Ah there you are my little dip shit," the man said. It was Bailey. "Are you still alive?" he prodded Gregory with a bloodied bayonet and the fine point pricked through the strait-jacket and his pyjamas into his flesh. Gregory squirmed away. "What a shame! I was hoping to find you dead." A new apprehension gripped Gregory that Bailey had decided to kill him himself. Gregory was at a complete loss to know how he engendered such feelings of hatred in this man. Fortunately another figure appeared behind him, it was his doctor, also in uniform, looking red in the face from the effort. She bent down and expertly unbuckled the strait jacket.

"Thank you," he said. He began to rub the circulation back into his cramped arms. Generally feelings were returning.

"Can you get up?" she quizzed.

"I will try."

"Hurry up," barked Bailey. There were sounds of gun fire getting nearer. Without warning an automatic gun began chattering and the doctor fell to the floor crumpling like a limp doll. Gregory groaned. Bailey was firing back at the attacker and with his free hand he grabbed Gregory by the hair, leaving no alternative but to go with him. "Don't struggle I want to get the reward for you."

"The doctor! The doctor!" he cried.

"Screw the doctor, she can look after herself."

"She's wounded."

"Shut the fuck up." Bailey's gun stock smashed Gregory in the face and he fell to his knees. Before he could move further a tremendous force threw him along the floor. Next Bailey and someone else landed on him knocking all the air from his body. A tremendous battle began between the unknown assailant and Bailey, they tumbled and tore at each other smashing away with their fists continually entangled with Gregory. One of them stood on his leg, tripped and fell heavily on him a second time. At one point Bailey tried to drag him once more by his hair but the other man got Gregory's left foot and pulled. Gregory became the rope in this tug of war. Frustrated by their inability to best each other they joined battle again. After an initial throw Bailey rushed forward and aimed a kick at the other soldier but the man ducked right at the last moment and with a countermove struck Bailey's other leg and brought him down with crash on Gregory's prone head. Something hard and sharp rasped across Gregory's temple and right eye and a sickening pain began in his forehead: his face had been crushed against one of the discarded weapons. Finally there was more firing and the enemies head exploded in a shower of bone and flesh pulp spattering over Gregory and Bailey. More soldiers arrived and dragged Gregory off by his feet with his head banging on the ground. The corridors were full of smoke and the noise of artillery was immense. Eventually he was in the fresh air and someone pulled him back on his feet. He was bundled up and pushed into a waiting helicopter. The machine took off immediately and as it whirred over the embattled hospital Gregory could see that flames were shooting high into the early dawn.

Gregory lay still on the empty cargo floor to keep the effect of the nausea, caused by the bucking machine, to as little as possible. Bailey, with several other soldiers knelt over him; he, Bailey, was drenched in blood but by his manner and triumph it could not be his. "The old dog came for you didn't I? You should have seen your face. Your worst nightmare. Well you're coming back to my Cathedral now mate." Then he punched Gregory as hard as he could in the face over his wounded eye.

"Steady on," said one of the other soldiers.

"He's damaged anyway," observed Bailey.

"Even so Sir." Bailey scowled, got up and went to the front of the helicopter.

"Disheartening for the troops aye?" Gregory had passed out with the pain.

```
[B5] The human image is so strong that
even the barest representations of it are
recognisable, not necessarily because of the
skill of the artist, but because of the power
of the image. Thus the crassest mystic, as
long as he is genuine and not in denial can
fumblingly portray something of the grandeur
of the divine spirit. This is because divine
spirit's presence/image/form is so superior to
humankind's as never to be lost. Thus we see
him in the work of his hands.
```

Chapter 25

Gregory was now very disorientated because, when he came around, he was back in his cell at St. Arburn's and it was as though he had never been way. He was attached to a drip and his head was swathed in an encompassing bandage. Gratefully he was quite calm and pain free. When he raised his head he found Little holding his hand and talking to another man who had a stethoscope around his neck. Little stared back at him and squeezed his hand. The doctor kept talking. "There is a lot of trauma to his face and we will have to wait and see about the sight of his eye." He got up and went.

"Welcome back," Little said, there were tears in her eyes. "I have been so worried about you my darling." Gregory liked the word 'darling' it made him feel good, like the first breath of a new day. He reached out his untethered arm and gathered her to his chest. She snuggled down onto his bed. "I wrote you loads of letters but I just knew that you would never get them." He shook his head.

"No it was impossible."

"I feel so guilty."

"Hush it's all right."

"No I must say this. I knew, when you had gone, that I had not tried hard enough to get you out of here. I know that I had no force but I was too frightened of the consequences of making other sorts of stands. I can tell from talking to others that there is a strong feeling for you and we can work together now to get you released."

"You mean that they are not going to let me go!"

"No."

"They found they had no need for me at Persfeld. They were going to kill me."

"Yes, I know we got information."

"From your relation?" She smiled at him.

"Yes, she told you?"

"What a coincidence."

She nodded. "Her practise is within their old cloisters, they rent them out, so when you were wounded taking you there, it was an obvious choice to call her first. I am grateful." Then she paused.

"Use that word darling again," he was trying to deflect the

conversation.

She sat up and looked down at him and said, "darling."

"I thought you were an old fashioned girl."

"Meaning?"

"Surely I should have said darling first or some other sweet meat."

"You'd never have thought of it - anyway you are too busy out and about making a name for yourself as a mystic." They both giggled and it felt good. She looked at him. "I noticed."

"What?"

"That you had changed the subject - my half cousin?"

"I am very sorry," he pulled her down to him again. "She was there at the rescue and she was shot and I didn't know what happened to her. Bailey would not let me go back to help." At the name of Bailey she stiffened.

"Things have changed seriously and Bailey is at the centre of it."

"I suspected by his change of dress."

"Yes he is an officer now." There was knock on the door and the Dean and Mercy came in. The Dean looked quite stooped and much greyer. His voice, when he spoke was quieter and less assured, there was a pall of self-pity hanging over him. Little sat up and back removing herself from Gregory's embrace.

"The wanderer has returned," the Dean said in an attempt at a light hearted beginning.

"Yes you've me back in your power again."

"Not my power," there was a gap for him to say some more, such as, "more's the pity," but there was a silence instead. "There have been some changes whilst you have been away. I expect Little has told you about them."

"She was about to. She tells me that I am to be confined to this cell again."

"Tough luck."

"What's the point now?"

"Even more point in some ways - and less in others. They are no longer worried about your words, your sermons don't frighten them like they did at Persfeld. We - our government - is made of sterner stuff apparently. They are going to treat you like an explosive - if you contain it it causes more damage. I am no longer to be in control of you, although I am to remain as your host at the Cathedral. You see I hoped that your presence here would bring the healing of the rift between the secular and spiritual, a new age of unity, a return to that which has been long lost, but tragically it has had quite the opposite effect."

"Are you blaming me?"

"No, I don't believe it is you, you have simply been the catalyst for all the old enmities, a new form of the membrane across which all the old vitriol has always been expressed." He sighed. "Now we are to become the institutional church of the state I am told. Wrecked my dreams for sure."

"It hasn't done much good to mine either."

"I acknowledge that."

"So what is to happen to me?"

"Bailey..."

"Not Bailey!"

"Bailey will have responsibility for you, yet not directly. Bailey has moved onto better things. We now have a ministry of religions. Each ministry has a military input. Bailey is to have that role in this new ministry. Although a Mrs. Ashford is in charge - she will be along to see you soon I expect."

"But if I am to be have the freedom to express myself, why cannot I be free?"

"As I indicated they are not averse to a disembodied voice but they are afraid of who might rally to you if you were more visible."

Gregory just shook his head. "This is so ridiculous. I cannot believe that you are talking about me. I cannot conceive how it has stirred up such..." He couldn't find the words. "And why I have suffered so much as a consequence. Why has it all been so hard?" The Dean paused for a moment.

"Somebody must have the short straw. None of us wants it, we all look for someone to deflect the consequences of our action on to. Why should it not be you? Why should the divine spirit not choose you. I know that I am being hypocritical here, but I am glad it is not me, and I know you will blame me for starting the whole thing going, but even so I cannot be sorry. It felt right."

"So if something feels right to someone else that is OK?"

"No it felt absolutely right. I am no spiritual man and I have never had the remotest spiritual feelings that I could have any assurance about until you came and the remembrance of that has not gone away. I am making it worse I know, I have a responsibility to try and rescue you from this but I would need the same assurance I had on bringing you here to know that it has come to an end."

"May the divine spirit grant you that assurance," interceded Gregory. He sighed again. "You needn't say any more. I cannot say that you were right, I sense some stirrings of integrity in you. And I forgive you."

"The Dean's head dipped slightly, "Thank you," was his reply in a barely audible voice.

All this happened whilst Mercy had stood just behind her father hopping about and looking as though she needed the toilet, with a sickly grim expression on her face. The Dean turned to her and took something she was holding.

"Gregory thinks our cousin - half cousin - was wounded when they rescued him," Little told them both. The Dean looked sad and shook his head. Mercy began to cry.

"That is very bad," was the Dean's response and then, turning to Gregory, "we have this for you." It was a large padded envelope. Gregory opened it with his stiff fingers and when he saw what was inside he beamed: it was his black book.

"How?"

"I honestly don't know - it just came by post."

"Maybe your cousin?" Gregory looked at Little for confirmation.

"I must go affairs of state - not any more - just running this ancient pile." The Dean disappeared. Mercy came forward, her eyes were bright with tears, and she looked as if she would burst. She came and knelt down by the bed and put her head in his hand.

"I am so sorry, please do not be cross with me." She pulled something out of her pocket, it was a wad of bank notes. "Most of them are still there."

"What are you saying," said Little impatiently. She did not like the way that Mercy was so close to Gregory.

"It was me - don't be cross. I gave them information so they could take you to Persfeld. I just thought that it would help you and get back at Bailey. They told me they would rescue you. I thought that I had done a good thing, but now I know they were cruel to you, even worse than here."

"I wouldn't say that!"

"Please take the money I cannot bear my conscience anymore."

"Yes I will keep the money - and it is all right - well it's all wrong, but it's part of this whole thing, one more small choice made by others on my behalf. Whether the divine spirit engineered it or he rescued me from something worse I am quite at a loss to say, but here I am. My theology sucks. Go on, just go away, just put it down now."

"Can we be friends still?"

"Yeah." Mercy kissed his hand and ran away. Little laid down on the bed again in Gregory's arms and he slept for a while. She was gently wiping some dribble from the corner of his mouth when a crash of the door heralded the arrival of Bailey. His eyes narrowed when he saw Little in Gregory's arms.

"The minister is coming to see you shortly. Susan will have to leave now. The door is to be locked soon." He turned around. "Come in," he commanded. An elderly man stepped around the bend in the stairs. "This man will watch you - he is my spy," Bailey said with relish, "and everything you do or say or even think will be reported by him to me. I will be watching your dreams."

"Why do you have to be so spiteful?" Gregory asked, "how have I hurt you?" Bailey's eyes flicked to Little but he had nothing to say.

"Out," he commanded Little and the spy. He stood over Gregory who tried to brace himself for the blow that would come when the witnesses were gone. "I won you, now your life is in my hands." Gregory did not feel afraid of such talk anymore.

"Actually I thing you are wrong," but he did not expand on his meaning either.

"I hope you rot away in here."

"So be it," he replied calmly. Bailey scowled and went away locking the door behind him. However, Bailey proved to be wrong as the minister did not turn up that day.

It became clear that the elderly man was to be his servant as well for it was he who began to bring Gregory his meals. Unhappily for Gregory he would not respond to any attempts that Gregory made to engage him in conversation either. More annoyingly he was subjected to this servant sitting or standing close his cell for long periods of time. He was obviously taking his duties seriously. It was only when Gregory started to read from the black book, looking and saying the words directly to the man that he withdrew.

Several days past whilst Gregory grew strong again. Unfortunately, he suffered constant headaches and his face itched like crazy as the scar tissue healed. His eye socket remained swollen and painful with all the colours of the rainbow displayed in the surrounding flesh. In addition, and of more concern, was that his eye would not focus at all. He could see light but had no resolution. Little came to visit regularly and they avoided outside matters as much as possible. Hesitatingly they began to speak more of their affection for each other and started to have 'what if only' type conversations about the future.

On one occasion they had a frank discussion centred on the worsening political situation between Persfeld and St. Arburn's. Both Little and Gregory were concerned for the future. It was clear that the possibility of civil war loomed.

On the Thursday Mrs. Ashford came gushing to his cell window. "Gosh you are snug in there," she said immediately pushing her head through the window space. "I bet you are glad to be back - we are for you. You are a bit like a national heirloom or should I say state heirloom. Look we are all dreadfully excited about this new ministry idea and in it we hope to bring together all culture, both high and low, and all the wonderful benefits that religion brings to society and the human spirit. Like the wonderful witness of this Cathedral." She looked around and up, lurching dizzily for a moment. Then she turned back to Gregory and beamed again. "Look, now you are here, we want your views on all kinds of things. We have had this brilliant idea that we can start to publish a series of government-sponsored monographs. So you will start to get paid for what you do. Great eh?" She rattled on without a pause. "Therefore if you would like to start putting your mystical thoughts to paper then we will provide you with secretarial assistance, and editorial help, to polish up for publication. It is always brilliant to see your own work printed. Wonderful experience. You are probably worried that we are going to alter everything you say, let me put your mind at rest on that score, we are not a government that balks at free speech, we see ourselves as very much serving the people." There was not a break between sentences. "Everyone should have their say from the humble right up to the famous celebrities - like yourself. Oh and we want you to preach a lot - what you say is dreadfully popular and you really have helped people get closer to spirituality and the like. Wonderful. Good, good. I'm sure we will have many more fruitful meetings. I will ask my under-secretary to come and explain in more detail the whole new initiative and what you will get out of it. Great to meet you at last. You mean so much to our department. Bye." And she was gone.

Gregory had not moved a centimetre during the diatribe and when it was finished he looked down at the pages of his book and returned to his own private thoughts.

"Wonderful isn't she," said the Dean, who appeared next. It's great to have her in charge now. So enthusiastic."

"Stop it," said Gregory, "enough." The Dean giggled. Gregory scrutinised him carefully, it appeared to be genuine. "Mmm, to what do we owe this change?" The Dean blushed slightly, which was also a unique occurrence.

"I have just had to give up in some ways," he sighed.

"Good," said Gregory.

Then more business-like the Dean continued, "So I have been told that you are to preach this Sunday and from now on."

"No."

"No? I thought that that was just what you wanted."

"No, I haven't got that much to say. They would have me exhaust myself with banalities. But when it is right then I will speak."

"They won't like it. Bailey won't like it."

"Hopefully, yet what can they do? I think even they are unlikely to torture me in public."

"Don't underestimate them," warned the Dean. "these are troubled times and nothing is certain anymore."

"Do you think Persfeld will try to get me back again?"

"No from what Little tells me. It's OK, she is still my daughter and she has not been indiscreet - it seemed that you had served your purpose for them. If anything they'll just be vindictive and I cannot predict what form that might take. So will you preach this Sunday?"

"Not yet, get someone else, like normal."

"OK," he paused," I am glad you have come back, this has always felt like the right place for you."

"I know."

"Goodbye for the moment." Gregory felt warmed by this new found courtesy in the Dean.

However, the news had a bad effect on Bailey who was there breathing fire within the hour. Gregory let him rant, threaten and blaspheme. Gregory bit his lip when Bailey said he would be cruel to Little, nevertheless Gregory's determination, formed by his suffering, was now much more robust and he was not so easily stirred. When Bailey paused to take breath Gregory said slowly and calmly, "I am sure the Dean has already explained that I do not intend to preach every week but only when I have something to say and that I will indicate when the time has come." Bailey began again, he was very worked up and had completely lost it. Gregory stood up, walked away down the stairs to his bathroom, entered, put down the toilet seat and sat down closing the door behind him. Outside he could hear the sound of continued shouting. Then another voice began to shout in return. It was the Dean, he thought so he wanted to watch. Gregory opened the door a crack to check.

"For goodness sake man pull yourself together." It was a tall thin officer who, with the Dean and several soldiers, had come to see what was happening.

"This is the house of the divine spirit," said the Dean smugly and much to the delight and surprise of Gregory. "This sort of behaviour will not be tolerated. Please," he turned the officer, "would you escort him from the building."

"You do not know who you are talking to," blustered Bailey.

"Maybe not," said the officer, "but I know when a captain is being insubordinate to a major. That is clear enough. If you have official business here then may I suggest that this is not the way to conduct it. This is disgraceful. I should not need to reprimand a fellow officer in front of..." he nodded his head to the delighted soldiers. "Go away and compose yourself - and if you must come back do so calmly as befits a proper officer."

"Sir!" spat Bailey and walked away.

"Completely lost it," remarked the Dean. "He is a very difficult man to work with, he is always angry like this and losing his temper, particularly with our friend here." He pointed to Gregory who had emerged out of the toilet cubicle. "I don't think it is the right brief for him."

"Hmm," said the officer. You could tell he did not want to be any further involved. The Dean took the officer by the arm and walked off with him. Gregory heard, "Major, look you work with Colonel Wesley.........."

A verse from his black book came into Gregory's mind:
> *O you who dwell in the gardens,*
> *my companions are listening for your voice;*
> *let me hear it.*

"Oh let me hear your voice," said Gregory. He sat down and took up a pen and paper and began to write his next sermon.

'O good spirit, O kindly spirit, O spirit of wisdom, O spirit of knowledge, O spirit of council and might, O divine spirit grant us all a mystical experience of your desire for us.

The divine spirit in his compassion for us, in his outreaching desire to share all of his riches with us, is angry. Can you hate the one you love, can you despise the work of your own hands, can you be so consumed with the pain of rejection that you cannot contains your words or feelings even for the very same person you would die for? The divine spirit's emotional life is as rich and as varied as the purest untouched verdant and virgin forest. It contains every single species and variation of emotion and feeling. The unique significance of one single tree does not diminish the whole or deny a different expression of another. They may live and grow in opposition and yet still blend into the whole. So we need to hear the anger of the divine spirit, the direct assertion of his rage at his rejection by us, without doubting the clearest expression of his mercy.

I beg you no longer reject the call of the divine spirit to join with him. Let him cleanse and draw you to himself. '

Gregory put down his pen and read it through. He was pleased with this beginning. There seemed a sense of rightness about it as though he was coming on line in some way and he determined to finish it later. He went to rest on his bed. The previous day he had removed the bandage from his head for the last time and the swelling was going done but he could not bear to put any pressure on it and it was making sleeping at night difficult. Consequently, he felt more tired in the day. He settled down on his mattress for a rest and a think. He reviewed his current stories and decided to go and see the crocodile.

When he got to the wooden lodge it was deserted but it was lovely day and the ozone on the sea breeze was particularly strong. With the sun being so very hot, he decided not to go down the estuary to the sea or even into the wood but to head north back up the slope of the entrance field to where the gate stood. He walked up the field and turned left. There was no sign of the gate at present but he did not mind because he did not want to leave. The field was in reality a meadow, or so it seemed now, and as he walked slowly up the rise he was greeted with the lovely sound of droning insects and the sweet smell of the meadow flowers and grasses. At the top of the hill was a deciduous woodland and he headed for that. The wood, when he got to it, was quite open and he swung into it along a well-defined path. He was surprised that there were no large animals around and faintly disappointed: he had come to depend on their companionship. Gregory was not quite alone because he could hear rustling in the vegetation alongside the path but nothing appeared to greet him. The trail swung round in a wide arc cutting through sunlit glades and deep shadows where the canopy was complete, until he could once again hear the sea. In time he came to the last of the trees which were now only a metre or so from the edge of the cliff. The brim was covered with a plush fine grass of about ten centimetres tall which, under foot, was like walking over a plush carpet. He gingerly approached the brink of the cliff and when he looked down he saw it to be a steep drop of several hundred metres. It caught him unaware that he had made that much ground climbing up the gentle incline of the meadow and wood.

In the distance he could see the sand bar and the end of the creek; his position being some quarter of a kilometre from the actual sea. Past the cottage, to the south, the cliff edged the sea but here it was more of a backdrop. He lay down and stared at the far ocean. There was not a ship in sight nor any further hint of land. He felt calm and relaxed, neither hungry or thirsty. His body did not ache nor was it filled with energy. A gentle lassitude hung over him and he submitted to its delicious administrations. In a few moments he fell asleep. He had no idea how long he was unconscious but when he awoke he was still on the cliff top. An albatross, which now squatted near him, had woken him up by its cawing. "Do you speak?" he asked it sleepily but the bird only contemplated him with one eye for a few moments before shuffling to the edge of the cliff and fell off. Almost immediately it swooped up back into his line of sight, gave a kind of nod and glided off.

"Hmm," he said to himself and got up from his bedding. Gregory checked the time and went for a quick wash and to clean his teeth. It was time for Little to come and see him. They had fallen back into the old pattern of her popping in to see him at odd times during the day and particularly when she got off work. She was on time but did not bring any newspapers with her this time.

"Oh before I forget," she remarked after giving him a kiss on the cheek as a greeting, "dad asked if you would like to start seeing pilgrims again."

"I didn't think I would be allowed - as I am a kind of pollutant."

"Not true."

"Yes I would, I am very bored waiting to see what will happen to me next." They both laughed. "And can you tell your dad that I have changed my mind and that I will preach on Sunday but only if I can come and deliver it myself." Little made no comment about that.

"How is your face?" He told her. "And your sight?" He gave her an answer for that question as well.

"I really wish," he said, "that we could have a more conventional life together and share the everyday things."

"Yeah that would be great but then you wouldn't like me anymore."

"Don't be daft. I don't know how I can prove to you - that I think you are special - not just as a product of me being in here."

"It's difficult," she said.

"I love you that's why." Gregory had never used those words in that deeper way before. Her face brightened; it was a significant moment for her.

She was about to respond when there was a cough behind her; their lives were constantly interrupted by other people appearing unannounced. It was like being actors in a television drama: the action all took place within the compass of the limits of the screen with other members of the cast appearing magically and often unwanted from another dimension - the green room of life.

This time it was Bailey. He was very dapper in his uniform and for once his face did not seem angry.

"I thought I would find you here," he said casually. "May I speak with you please." At first they both thought he meant Gregory but as he continued to look at Little it became obvious who was the object of his attention.

"Yes go on," she said blushing.

"Privately if I may."

"Well I don't have anything private to keep from Gregory."

"Well I do," countered Bailey. Little looked towards Gregory for advice.

He instructed her quietly, "Go somewhere public." She got up and went off with him. Gregory did not know what to think, he had no sense what this might be about. After about ten minutes she returned. She looked very pale as if she had been given a shock. Little came, sat down and put her hand through the window so that Gregory could take it. "What," he said impatiently.

"Bailey wants me to marry him."

"My God!" Gregory was immediately angry.

"No calm down. Don't make your reaction bigger than mine. You haven't heard it all yet. His manner was remarkably human. He spoke very quietly."

"How old is the creep?" Gregory was responding badly.

"I don't know - forty. It's a guess. It was classic romantic literature. He told me how much he had always admired me and that, although he had felt very fatherly towards me at the beginning, with being around when I was growing up, now his feelings had changed. It was true he could see that I was very attached to you but he wanted to speak before I made my mind up about you finally in case I had never considered him in that way. He knew that he has a problem with his temper but he felt he could deal with it for my sake and he asked if there was any chance I could return his affections." Gregory was about to speak but she put up her hand to shush him.

"Preposterous!" Gregory could not help himself. "You don't seem very upset."

"No, that's the strange part, I have seen it coming for some time and feared it, but now it has happened - you're right I feel calm about it."

"You said no of course."
"No I didn't."
"What?"
"Listen Gregory - please. I need you to listen to me." Gregory put his hands on his mouth. In this pale calmness she looked so beautiful it was as though they were living through a bewitched moment and he did not know how to respond. A stillness had descended on the whole Cathedral. "He went on to say he was in a position to help me over a number of things - and for my sake he was prepared to do them regardless of my feelings for him - yet he hoped that they would persuade me of his good intentions. He told me that the daggers were out for my dad, that the debacle over your capture was going to redound on him and that he was going to be dismissed by the Cathedral board. He told me that Mercy had got herself into some serious trouble and that the net was closing around her - he knows about the money - but he could use his influence to help her. And finally he said that he would help you escape. He was a completely different man from the one we know and he did seem genuine."

"Too suspicious."

"Well I don't care for him at all and I never have. He has always been a bit spooky, more machine than man, but if he can really help with those things we should let him." Gregory sat back. It smelt very bad he thought.

"Are you telling me that he didn't want anything from you?"

"No, well only that we meet again for me to give him my answer."

"How very bizarre."

"What should I do? It is so completely out of character that I can only ask what is his game now?"

"Tell him to give you a month and that he can prove his good intentions by showing this new altruism and tell you dad tonight."

"OK." So her mood lightened now a decision had been made. Now she looked at him mischievously. "Did I detect earlier you using the 'l' word for the first time. He laughed.

"It must have slipped out. I can't remember what word it was now. Longevity, lassitude," he was pulling her towards him by her hand. He had not relinquished the hold on it since she had given it to him earlier. She was so slight that her head and shoulder could be pulled through the gap between he stanchions. When he had her as close to him as he could get her he kissed her on the lips and she struggled to get even closer.

"Oh put your arms around me," she pleaded. He tried to, putting them out through the bars on either side and around her back and shoulders. They embraced thus with the cold stone pillars between them. Unbeknown to them Bailey was leering around the corner of the Presbytery just showing the merest slice of his head and the edge of his eye, so he could observe them secretly.

"Fuck you both," he said quietly to himself. "You two little innocents."

"What are you doing here?" asked the Dean behind him.

"Spying on your protégé old man," came the slick reply

"Why have you become so beastly?" asked the Dean.

"Quite the opposite sir," he said quietly, "I wish to fulfil my responsibilities to you, your family and this Cathedral." He was nodding to himself as he walked off.

"Mad," said the Dean when he was out of ear shot.

Chapter 26

```
[D5] Can not even the stones of walls cry
out about the divine spirit should they have
cause? Maybe they whisper even now.
```

Gregory enjoyed the next day because he was allowed to see pilgrims again. It was as before except that there seemed to be a greater military presence in the Cathedral. Not only were there more soldiers around generally - some came to him as pilgrims - but he now had a discreet guard standing at the furthest limit of the presbytery. It felt uncomfortably like Persfeld.

After the pilgrims, and before lunch, a strange man appeared saying he had been sent by the Dean to show Gregory his catalogues. After a few moments of confusion, and once the catalogues were proffered, it became clear what his intention was: he was the representative of a clerical outfitter and he had been sent at the Dean's behest to ask Gregory if there was anything he wanted. Gregory took the catalogue and began to flick through it.

"I understand sir," said the man in a confidential tone, "that one is to be allowed to preach this Sunday at the main service. I believe that the Dean would have you dress appropriately for the occasion and to take into account the tradition of this temple."

"What tradition is that?" enquired Gregory.

"High sir."

"Meaning?"

"With feeling, symbol and pomp - and with help from my catalogue sir."

"But I am not licensed in any way."

"That's correct sir." It sounded like a criticism but Gregory ignored it. "Perhaps you would cast your eye over the pages sir."

"I won't be able to concentrate if you stand over me. Come back in ten minutes."

"Certainly sir," and he was gone. Gregory flipped casually through the pages. It was true he had very little to wear and certainly nothing for a formal occasion. He deduced from the man's appearance that his request, or demand, to preach in person had been heeded. He couldn't guess at why.

Gregory could not make up his mind whether being a mystic meant he had to look as shabby as he did. The clothes he wore had been found for him from some charity shop. Feeling pleased at the thought of having some new clothes he chose some black trousers and a jumper from the back of the catalogue. Then he looked again at the more formal clerical wear. There were cassocks, albs, surplices and even a habit for a monk but none of these felt right. After these, in among the black overcoats, he discovered a cloak with a hood and he just knew that he wanted it. The man came back bang on ten minutes and wrote the order down in a small note book. "Is that all sir? Surely you will need more than one pair of trousers. I understand the intention of the Dean is to kit you out. Money is no object, so to speak, you need not stint yourself."

"OK can you get me underwear and so on?"

"Of course sir." The order was amended and multiplied. Gregory also added shoes and three white shirts. He felt touched and pleased with himself when the man had gone. This was the first bit of vanity he had been allowed since his incarceration. The measuring had been fun with Gregory having to do it himself and call out the measurements using the proffered tape measure.

He told Little when she came at lunch time and she was pleased, eventually, after questioning him as to whether it was not some sell-out to the establishment. It was only when he said that it did not feel like it that she stopped questioning him. "Don't you want me to look smart?" he asked.

"Of course I do." She changed the subject. The Dean had been delighted at his decision to preach and cast down by Bailey's attentions. Although he had acted cross he seemed very worried by it. She had also sought our Bailey and passed on to him what had been decided. He had once more been very pleasant and repeated that he had only mentioned his feelings, even though he knew she was so fond of Gregory, so that he would not regret taking the chance whilst there was still time. She had also dared to say that, as he had noticed, Gregory and she were sweet on each other, so he must not hold out any hope at all, however as he had the courtesy to speak so plainly and calmly to her she would consider his words. Gregory was not sure Little had done the right thing and wondered if they were not being drawn into some new game but he kept his thoughts to himself.

Gregory was surprised to find his order delivered the next day. Everything was boxed and wrapped in tissue. Gregory had a delicious moment of anticipation before he began to open them. He wondered for a split second whether to keep it all until Little was there but his hunger for the experience made him go ahead. The shirts were crisp and beautifully tailored. He recognised the name inside. The black jumper turned out to be a real Guernsey and it fit him like a glove. In the largest box was his cloak. It was made of a fine woollen material lined with maroon silk and with a detachable hood of the same woollen material but lined this time with black. He put it on and swirling it around him sat down in his chair to luxuriate in it.

"Ahh, splendid," said the Dean. Gregory had been so engrossed that he had not spotted his approach. "A sensible choice, it gives you that extra touch of dignity and authority for a public occasion and yet does not imply any traditional function. Well done." The Dean seemed so pleased that Gregory wondered for a moment if Little had not been right and that he had sold himself out.

"Beware of gifts," he thought to himself.

"You are wrong, it has not diminished your integrity," said the Dean in an unusual moment of insight.

"Good."

"I was wondering if you would also be prepared to wear this?" He held out a small wooden black box that Gregory had not spotted in his hand. "We are very different here from Persfeld we take our liturgy more seriously, we maximise the visual aspects of it more."

"What is it?" Well it is very old an heirloom of the Cathedral. No one knows where it comes from and of course it can never be yours whilst the Cathedral stands. It is one of our vestments, so to speak, but one that has lost its history and one for which we have no use at present. Well - perhaps until now. On our inventory it is called, 'The Chain of the Office'. We don't know which office. Maybe it can become the chain of the office of mystic. He passed it through the grating. Gregory took it and opened the box up. In it was a very long ornate gold chain. Firstly he noticed that there was no medallion or symbol hanging as a pendant. The chain itself was made of three separate lengths linked together by enlarged gold rings. It was very heavy. Every fifteen centimetres or so there was a gold decoration separating it from the next length of chain. These ornaments, which were all identical, were like small elliptical boxes with carved apertures one each side to allow the light through. Although the chain was not fine neither was it grossly large but had a balance and symmetry to it that were pleasing to the eye. He weighed it in his hands. Gregory lifted the chain over his head and it fell uncomfortably down too his belt buckle and the weight made it cut into the back of his neck. "Hmm I can see why nobody wears it," he said.

"Think about it anyway. I will leave it with you."

"Cheers." Gregory could not cope with the new found pleasantness of either the Dean or Bailey. He was fearful that neither could last. After the Dean had gone he experimented with the chain. First doubling it, but that meant that the weight pulled one loop inexorably larger and the shortening one strangled him. Eventually he slung it over his shoulder so that the long loop fell to his side, that was the best, he left it there for a while before stowing it safely away in its box. From time to time in the day he took it out and fingered it. The chain had a wonderful glow: its lustre, the skill of the workmanship and the ornamentation gave him pleasant feelings as he ran it through his fingers.

When Sunday came he dressed in his new clothes, hung the chain across his shoulders and donned his cloak. A message had come that he would be escorted to his seat a few minutes before the service. His new valet, who passed on the message, was at great pains to tell him that his escort would include two soldiers who would be armed and who were there to prevent him escaping. But the message came out as rote making it clear to Gregory who, despite his present pleasantness, was the source of it.

There had been the noises of an arriving crowd for up to an hour before the service but even so Gregory was surprised at the density of faces presented to him when his escort took him through the presbytery into the Nave of the Cathedral. He was given a seat under the pulpit by the Dean who was also participating in this ceremony. An order of service was on his chair. He scanned it quickly to find when he would speak. His slot was about two thirds of the way through. The office was a mixture of songs and responses with drama and poetry reading. Gregory found it dull and unsatisfying. He looked at the crowd but could not spot Little and wondered if she was there. The Dean sat like a block of wood throughout it all. When it was his turn. Gregory took off his cloak and laid it on the chair and then walked up the stairs of the pulpit, there being no other option left for him for all the other directions were blocked either by his armed guard or the Cathedral servers.

He read slowly and carefully the sermon he had prepared a few days before. There was a kind of shiver that ran through the congregation when he had finished because it had been too short and it was obvious that people were just settling down to hear his main points. He was about to come from the pulpit when the Dean was on his feet. He was staring up at Gregory with a grin on his face. "That was so succinct," he said and his voice boomed through the loudspeaker system: he must have had a microphone on him in for emergencies, "that perhaps you would do us the kindness of repeating it for the sake of those of us who are slow to begin to listen."

"There was a murmur of approval by the crowd. "All right." Gregory read it again and he could tell that people were listening more carefully.

The Dean had remained on his feet during this second rehearsal and said at the end, "Thank you very much." Gregory came down the stairs, put on his cloak and sat down. The service continued in its meaningless way. "That will set them talking," observed the Dean. "By the way, how do you know the divine spirit is the source and the means of all good and that nothing happens without his involvement?"

"I don't completely - I believe it and I know it intellectually but I don't really feel it in my heart yet. I wish I could."

When he got back to his cell Gregory found that the words of the Dean had made him very angry with the divine spirit. "I hold you to blame for all of this," he whined angrily at his cell walls. He fell into a black mood that lasted for several hours and filled him with doubt and dread. It made him think that he had been defending the indefensible. "What is the point, what is the fucking point!" Was all this some kind of test or was it some kind of refining process to make him a better person? He began to feel that it was neither. Perhaps the divine spirit is so full of himself that he is beyond arrogance and really is never able to put anyone before himself? This, and a myriad questions and other angry responses surged through his brain and cast him very down. When later Little came to congratulate him on his address she could not get anything but monosyllabic answers out of him, so she withdrew and left him to his gloom. Towards the end of the day his spirits began to lift, even so the questions and doubts remained un-answered. In the end he went to bed and tossed and turned for several hours before sleep came. It was as if the divine spirit had just upped and left him.

  Little came to see him early the next morning before she went to work; this was unusual but he was still unable to explain to her what the matter was. She sat and held his hand for a while and kissed him tenderly on the cheek before going off to her job. She left him a pile of newspapers to read.

  On the front of the national tabloid was the picture of an old fashioned army drum: the sort used to beat time as the soldiers marched. The banner headline was not unsurprisingly, 'The drums of war'. As he read the articles in all the newspapers and compared and contrasted them he became even more gloomy. There was fear in the air. There had not been a civil war in his country for years and now there was every possibility of one starting. The two main proponents where to be Persfeld and St. Arburn's, but other city states were already involved in diplomacy and choosing sides. The remnant of the old central government, now a toothless wonder, was vacillating dangerously and making the matter worse. It never actually said that Gregory was to blame but there was a clear understanding that the two armed incursions into each other's territory, to kidnap and recapture him, were the basis of the present difficulty. His previous day's sermon was printed in full but took a secondary place to the national situation. It was simply printed under the caption, 'Gregory's latest sermon' and without comment. More strangely there was a short section on the fashion page about what he wore and a prediction that he could well become a leader in that field as well because several of the major fashion houses were taking an interest in a retro clerical style. The most worrying aspect of the whole scenario was the news that check point controls were to be strengthened and that both City States were sending their militia on training exercise near their shared border. The editorial in the broadsheet made a passing comment as to the various military strengths of each city state. It was clear that St. Arburn's had not fared well in the share out of the national forces.

As he reached the bottom of the pile that Little had left him he found an open brown envelope addressed to Little. Inside, without any note, was the Cathedral news of Persfeld. On the front page was a letter from their Dean. He was shocked when he read it. As he was finishing Little came running back. "I gave you my post by mistake. You have not read it have you?"

"Just."

"Oh sorry, I wasn't going to hide it from you but you seemed so depressed that I was going to save it. It's from my half cousin I recognise the handwriting - so it means that she must still be alive. Let me take it away."

"No I must hear it and bear it."

"Oops," she was grimacing at the pain on his face. "I must get back to work. Sorry, I'll come at lunch time." As it happened he could not dwell on it as the first pilgrim arrived shortly afterwards but it was all too much on his mind for him to concentrate effectively. When they had gone and his lunch arrived he sat down to read it again.

'Dear Brothers and Sisters in the divine spirit, we have been terribly misled by that sinner Gregory. We brought him here in all good conscience to feed our spirits but he turned out to be an evil presence masquerading as a spirit of light. Apart from his descent into mental illness during his time here, he inveigled himself into our hearts by the most diabolical means. I urge all of you who had anything to do with him to expunge from your minds anything he said to you. There will be counsellors available in the sacristy all this week if any of you want help and prayer to rid yourselves of his influence. This is a very serious matter and as guardians of the Spiritual for this city we are ashamed that it was because of us that we brought such a pollutant into our midst. Without going into particular cases we have since discovered various other debaucheries he indulged in without our knowledge and he has wrecked many young lives by his predatory behaviour. He cannot be forgiven for these last acts and only his complete removal from any sphere of influence is acceptable. We at least are well rid of him. Those who now harbour him compound and endorse his crimes. It casts an enormous shadow over the spirituality and conduct of the Cathedral at St. Arburn's who, having so embraced his wisdom, have corrupted themselves. It would be a mercy if his evil influence could be removed completely and anyone who were to return our sister Cathedral to a right path will win lasting thankfulness from the divine spirit himself. When you read this please join with me in this concluding prayer. Dear divine spirit, blot out all the evil influence of the illegitimate, so called mystic, Gregory. Punish him for his vile untruths and take him to your eternal punishment. We ask this in the name of our holy Cathedral at Persfeld. Amen.

Gregory felt sick to the stomach. He called to his servant to fetch the Dean. He was brought within fifteen minutes. "Yes what is it?" he asked distractedly.

"Read this," Gregory thrust the magazine into his hands.

"Wherever did you get this?"

"Never mind that just read it." The Dean did dutifully twice.

On completion he inquired, "Well quite apart from it being completely defamatory."

"She is trying to stir them up to kill me."

"Nonsense you are reading too much into it. I will counter it all in our next magazine. It is not serious - just posturing twaddle. They would only make it worse if they martyred you."

"It would be an excuse to start a war," Gregory suggested.

"That I fear will come without your involvement. This is about power now. No sooner than they have turned the country into City States than one of them wants to be the national government again. The whole devolution was just a ploy to take over the country," the Dean said cynically. He was looking much older now: his cheeks had sunk and there were wrinkles around his mouth. When he spoke the spare flesh on his face flopped. His eyes also looked duller and there was some brittle sleep in the corner of the left one.

"You've changed your tune."

"I wish we had never got involved, we should have stuck to what we know best."

"Sour grapes," said Gregory.

By contrast Gregory's features had fleshed out. The increasing length of his beard and hair gave him a patriarchal appearance and he spoke assertively with obvious intelligence. The posture of his body revealed a continuing growth of strength of mind. Like a lion who had outgrown his cage so his intellect now emanated beyond the bounds of his cell.

"Yes and no. I really thought that the spiritual and the secular could be brought back together - but they just argue too much."

"I hate to say this, as you are in such a reflective mood, and that is new to me, but I think you are being too pessimistic."

"Maybe but my hopes have been dashed."

"You have put them in the wrong thing."

"If you say so. Anyway," he waved the magazine, "better not take this to heart. It is all hot air. They were left with egg on their face and don't want to lose face anymore."

"Perhaps," replied Gregory and the Dean smiled.

"I've wanted to let you go," he said," you must believe that but they won't let me. You are a trophy to them. That's odd isn't it? You were a trophy to me at the beginning and now you have become quite a different one to them." He did not elaborate. "I have begged for them to let you go, but, well, you know Bailey, he hates you so much."

"Because of Little?" asked Gregory.

"That's a part of it but there are darker things there as well."

"You will protect her from him won't you!" Gregory said forcefully.

"Naturally, I am her father." Gregory was not reassured.

"What should I do now?" Gregory asked him.

"You must act on your own truth," the Dean replied. They chatted for a while and the Dean asked him for his plans for another sermon but Gregory was not able to tell him. After he had gone Gregory read the article again repeatedly several times and became a little calmer. He was very struck by the change in the Dean, although wise enough to see that the Dean was still being quite naive, nevertheless he liked his last statement about acting on his own truth. Gregory prayed for a while and asked particularly that his truth would be a reflection of the divine spirit's truth. As he interceded the uneasiness returned again. It seemed that his contact with the divine spirit was making him more unsettled than with the Dean his old enemy. Had the divine spirit become his enemy? Or was it that he was just upset. Could the divine spirit be upset, out of sorts? Had he not just said so in his last sermon. There was strange sort of deep vibration within the fabric of the Cathedral as though someone were drumming their fingers somewhere. This was very uncomfortable. "Cheer up," he spoke into the air but there was no respite. The essence of this deep spiritual disturbance was numbing his brain and a new gloom about his future clung to him. There was a bad feeling in the air and it was about him. Is my end coming? Was the divine spirit is trying to warn him? "Will you be kind about it?" he asked aloud. "I'm the mortal one. Spare me this oppression. Show me what to do. He picked up his black book for an answer.

> *How the gold has grown dim,*
> *how the pure gold is changed!*
> *The sacred stones lie scattered*
> *at the head of every street.*

His old guiding shiver drew him to this strange verse. There was no escaping it, there was trouble ahead. If the diagnosis was true - the prescription must be cashed and the medicine drunk. Somewhere the gargantuan spiritual tide that undergirded reality had turned and begun to flow inexorably in the opposite direction. The very fabric of the building seemed to shudder a second time and Gregory felt cold with sweat. And so with the turn of the tide, the wind veered and he was buoyed and lifted from his chair by some unseen force to be thrown crumpled down onto the floor.

That night he felt ill and could not stomach his food, by the middle of the night he had a full blown stomach bug and spent the early hours retching into his sink and sitting on the toilet. The following day he despatched his servant to get some stomach tablets and then, taking them instead, refused his food. Now weak and listless, his appetite gone, he spent the time flicking through the black book but with little concentration.

Towards the evening his appetite returned but there was an unusual impulse not to eat. Instead he wrote some prayers to the divine spirit about the national situation and drank several glasses of water. By bedtime he felt hungry but still he resisted the temptation to eat. The following morning he awoke with a headache and bad breath. Gregory was embarrassed about kissing Little when she popped to see him at her lunch break. When she asked him why he was not eating he prevaricated and pretended that his appetite had not returned after his tummy upset. She offered to get a doctor for him but he declined. He found it very difficult to pray or concentrate on anything. During the next twenty-four hours he was cold and trembly with a persistent headache. All sorts of anxious thoughts began to trouble him and he twitched at the merest sound.

On the third day the Dean turned up with his breakfast himself. "They tell me you are refusing to eat dear boy. This is not the beginning of a hunger strike is it? It won't work, Bailey would be glad to see you starve to death and wouldn't lift a finger to help you."

"No it's not that. I have begun a fast," he said clearly and thus having owned it began to feel better.

"I see." The Dean was at a loss to know how to respond to such strange behaviour. "Good for you, there is certainly a long tradition of it in the past. Never heard of anyone doing it recently by choice. We are more into celebration at St. Arburn's - trying to rejoice in the good things that the spirit provides. Delaying gratification, although worthy, has never really proved much has it?" It was a question.

There was no need to respond to this interrogation and neither did Gregory particularly want to articulate any answer to this man, once a sworn enemy, now a more benevolent drogue, nevertheless Gregory stammered it out, "I think...believe... the divine spirit wants me to do it."

"Mmm, no choice then," admitted the Dean reluctantly. "I wish I had a hot line, like you, to the spiritual world."

"Join me."

"In the cell?"

"No in the fast." The Dean chuckled.

"I know it wouldn't do anything for me. Sorry. We'll let you represent the Cathedral."

"Someone needs to." The Dean ignored the barb. "So what about your food should we stop sending it?"

"Yes, just drinks until I say." When Little came at lunch-time she was very cross with him. "I just can't understand why you are compromising your health like this. You will need your strength for..."

"The trials ahead, yes. I believe this will give me strength." She could not remain mad with him for long. It was becoming clear that she had fallen in love with him. As if he were some malignant repetitive, interruption of their lives Bailey arrived adding one more to his tally of silent and unwanted approaches. He was sporting a new pip on his epaulet. More promotion. He expressed unctuous solicitude and showed himself relieved that Gregory was only fasting and not starving himself. His presence gave both Gregory and Little the creeps and they shuddered in unison when he had gone. Even so they did not feel able to voice aloud their thoughts because they were not sure how far their voices could carry or how near he was lurking. Later in the conversation Little told Gregory how Bailey's and her paths crossed with increasing frequency and how he continued with the slimy charm he had just demonstrated. They both felt more anxious about his change than they dared admit to each other.

Chapter 27

I came around a few moments later on the embankment. There was huddle of men around me and some cars parked on the hard shoulder with their lights flashing. My wonderful car was in flames. I tried to get up but one of the men, who I now saw was kneeling beside me, told me lie still. "Are you cold?" he asked further.

"Yes." And then a sudden realisation that there was something wrong with my left leg. "My leg?" I queried.

"Some damage," he returned. "You're lucky not to be trapped in there. The impact brought the engine back," he told me in a matter of fact way. "We've put a tourniquet on it." He could have been talking about the engine. I remained prone but looked along my body. In the dim moonlight I saw that there was black on the cloth and I could not see any lower. Suddenly, the pain overwhelmed me and I fainted.

What happened next was a blur. Strange faces asked imperative questions and I discovered later that I had had to have an operation on my leg: both the knee cap and the thigh bone were broken. It was a couple of days before I came around completely, although a nurse told me that I had been quite lucid immediately after waking for the first time, from the operation. I didn't care until she told me that the police would be coming back the next day to finish their interview. "They saw me after the operation?" I asked urgently.

"Yes."

"What did I say?" I inquired forlornly. She shrugged and went off with my bed pan. It was a very stressful twenty four hours and I worried the staff because my blood pressure suddenly took a high. I tried to work on my story but the thoughts would not hang together. I tried to think of all the mistakes I had made, the things that my girlfriend had spotted to make up her mind. Then with a cold shiver I remembered the handbag. I had thrown the map away and nobody who found that would see any relevance in it. But the bag - maybe that was not destroyed in the fire. Forensic science can tell all sort of things from the smallest specs of matter. They tranquillised me in the end and when the police did arrive it was on the understanding that it was for five minutes only.

The main policeman was small, robust with leathery skin. He had a firm but kindly face. "I am sorry for your double tragedy," he began "and we are sorry to trouble you again - but there are some matters to clear up from our previous chat."

"Oh what did I say?" trying to sound as innocent as possible. However, he had been a policeman too long. He just smiled.

"If I understand this right," he began, and then paused to take a notebook from his pocket. "You were travelling back up North with your girlfriend." He gave her name. "Because, sadly, her parents had just discovered that their other daughter had been killed - maybe even murdered," he said with some relish, "and left in a ditch on the A.... They are very distraught to lose two daughters in twenty four hours. Perhaps when you are well you will go and see them? I understand they are not coming down here. They don't travel too well." Then for just one short moment I felt as guilty as hell: I had killed both their daughters. But it passed. Grief for them was not on my agenda.

"Do you know why you crashed sir?" he asked directly and suddenly, presumably to throw me of balance.

"I fell asleep at the wheel."

"But you had just drunk a cup of coffee. You were remembered at the restaurant."

"I had already driven eight hundred kilometres that same day."

"We are aware of that sir."

"It was understandable then that I should have fallen asleep."

"Possibly you should not have undertaken the journey if you were that tired?"

"I felt good when I set off and I wanted to help my girlfriend. As you've said she was suddenly bereaved and not in a fit state to travel alone to comfort her parents."

"Perhaps you could answer then, sir, how you fell asleep when there appears to have been a large quantity of Idelmadol in your blood? This is an illegal substance - but we will leave that at the moment. However, it is fairly well documented that it heightens awareness temporarily rather than dulling the senses or making you soporific." This unusual word brought a smile to his silent colleague, who stood behind him. I guessed that this was a well-known example of his eccentricity at the police station: the use of rare words. I could not help myself.

"Soporific?"

" Sleepy," he said bringing another smile to the face behind him. "Anyway medical evidence might suggest that it is impossible to fall asleep on the amount of that drug you had consumed."

"I have no other explanation. Why would I want to crash my car. I had just spent months building her, she was my pride and joy."

"Your father-in-law, partner-in-law says he noticed that there was some damage to the nearside door."

"Yes." I flushed. "Damn the old sod," I thought. I told the officer that lie about the wind.

"OK. Perhaps we should move on to the main issue. What is rather bizarre is - that the other daughter's, your girlfriend's sister's, handbag was found in the car. Fortunately, the fire brigade got there before the fire had consumed everything. By the way we have your car, it has gone for a forensic examination, just routine." I nodded slowly but made no response. "The hand bag sir," he pressed me.

"Yes, it was like this. My girlfriend was in contact with her sister about the visit. She had told her not to expect her at home because she couldn't stand the thought of being with her parents - they were always onto her about her lifestyle - but that she needed her handbag brought down to her, back to London." It sounded unconvincing to me.

"I see." The officer consulted his notebook, then stood up and walked off with his colleague.

The nurse came in and asked, "Shall I send them away? Are you tired?

"No best to get it over with," I reassured her.

"They have no right to bother you," she declared angrily.

The officer returned. "The thing is her parents had no recollection of her leaving her handbag in their house." I began to sweat. The officer was watching my face intently as he had all along. "All right?"

"No, just my leg paining me."

"Shall we leave?"

"No go on."

"In addition, there does not seem to be anything of real value in the bag that she could not do without. What's more, there is a city bus ticket in it dated a week ago. Which you must see, from our part is very strange, because how did such a ticket get into her handbag hundreds of kilometres away? She had not visited her home there, by all accounts, for a year or more." I shrugged but then I had a thought. I told them about my girlfriend rummaging in the bag for tissues and I acted out how I suddenly remembered when she put her own purse back in it by mistake.

"I remember clearly now," I reassured them.

"Very useful," nodded the policeman. "Well you have been most helpful." He got up to leave. "We have several avenues to enquire down. I hope you feel better soon sir. Back on your feet. May I suggest you stay off the Idelmadol. They say it messes with the mind."

"Thank you." He reached the end of the bed.

"We might need to see you again."

"Good," I responded, "you may be my only visitors." He took another step and turning apologetically delivered the coup de grace.

"You will be interested to know that she actually set off for the North - your girlfriend's sister, that is. Her fellow squatters told us that she meant to go. Set off on a bus from Museum Street."

"Oh my girlfriend works - worked - near there." I said.

"Really." His eyes were like diamonds. And he was gone.

But he did not come back and the following week, the

day before I got out of hospital, there was a Coroner's Court. Many of these same issues were raised but without resulting in good enough answers either to clear or substantiate any of the worst unspoken suppositions about why the car had crashed or even what had happened to either sister. Nevertheless, I discovered something unusual in the report of the proceedings - I had not been able to go - and it was that they were actually non-identical twins and that my girlfriend's sister was in reality the younger sister, as they had always called her, because she was born second. It transpired that, because they had none of the psychic connection of identical twins, nobody had thought it worth mentioning to me.

It took months for me to get better properly and before I could contemplate work. There was talk of prosecuting me for dangerous driving or being under the influence of drugs. However, the research on Idelmadol was in its infancy, so I got off that as well. Unfortunately, the whole thing took its toll and, well, as I sit here writing this, I have become the first person to be certified as a result of overuse of that same banned substance. I don't understand what it's done to my brains, the technical terms do not mean much, you see after the accident I became very dependent on it, taking it a lot regularly. In fact it took all of the insurance money so I never even got another beautiful car again. But then I don't go anywhere now. Sad eh. or what? Of course I still like making up stories: my favourites are mystery, mysticism and madness.

Chapter 28

So as the days passed Gregory's concentration and mood improved. His breath and skin cleared and there was a new brightness to his eye. There were changes in the pattern of his day as well. He felt more able to sit still for longer periods, not just because he was weaker and thus less active but more that his own internal, anxiety-driven activity had damped down. So he mediated for long periods on the disconnected and puzzling verses in the black book. In addition, he wrote long and detailed prayers, repeating and refining them day by day. He focused on the civil tensions in the country, poring through the newspapers for subjects to pray for. He prayed more directly and authoritatively for his pilgrims.

The news however was not good, diplomatic initiatives by the other City States had failed and the rhetoric of Persfeld and St. Arburn's was becoming more rigid and uncompromising. The mood was pessimistic.

As Gregory deliberated, reading continually between the newspapers and the black book an increasing burden of sorrow and grief gripped him for the situation. Neither was it entirely his own bad feelings surfacing but rather a resonation with the mood of the divine spirit. As his fast deepened so the pitch and amplitude of these echoing chords also increased and he had to sigh aloud to himself in order to release them. Tension gripped his lungs and made his breathing shallow. At times he felt as though he were drowning in the answers to his own prayers. There was no escape, he was simply not hungry and therefore he continued in his refusal to eat. The Dean and Little were beginning to express their worries for him more strongly. They even brought a short note from the President urging him to desist. However, when Bailey came near he simply grinned wolfishly. Apart from this, his life was ordered and he felt fruitful. The only extra burden was a resumption of visits by Mercy.

Her first visit, after such a long absence, brought a much changed Mercy. The deep contrition resulting from her having sold him to Persfeld remained with her and there was real hesitancy in her speech. They spoke first of trivialities and Gregory waited, without prompting her, for the real reason to her visit. After a particularly long pause she confided. "Do you remember all those months ago you said you would help me?"

"Yes."

"Is the offer still open?" her voice caught

"Of course. What is it you want from me?"

"Somebody to listen really."

"I am not a priest."

"I know, but like with the money, I can't get rid of some of this stuff without saying it out aloud and to someone else."

"OK. Let's make a start. Are you with a boy at the moment?" He already knew the answer because Little kept him up with the news.

"Not at the moment. Many boys want me. They can be very hectoring and crude but....No - nobody."

"Tell me how it all began." And she did. For several days she came back for a half an hour here and there to rehearse it all. Gregory listened patiently to every detail of every sordid encounter. At the end he asked, "Do you want me to do something?"

"No."

"We haven't looked at what caused it all yet." Mercy nodded sadly in response.

"I am not ready for that yet. One day perhaps. It wasn't my dad. There is some shadowy figure there in my dreams - who knows. Thanks for listening. Now forget it all - please."

"I will."

"Can we be friends?"

"Only friends - let's not make Little jealous."

"She's bearing up well - me coming here to see you."

"True!"

Towards the end of the twenty first day of the fast a deep hunger arrived. As he sat in his chair, at the end of one of his times of meditation, study and prayer, his gaze was drawn to the ceiling of the cell and he nodded to himself as though in response to an unuttered statement of the divine spirit. "I will eat tomorrow," he acknowledged to the air. "I can see now," he continued, "that I cannot blame you for all of this." He swept his hand around the cell. "You've done enough to create us and sustain us - me, I mean." A pause. "I wish to continue as your servant." As Gregory sat slack and calm in his chair, savouring his decision to give up his fast and looking forward to assuaging his hunger, a warmth began to creep into his limbs. First, the unnatural heat began to make his fingers drum on the chair arm. Then a tremor pulsed from his twitching digits up into his forearm and into the muscles of his neck. He began to feel as though he would need the toilet but the warmth continued to grow. Now it started in his feet which also began to tremble. These were not pleasant sensations and he began to get scared. Gregory brought his shaking fingers to his collar and unfastened several buttons to dry the burst of perspiration that now ran on his chest. His mouth was rigid and his throat could not swallow without difficulty.

Then a light began to grow in his room. There was no focus to it, more a general increase in the luminescence. He stared around wildly and sprung to his feet - pacing around his cell. He began to tear at his clothes with the heat of it and he tore his shirt in the hurry to remove it. Gregory felt a headache start and his eyes grated in their sockets. When he looked at the floor it seemed to have a hole in it like when you get the visual disturbance of a migraine but there were not zigzag lines to accompany the sensations. His knees buckled as a strong sweet smell swept over him brought by some unseen wind. Now he was trembling all over and sweating profusely. To an observer he would have looked wild and deranged with his clothes half torn from him. And still the light continued to grow. There was pain in his heart as if something terrible was going to happen and he fell forward onto the floor as he lost all control of his physicality. In a half swoon, half-awake dream his mind bolted from his normal sense like a young horse freed from the confines of its stall. Gregory managed to turn on his back and he felt wet as drops of moisture fell from the roof of his cell. One that fell on his hand, he drew with painful effort near to his face to examine: it was brown and it gave of an odour of heavy sweet scent. When he sniffed it up, it went straight to his mind like a translucent smoke. The drizzle of drops continued soaking and anointing his skin with a divine odour. Without warning his heart lurched and he knew that someone was in the cell with him. He tried desperately to turn again and look round but his body was desperately paralysed. The fear continued to increase until he swooned away completely for a few seconds with the shock of it.

As he shook his head to clear it, the emotional atmosphere of his cell changed seamlessly to one of a deep satisfaction and then on further into a kaleidoscope of feelings from the most exquisite pain to such a feeling of joy that he felt that his whole being would burst. The roller-coaster drained him of every last resistance to this experience that had kidnapped him. For a moment he was back in his mind when suddenly colours began to drip from the cell roof directly into his eyes. Pictures began to form and as he reached out for them his hand came across a feeble resistance as if encountering insubstantial borders of the objects he saw. Gregory blinked hard.

And then he was sitting in his chair contemplating the prone shape on the floor. Now there were words. "Lover." It came twice and the image of him was picked from the flagstones and manipulated by some unseen force. The image looked placidly towards him as the vision began to distort. Immediately Gregory felt the force as well and it was him that ...

Gregory's mind could not conceive what had hold of him: it was so immense as to be indescribable. He felt an assertive and creative presence that worked on him purposively. He could not resist. There would be no way to stop it. It was like a surgeon killing to cure. His limbs had become clay and the Divine Spirit - he suddenly know it was the Divine Spirit had him in its grasp. It was remaking him. Gregory was so desperately afraid that his senses couldn't register it. There he was the centre of an intense scrutiny and the object of a unique creative process. His voice began to make noises on its own; he groaned and cried and prayed and swore. The hands that held him were like steel, as warm as flesh but as sharp and as antiseptic as salve. When he tried to look at his own hands they were gone. As he was turned this way and that - gently but forcefully rotated in the air - he caught glimpses of his own extremities. The images were appalling, his arms and legs had become living pillars. Once more these hands plunged into him and pulled out his organs. They formed them into decorations of alien fruits on the base of the pillars where his hands and feet had been. His whole torso became a roof and ...

Oh then an awful pain. He cried out with it, "Oh the pain. Oh the pain. Divine Spirit I love you but you are killing me." He was squashed, crushed, flattened onto the floor so hard that his flesh took on the imprint of the ridges and edges of the floor pavement. "You are bruising me. Hurting me! Speak to me. Reassure me! Be patient. I will yield. I will yield." But there was no answer. It all just began again. He was pushed and pummelled and stretched and cut and shaped. Now a house, now a temple, now a bridge, now a dam. In a blur of almost ferocious zeal the divine power played with him and Gregory screamed and shrieked with terror, pain and delight at each bold stroke and change. Finally, the Spirit put him back together as himself. Nevertheless, he was not the same: the work had caused a permanent damage to his whole being. Not a simple physical metamorphosis but a deep psychological and physiological change. The old Gregory was ruined. The Divine Spirit had played with him too hard - he would never be the same again

So he flew, drifting upwards, resting now on the back of the hands that had recreated him. High and deep into the universe Gregory went and the Spirit spoke to him, whispering contentment and secrets of purpose into the ears of his heart. Such things he saw that no words could express, that only colours and light could hint at and which any physical object could barely imitate. Such thoughts that human words would fail to bring meaning to them. He drifted for an eternity on the hands of the Divine.

"Look at this lover," the Spirit said over and over, out there through time and space and meaning. "Come here lover. Stay with me lover. Let me serve you lover. Be mine lover." So safe. So sure these hands. There was no fear that he would roll off. No cold or damp. No noise too loud or star too hot to touch him - even in their centres. No planet too lush to hold his curiosity so as to give up his own hold on his Lover. There was no need to leave, no argument, no force, no point that would ever make him return to his old life. This was essence.

It broke his heart to come back to his cold damp cell. He wept with unimaginable grief as the Spirit laid him on his pallet and the light and heat receded, flowing and ebbing away as a tide.

It was Little who woke him up with a new bottle of water: she had been bringing him bottled water for the last week. This was a treat he felt able to receive; the water in his cell always tasted tainted with the mustiness of the fabric. He was not able to tell her what had happened to him. It would be some time before he would be able to speak of it. The experience was far too raw. Instead he said, "I am going to eat tomorrow." She looked very relieved and, for the rest of their time together, they had an animated and funny conversation about a program on the TV that Little, having watched the night before, now recounted to him.

By the morning he felt quite ravenous but there was no response to his call to his servant who had become noticeably absent during the fast. Now that he had decided to eat and he could begin immediately Gregory felt a bit irritable. However, he was distracted by the arrival of the President who sat down and perched on the edge of the chair that was now left permanently in front of Gregory's window. There were several armed soldiers well behind him keeping their distance. "My you look very thin," he began, "quite a change from when I saw you last."

"You also," said Gregory. The President pulled his wrist from his shirt and spanned it with his hand.

"Yes, stress is the best known cure for obesity. But my weight loss has not been at my own instigation. Any way. How is it going?"

"My fast?"

"No our situation. I have come to visit you so you can tell me what your judgement is. It looks bad - I mean," then he hesitated from using the words, "the divine spirit's judgement.

"I believe he is sad it has all come to this. He does not support strife."

"Will we win though?" and before Gregory could answer, "Is he on our side?"

"No!"

"Which?"

"Nobody will win - we will all lose."

"Does he speak in riddles?"

"Look I cannot tell the future. I am not able to give you the satisfaction that your own conscience doesn't. The divine spirit is not a foreign country. I'm not a diplomat or courtier who can act as a go between for you. I am more like a coach. Here to encourage."

"So you cannot give me an answer?"

"I have given you an answer!"

"Bah. You are useless. I always regret coming to see you." The President stood up testily. "The Dean is as stupid to keep you as he was to get you in the first place. You are not even entertaining anymore here in your little cage."

"Why is it," observed Gregory as he man turned to go, "that everyone feels free to abuse me when they cannot force me into giving the answer they want? Why turn on me when I genuinely do my best for you. I don't lie. I am just like other men I have feelings too." The President turned, and looked back for a moment, he was thinking.

"Yes, but this is where you are. We're all stuck in this with our own part to play. I must do mine now," and as an afterthought, "Thank you for your time."

When his food came it was greasy and Gregory ate too quickly and was immediately sick and then suffered several hours of bloating, gas and discomfort. He did not try to eat again until the evening by which time he had enlisted Little's help to get some fruit juice, fresh vegetables and plain bread. He ate carefully, chewing slowly and managed to keep it down, he reserved most of it for his next breakfast. The food made him quite wretched for a while and he kept passing wind. It was a while before he fell asleep and even then it was not deep, and for the first time without choosing he fled to his cabin.

It was wonderful to be back, the animals greeted him enthusiastically and he spent a wonderful day in their company. Towards evening he was walking by a new freshwater lagoon which he had either just found or it had found him when he came across the old crocodile. He saw him in the near distance waddling purposefully in the other direction. He imagined that the reptile had not seen him. Gregory hallooed after him and the crocodile turned its long snout to look back at him before coming to a halt. The animal waited until he caught it up. "Where are you going?" Gregory asked it politely.

"There has been an unexplained event," the king of the animals said slowly with sadness. "There has been some..." it could not bring itself to say or rather think the next word. It was possible the crocodile could not remember it. Eventually it came out, "trouble." It was a chilly sort of word in that place and Gregory had never heard it said there before. If they had a dictionary Gregory imagined, then there was no place for such a word in its pages.

"What sort of trouble?" he asked.

"Follow me please," replied the crocodile and set off again at its slow gait. There was no more conversation and all sorts of morbid thoughts went through Gregory's mind. Why he wondered was the crocodile walking, when their route took them around the curved edge of the lagoon, which the crocodile could have swum across more easily? After many moments of silence and the increasingly laboured breathing of the huge creature he plucked up the courage to ask.

"Where are we going?"

"You'll see when we get there."

"Why are you walking?"

"Why not?"

"It would be easier for you to swim. Don't feel obliged to walk for my sake."

"All right I won't," the creature answered. It was painful to watch the creature struggling so and it seemed to be getting older and wearier as they walked.

"Would you like to rest?" Gregory tried again.

"It would make no use, whenever I was to come here it would make me old and tired." They trudged on for many more minutes until they took an abrupt left turn. Well the crocodile did, cutting across Gregory's path and almost tripping him up with his tail. It looked plaintively at him but did not apologise. They plunged into the forested fringes of the lagoon and walked on for several minutes. Eventually they came out into a natural glade in the woodland. The crocodile came to a halt. He said panting heavily, "you look and tell me what you see." Gregory walked around the glade.

"It's quiet," he thought but did not speak.

"Yes all the creatures have gone." There were some broken ferns on the ground as though something had trampled them. Gregory stood for a while and scratched his head. As he looked down at his feet he saw two small feathers on the ground, he picked them up. They were stuck together at the quill end with some gooey matter. He turned to the crocodile who, when he saw what was in Gregory's hand, nodded sagely. Gregory looked at him expectantly. You can't smell the blood then," said the crocodile who had now regained his composure a little."

"No, not at all."

"There is not much, but there is some - a creature was torn here and didn't leave but it's not here."

"What a mystery," said Gregory light heartedly. He was in too good a mood to see what all the fuss was about.

"You do not care then - you from that other world who only visit us here."

"No I do care, I just don't see."

"That's true, you have lost the ability to see. I will show you." Gregory was looking around to see what the object of his lesson was to be when the image came into his mind. It was the shock of his own foot stepping unknowingly on broken glass and the pain, the anguish and shock and the smell of the blood there in his head. He felt weak, and faint, and his head dipped and he was sick to his stomach. He shook with the trauma of it. A cry escaped his mouth. Then even worse followed, horrible abusive images dredged from his own subconscious, sick perversion and the venial smell of them. He gagged. Then it all ran away as if it were sand in an hour glass and he regained his equanimity.

"One day," said the crocodile, "you must tell me what you saw - but later I can't get over this yet. I will need to grieve awhile." Gregory could not face the long walk back, or the jollity of the cabin, or even the sombre crocodile so he went back to his own pallet and slept the night away.

[F5] The divine spirit in his inspiration of human creativity also judges and validates the product. By his word he sets boundaries and gives values to the human effort. He helps and directs those who are open to his influence. Human creativity is bad when it stops being that for which it was called into being.

[I5] The Urban Mystic prays about everything, especially his own city. He looks to its welfare and it prospers because of his interest and care.

Chapter 29

Gregory was most puzzled by this dream version of his own fantasy 'think' and although he lay down in the day and tried to repeat the vision he was unable to access it at all. However that night, as he drifted off to sleep, he did return and found the wicket gate - however, it was all slightly different. Although the meadow looked the same, this time there was a heavy dew persisting on the grass even though he guessed it was almost noon. By the time he got to his lodge his feet and trouser bottoms were soaked. He was pleased to find that the animals were there to greet him in force yet they all seemed a bit frenetic and the zebra accidentally pushed him over as they crowded around. Needless to say the animal was most apologetic.

In addition, the greeting seemed to end more quickly than normal and the animals soon went back to their usual occupations. He spotted the smaller of the two brown bears stretching and rocking over by the entrance to the forest trail. It appeared oblivious to him. Inside the cabin the fire had died down to its embers and he had to rake it through and fetch more wood from the pile behind the shed. The larger animals in particular drifted off very quickly so he sat down to pet a small antelope. "Is there something wrong? he asked it. It did not seem to understand the question. "Are the animals unhappy," he tried again.

"Yes."

"Why?"

"We are like the crocodile," it struggled to find long unused or unknown words to express abnormal concepts. The animal liked his soothing touch and in time it tried to speak again. Gregory sat patiently waiting for something to happen. "We are not comfortable," it said eventually. He tried to pin it down as to the particulars but it and the other small animals that he questioned did not have the intellectual capacity to satisfy him. Gregory got out of his chair and strolled outside. There was a group of the larger animals standing in a circle some distance away. He headed for them but as he approached they split up and nonchalantly wandered off. "Please wait," he called out. An old horse stopped and turned to face him. Gregory went through the same interrogation, this time the horse did not attempt to reply but shook its mane sadly until he asked "Do you feel uncomfortable like the other animals?"

"Yes." Gregory waited expectantly for some expansion of this answer but again none was forthcoming. Instead the horse sniffed the air and pricked up its ears.

"The king is coming, he will talk with you." The horse shuddered and backed off a distance. Gregory walked back towards the forest path and when he looked behind he saw that the animals had turned and were following him also.

It was shock to see the crocodile - it had visibly aged and at first sight seemed to have turned grey. The animals behind Gregory were making strange whimpering noises and the smaller ones were streaming from the lodge to join them. Now, as the crocodile drew closer, he saw that it had something in its huge maw. With a jolting shock his brain and eyes resolved it into a recognisable shape - it was a dead dog. The crocodile's eyes were glittering and there was blood on its muzzle. Gregory froze and a wild fantasy that this king of the animals had reverted to type flooded into his blood chilling it on entry. He would have run if the horse had not pushed him gently forward with its muzzle and the crocodile had not laid its burden down carefully at his feet. Only then did his fear disperse.

"What is it?" asked the zebra by his elbow.

"It is a dog," said a reindeer.

"Not a real dog," commented a rabbit. There was a palpable sense of doom and foreboding in this creaturely gathering.

"My children," said the crocodile, addressing the crowd, "it is," and he gave a name that Gregory could not catch, "and she is dead. There has come another who has robbed her of her spirit." There was a gasp.

"What is dead?" a small voice asked behind him and it was hushed by a motherly tone. There was silence.

Gregory felt impelled to say, "It wasn't me." None of the animals answered his declaration - it being irrelevant to them.

"We are not familiar with dead," continued the crocodile, "but you've experience of it, what must we do?" Before he could answer they were all distracted by a strange mournful noise that came floating from some great distance along the coast.

"Look for what has done this."

"No!" said he crocodile. It brooked no opposition. "What shall we do with...." and there was that name again.

"We should bury it," announced Gregory," in a good place. I will get a spade and you choose a spot where when you walk past you would want to see ......" he could not say the word, ".........our friend again." He walked off feeling bad.

In the shed, behind the cabin, he found a set of well used garden implements and returned with a small spade. The animals had moved off and were gathered around a grassy hummock close to the beach. "We would like to be with her here," the zebra articulated for them all. Gregory began to dig and the animals backed off to give him space. Fortunately, the sand was easy to dig and the loam underneath also quite friable. He dug steadily for fifteen minutes and then came up against bedrock and shingle about four feet down.

"Shall I put our friend in the hole?" Nobody answered, they seemed mesmerised by what he was doing. He gently lifted the dog. It had been badly mauled, either by its attacker or by its journey in the crocodile's jaws, and Gregory carefully lifted it into the grave. After he had put it down his hands were besmirched with blood and he rubbed them clean on a handful of sand. As he began to fill in the hole all the animals started to cry. Gregory also, overcome by the moment, blubbed as he worked. On completion he stood back and waited quietly for further instruction. With the absence of any response, except the continuing tears, he offered, "Some words?" The crocodile nodded. But none would come to his mind so he turned away, walked back past the cabin and through the meadow, nobody followed. As he shut the gate behind him - he was in bed.

```
[N5] The Urban Mystic is scared of being
thought heretical or straying into heresy. By
the nature of her mysticism she is pushing
back boundaries and frontiers. Thus there is
the temptation for her to be thought of as
extra canonical in that which she saying.
However, it may be that her sayings are
prophetic or simply that, by her insights, she
is interpreting particular verses of scripture
to their limit. The real and genuine heart of
the Urban Mystic is always directed towards
```

purity and orthodoxy. She wishes to avoid
being corrupted by the world.

When Gregory woke early the next morning he picked up some paper and began his next sermon.

The verses from his black book had been accumulating, during his fast, a new significance which attached itself to the sparse words. He wrote them down first at the head of his paper:

The ,,,,,,,,,,,,,,was angry! So he disgraced.,,,,,,,,,,,,

Enemies have stretched out their hands
over all her precious things;
she has even seen the nations
invade her sanctuary,
those whom you forbade
to enter your congregation.

They of the west are appalled at their fate,
and horror seizes those of the east.

How the gold has grown dim,
how the pure gold is changed!
The sacred stones lie scattered
at the head of every street.

He began with the words, 'We are to be disgraced and humiliated because of our inability to free ourselves from our obsessive need to believe that if we were given a free reign to rule the universe we could make it better.'

He went on to discuss the problem of human evil and the Divine spirit's reaction to it. He concluded by saying, 'I have a bad feeling about the future. I sense that these verse I quoted to you from the black book are to be taken as prophetic for our day. I fear what they should mean in reality for us here at St. Arburn's. None of us can rely on the divine spirit's patience being everlastingly elastic. We must take steps to placate him before it is too late. I urge you to join with me in grief at our presumption before him. How? Only by reaching out to him both as individuals and corporately. I will discuss with the Dean afterwards how we, as a Cathedral, may show

how the tide can be turned. May it be never said of us.
> *They of the west are appalled at their fate,*
> *and horror seizes those of the east.*

So be it.

Later that day he sent his servant to tell the Dean that he would preach the next Sunday. For the rest of the week he worked quietly, spending time with the pilgrims and organising for some of them to return after hours for longer consultations.

His sermon was listened to respectfully on Sunday but without much reaction. He was taken back to his cell afterwards and locked in. He felt tired and empty, as he did after every time he preached. It made him feel so vulnerable speaking out into the air the sense of what the divine spirit had given him. If he was wrong and it was just the result of some physical anomaly of his brain then it was all a colossal waste of time.

As bed time approached he heard a strange noise in the distance. It must have been powerful for it was carried loudly from outside through the fabric of the Cathedral. Gregory could not place it at first; it was a mechanical wail. Eventually it registered that it was an air raid siren. He had heard one as a child. The siren ululated on for several minutes before coming to a strangulated stop. All was quiet and still again. The Cathedral was empty, Little had gone several hours before, and the night watchman would be snoozing in his office just inside the main door some distance away from the presbytery where Gregory lived.

Without any warning there was a tremendous explosion and the whole building shook. Gregory's pallet on which he lay shuffled along the floor and the whole structure gave a groan of agony. Gregory's ears continued to ring after the first blast and when he stood up to look out of his window he saw a ghastly swirl of dense dust and smoke billowing from the Nave into the presbytery. He panicked immediately in case this heralded the beginning of an fire and that he was trapped in his cell. The siren recommenced its wail and in addition there were strange loud noises from the other end of the Cathedral, both of which drowned out Gregory's cries for help. Paralysis followed for a moment as he feared another explosion would come. In a panic he went to the door and, forcing his fingers into the gap between the door and post, pulled with all his might. It flew open easily catapulting him back onto the stairs. The lock hole had crumbled in the blast. He walked out cautiously, there was nobody around. A thought struck him and he went back into his cell closing the door behind him. On testing the cell door cautiously he found that it still held to the casual inspection but with only a little force it would open whilst the lock bolt still protruded. He went back into his cell for a second time and fetched a piece of paper which he used to wedge the door more tightly shut, so as to give the impression that it was properly locked. Now anyone testing it from outside would be fooled into thinking it was secure. A smile ran onto his face, the fear of further danger driven away by this unexpected news. Now he had grown too cautious to act on it immediately; a new mature Gregory kept the news to himself. The siren stopped again and he couldn't help cringe at the thought of another bomb. There was shouting and noises in the distance and all the Cathedral lights came on. He sat down calmly to wait for something to happen. It was Little who came first and she was bloody and in tears. Her appearance gave him another fright but she was more pleased to see him safe than concerned for her own injuries. Gregory was so disturbed at the sight of her that he was almost ready to give up his secret just so he could hold her in his arms properly. He resisted the temptation. It transpired that what had happened was that a single bomb had been dropped on the west end of the Cathedral and had demolished the main door, killed the porter and brought down some of the west end. The blast had also shaken the Dean's house, that was nearby, and Little had been cut by flying glass.

    She had some small cuts to her face and her arms. There was one that looked quite deep to Gregory, on her knuckle, but she did not seem bothered by it. He urged her to go to the hospital but she refused saying she would rather stay with him. They sat together holding hands and soothing each other for a long time. There was a lot of noise in the distance - fire and police car sirens. At one point the Dean came, he had survived unscathed, his bedroom being situated on the other side of their house. Even Bailey appeared tentatively at the edge of the presbytery.

    Later still someone tested Gregory's door but it did not give and Gregory smiled wryly to himself. He guessed that it must have been Bailey. The Dean also urged Little to go for medical attention and eventually the pair of them prevailed on her to go and see one of the ambulance crews that were standing by, near the main door. The Dean told Gregory whilst she was away, that they did not expect any more strikes for the meantime and that the army believed that this was in the nature of a warning shot.

"We have no air force," said Gregory.

"True." The Dean did not stay long he was very upset about his beloved Cathedral. Little returned soon after with her wounds swabbed and with tape pulling the edges of the deep cut together.

In time, Little began to nod off in her chair and Gregory was able to send her home. After her departure he dithered for a while as he pondered whether he should try the door again and make his escape in all the confusion. He could send for Little later he reasoned. In the end he felt so jaded that he decided that some rest would be better and that perhaps he needed to hoard some provisions before he ran. However, he remained worried that his secret would be discovered before he had a chance to utilise it.

Chapter 30

Little turned up very early the next morning with the newspapers, despite falling asleep quickly, the pain and discomfort of her abrasions had woken her. The papers told them, as the Dean had intimated, that the bomb had been a warning shot and a threat. 'We have superiority in the air,' Persfeld screamed, 'do not mess with us.' And more arrogantly, 'we all know that air superiority wins wars.' The editorial columns in both the nationals and the St. Arburn's local paper were all loud in their condemnation of this act of aggression. However, some journalists writing in the body of the Nationals were more hopeful that this a deplorable episode, would be the end of it. 'We can all see,' they declared, 'what destruction even such a minor incident can cause.' They lamented the damage to an historical building but wrote that there was hope that it would have a sobering effect on all the hotheads by showing them plainly the consequences of any further posturing.

That night all was peaceful again. Gregory had ascertained from the Dean that the damage at the far end of the Cathedral was secure: he did not want the Cathedral to be invaded by prowlers in the night. The Dean reassured him that a new secure, temporary wall and gate-house had been erected in the day. In the context of this discussion, Gregory asked innocently about other entrances and exits to the Cathedral and discovered that there were four, none of which were alarmed. However, all were locked, save one fire door, which could be opened without a key. Gregory yawned at this unnecessary information and the Dean changed the subject.

Gregory decided to give it one more day to be safe and went about his routine normally, kindly dealing with his pilgrims. They were all very anxious now as to what the future would hold and Gregory felt sorry for them. They had so much to lose, whereas he had nothing. He even felt some regrets as to how they would manage when he had gone. The normal Cathedral structure, although it provided counselling for them, gave them nothing like the spiritual direction he did. That night he went to bed early and willed himself to wake in a few hours, which he did. It was about 3am in the morning. He had dismissed in his impatience his plan to stockpile food.

    Gregory wrapped his black book carefully in a clean sheet, hesitated over the chain of office, finally making up his mind to leave it in the cell. Dressing warmly he swung his cloak around him. He was trembling when he reached the door of the cell but he removed the wedge immediately and let himself out. Turning around and kneeling down he pushed the folded paper back under the door so as to fool a cursory check of the security. Gregory hoped he would have several hours to get away before he was missed. He headed for the cafeteria and the toilets, one of the fire doors was beside them. Unfortunately it was very stiff and although he should have given the bar a good sharp blow he dare not for fear of the noise drawing attention to himself so he had to push hard for several minutes before it clicked open. Then he couldn't shut it again from outside but forced it too with the vertical bar dragging on the concrete. His only chance was that this also would go unnoticed for a while.

    He looked around cautiously; he had come out near to where the old refectory had stood. In front of him were the preserved walls of the old monastic buildings. When he looked up there was a strong moon and taking a deep breath he revelled in the wonderful cool scented air of a spring night. It was enchanting. Here in the dark lee of the Cathedral, he caught his first glimpse for months of the stars, they worked their old magic on him. Gregory moved cautiously forward and squatted down by one of the medieval walls. Although he was desperate to leave he made himself wait patiently to see if there was any guard of any sort. Fortunately not a soul appeared and he guessed that the Cathedral was not the sort of military target that the army would bother to guard. Standing up he walked across the grass, downhill towards where the river was: he had remembered Little's imaginary guided walks around the city. As he reached the bottom of the slope and stepped on to one of the gravel park walks he looked back at the Cathedral. From where he stood he could see the damage at the west end. It looked very bad and he let his eye run down the untroubled length of the Cathedral. Yet in response, instead of sorrow at its plight a smile of joy came to his lips. The beauty of the Cathedral overcame him, even the damage did not really detract from its imposing profile, a black shadow against the sky. And not just the building but the whole situation, here like a guardian of the soul of the town beyond, towering majestically over the fall to the river below. He stood transfixed for some time until it occurred to him that this was not only his own emotional reaction to the Cathedral but the divine spirit's. "Lovely," they breathed together.

His original plan was to head for the country but now as he stared past the Cathedral he heard the city calling him. If they send dogs after me surely they will be confused by the smells of the city, he reassured himself. Maybe they will just say good riddance. He tested himself by taking a few steps away from the city but a strong magnet arrested his progress and he turned both reluctantly and with a thrill towards the city. He edged himself, by way of the lower slopes of the Cathedral mound, in a wide arc around the west end of the building: he knew there was a night watchman there. After four minutes he came to one of the minor gates out of the park. His feet were soaking from the damp grass, he noticed.

Gregory pulled his hood up and wrapped the cloak around him. There was some minor traffic on the road and he walked up into the main shopping street. He kept his head down and although a few night owls walked past him they said nothing. There were no soldiers about and the only person to speak to him was a drunk who asked him for money and became abusive when he had none to give. The heat of the unaccustomed exercise made him take off his cloak. He folded it up and held it in his arms. This had the effect of making him look a little more normal. He prowled up and down the main street looking in the shop windows but he dare not enter the shopping centre for fear of a whole mix of emotions. He could not understand why he was not making his escape. Inside himself he was frightened as well as worried by the returning responsibility to care for himself that his months of captivity had denied him. Beyond that there was something more - the faintest recognition that this was actually his place to be. He looked up at the Cathedral in the distance, where he could still see its central tower dominating the sky line.

Walking on he forced himself to take a side street and moved from there through the specialist smaller shops into the beginning of suburbia. He thought of all the people sleeping in the houses and he began to pray quietly for their safety. It was no good, he sighed in despair. He could not leave. Was he too frightened to leave? It was the most horrible dilemma he had ever had. The fear for his own safety was greater than the divine implication he should remain, but to acknowledge he should stay for his own fear was depressing. He was so unworthy of this awesome calling he had. Why did he end up always doing what he should by circumstance and not by choice so much of the time? He fled from that spot and turning his feet towards the Cathedral hurried back, retracing his steps until he came to the gate into the park. By now his heart was beating strongly from the exertion and the fear of returning. Continually he was obstructed by invisible walls of resistance. Now the fear was greater about returning and incarcerating himself in the cell again. "Why could I not stay, but stay in freedom," he moaned to himself. The answer would not go away. "Shit, shit, shit," he said. He felt ill with the effort and the mixed feelings in his breast.

As he skulked down the hill, returning towards the cathedral grounds, keeping to the shadow of the retaining wall, a chill breeze picked up and dried the perspiration on his forehead. Gregory donned his cloak, swirling it around his shoulders, and continued to the gate. But as he drew nearer a pain developed in his back and he could no longer lift up his legs easily: it was as if he were struggling through some viscous fluid. In every part of him but his spirit there was a hunger to flee.

He looked around nervously. Was someone following him? A fanciful notion infiltrated his mind. Was there a presence on the other side of the high wall? He dare not pull himself up to look. Was that a whisper? A whining, thin voice telling him not to go back. "You owe them nothing," it said. "You would do more good to leave and establish yourself somewhere else. I will help you," it cooed.

"Who are you?" his spirit asked in his mind. There was a sigh; a lonely, awful, simpering sigh. Gregory shook himself. Could he smell decaying meat? He moved anxiously forward and, entering by the nearest gate, he glanced back up towards the stretch of wall he had just passed on the other side. There was nobody there, only an eddy of debris twisted lazily by the slight wind. It had been a spooky unnatural moment and he did not want to investigate further. Up there by the wall was a clearing, not unlike a clearing in a dream of not so long ago. He did not want to go there again - his mind was still sore with the residue of that insight into the abnormal murder and of the vision of his own wounded feet. Gregory hovered by the gate.

In the distance he heard a car coming fast up the hill and when he turned to look his eyes were hurt by the headlights which were on full beam. It was hurtling on, accelerating hard up the incline. Within a hundred metres of where he stood the driver applied the brakes sharply and the car shuddered and slid, with a quick pulse of blue smoke, to a jerking halt level with Gregory. It was a large luxury saloon. The smell of acrid rubber reached him in seconds. The driver, a man of his own age and not dissimilar in appearance, looked expectantly at him. Gregory did not recognise him and did not move. The man scowled malevolently back - his mood changing in an instant - and turning to look forward he drove off sharply with the wheels spinning. Gregory followed the car's progress with his eyes and saw it take the junction at the top of the hill at speed sliding around on the bend. The car back-fired and it was gone.

He felt very cold, touched and scared by these two strange incidents. His mind was bruised by all these thoughts.

He looked up towards the boarded windows of the Deanery and Little. No he had to make this choice on his own. "Dear kindly Spirit," he addressed the air through chattering teeth, "please do let me be trapped here for ever. I give up my freedom to you, preserve it please." He strode through the Cathedral grounds, taking the circuitous route once more until he stood at the fire door. The locking pole was grinding gently on the concrete. With a heavy breath he was carried over the threshold and shut the door carefully behind him. With dragging feet he returned to his cell and after letting himself in, made the door secure behind him and lay on his mattress. His cell smelt of his own sweat and his troubled sleep when it came included giant crocodiles, crashed cars, aliens of all sorts, body parts and swollen sexual organs. He loathed his own weakness and berated his own strength.

```
    [R5] It would appear that each Urban
Environment responds to the witness of the
nature that surrounds it both organically and
through the creativity of the community that
built it and maintain it. A coastal town may
```

be influenced by the sea and an urban conurbation by its parks or lack of them; and the heavens above, the geology below and the seasons.

[S5] An artist uses a whole arsenal of gifts - his emotions, his psyche, his eye sight, his heart and head, his materials - everything he has got - to examine that which is before him or in him. This is in order that he can interpret and comment on those things in his work and art. So the Urban Mystic, as an artist theologian, uses all those same things to draw out the truth, the essence and the meaning - then describes his perception in his theology.

[U5] The Urban Mystic accompanies God on his second visit to Babel.

Chapter 31

It became a habit for Gregory to sit on one of the park benches at the side of the market square. After an initial encounter with a police officer he was left alone, attracting only the occasional nod, from the local constabulary after that.

The black book was too precious for him to carry around but he took his cloak and sometimes extra clothes to guard himself against the chill of sitting there during the night. On arrival he usually caught the end of the late revellers going home and so for the most part he had to imagine the square as it was during the day. It was a frustrating time for him because he had a strong sense that the divine spirit wanted him to take a greater part in the real community. However, it was impossible at that moment. Gregory could not decide whether it was gracious of the divine spirit to communicate what he wanted you to do well in advance or some cruel new test of faith. The pain of wanting his life to be different, and believing strongly that one day it would be, was immense. And of course there was nothing in his present life to suggest it would ever happen.

For much of the time sitting there in the dark of the night underneath the street lamps he would curse himself for his stupidity in returning to his cell and prison after each session. In the moments in between his times of doubt there were calmer periods when he puzzled through what it might mean to be a mystic in the world, here in an urban situation. For this season of his life his imagination had to make do in place of an unachievable reality.

All he could do was to ground himself in the people-free reality that presented itself in the quiet market place and the sleepy streets that he patrolled in-between times. He may have wandered aimlessly at times but he always stopped with purpose, standing still before some artefact. He drank in any changes from night to night and examined in detail all the furniture of the city landscape. With determination he interrogated himself to an object's significance and burdened himself with lists and categories of usefulness and goodness. "Where are you in all this?" he asked the spirit often and occasionally had a sense of him allusive and coy at the edge of his sight. "Stand still," he would say irritably to his God. "Walk with me, show me what pleases you," he would beg the air.

Gregory would rest his hand on the cornerstones of a public building, he would admire the lines of the latest public telephone box and he would notice the moss on the drain covering. This new world, far from the restrictions of his cell, even at night, was a wonderful release from him. At the art gallery he peered into the windows and caught the shadows of the old sculpture and longed to go in. The shop windows delighted him with their enticing displays and he meditated on how each item had been wrought from some raw material to present itself, now refashioned by the human hand, so appealingly to him.

Sometimes he would walk past houses where the lights continued to burn into the night and warmed himself at the flickering movements therein. Once he saw a fox, often he hear the cry of babies and occasionally cries of pain or pleasure. He had rediscovered his world through his own separation from it and now he longed for it even more.

Frequently he would reach out of his own soul and look around, as would a fretful child for its mum, to check he had not been left behind by the spirit.

```
    [W5] In his writing the Urban Mystic
knows that what he commits to paper is not
scripture - that task is complete - but he
believes that there are still echoes today of
the faculty that enabled those early authors
to fulfil their task. So he trusts that his
written insights may express the contemporary
vision/feelings of God to her urban
townscapes.

    [X5] Unrepentant soul, like a river too
little satisfied by its own meandering. Only
the farmer comes when you overflow your banks.
You had a mighty purpose to aid the rain in
its retreat to the sea. Now you hide in
impervious rock and rush hard and fast to
avoid your loving tributaries who would give
themselves to you. Beware you dry to a wadi.
```

```
[Y5] The Urban Mystic is looking for the
true artisan's work in the world of human
creativity.

[C6] The very worst form of evil is when
it can pass itself of as good.
```

The time was up for Little to respond to Bailey. Firstly he had not been much in evidence of late, presumably his military duties took him elsewhere. In addition, now the Cathedral had been side-lined again, the politicians did not need it for a cloak to their ambition anymore.

Nevertheless, Bailey turned up dutifully at the Deanery the day before and asked to make an appointment with Little for the morrow. Gregory and she had already discussed how the situation could be managed and at Gregory's suggestion they had come to the conclusion that the interview should be conducted in the presbytery in eye sight of Gregory but out of earshot. When Little proposed this to Bailey he agreed immediately and excused himself until the appointment. Little felt that his rapid promotion had had a beneficial effect on him but there was no romance there at all. He had been too cruel to Gregory to ever forgive. In addition, and not unexpectedly, he had made no attempt to fulfil his boast to release Gregory.

The appointed time came and Gregory drew his chair back into the shadows where he could watch and keep out of sight. Bailey turned up punctually dressed in his full dress uniform. Little was sitting shyly on the cell visitors chair close to the sanctuary rail. Bailey began immediately remaining standing and speaking with head bowed to Little's downcast gaze.

"Even if you were to look at me," he began, "I know the answer you are likely to give me yet I ask of you the courtesy to hear me out."

"Certainly," she replied quietly.

"I am sorry to revisit old ground," he continued, "but there was a time when I think you had positive regard for me in that I was a sort of surrogate father when your dad was very busy."

"That is true," she said.

"But we have both altered since then."

"I know we are both adults now and the difference in our age has disappeared."

"It is not just that," he sounded a bit irritable but he controlled himself. "I had hope that those strong feelings may have matured into something less platonic."

"I know you want to persuade me of this but to save you hurt and embarrassment I have to interrupt you."

"Very well."

"You have become a person I don't recognise any more, and on top of that my heart is fully engaged elsewhere. There's really no chance of what you hope for and I hope you can believe that and accept it. You must not nurture any future hope that I will change my mind. I have taken this period of time to think it through, as you asked, but really nothing has changed over the month. Even if Gregory were not here and I had no love for him I would not be looking to you. I don't say that in any cruel way. You do need to put it down and make another life for yourself. I am sure there are many women out there that would respond to you in the way you deserve."

"I don't think so," he said petulantly. "Your childhood was so precious. How can I find that in an adult."

"It is not possible. I must ask you to go away now and again press you to accept my no as a genuine one but without any malice."

"Very well," he said stiffly and went away immediately. Little carried her chair back to Gregory's cell and holding his hand wept a little with the stress of it.

"I hope that's the end of it," she said eventually. Gregory said nothing.

That night she did not turn up for their usual bedtime chat but it was not unusual so he dismissed it from his mind. He had been increasingly going out earlier and earlier, therefore, on completing a wait of a half an hour, Gregory felt sure she would not come. It was not like the previous evening and because of an unnatural tiredness he returned early to the Cathedral, at about midnight. He had become quite bold once he was inside the building and was now used to wandering around it at night and exploring all of its secrets. He wandered for a while around the north transept reading the inscriptions on the tombs in the dim light when he was startled to hear a distant voice calling his name. The sound made him freeze and he looked around for the noise before discovering that it was coming from the presbytery. He made his was cautiously back to the crossways of the Cathedral. As he turned left he saw Bailey stalking up into the central aisle. As he moved forward he could also see Little standing by his cell and calling his name gently. He watched the drama unfold.

Bailey, cat-like, pounced on Little who gave a startled cry. He put his hand on her mouth and lifted her easily up from the ground. There he held her swinging like a pendulum and she put up no resistance at first, so shocked was she. "Come out you wild, dirty little beast," Bailey cawed at the cell. There followed a torrid scorching flow of filth and abuse. The old Bailey had returned with a vengeance. At this Little got over her shock and began to fight back. She was kicking his shins. Bailey dropped her unceremoniously to the floor winding her. "Come out you fucking amoeba and see me fuck the shit out of your woman. If I can't have her then neither will you. You can watch from there - stuck in your cell and savour what could have been yours. Answer me you bastard! He doesn't even care love," he said as an aside to Little. "Take your clothes off." She was standing up looking defiant. Then Bailey stepped forward and gave her a violent back hander which sent her sliding across the floor. With a bellow of rage Gregory started forward and flung himself on Bailey. Before their heads cracked together Bailey half turned and registered the shock of seeing Gregory free from his cage. Both men were stunned by the collision, like two rutting males they rebounded off each other and scrabbled back to their feet quickly. Bailey obviously had some combat training because on their second encounter he easily turned Gregory and threw him. On a third attempt Gregory caught the epaulet of Bailey's jacket and was not thrown completely. As both men struggled Gregory put his hands on Bailey's throat and with his superior weight wrestled him to the ground. Bailey was slashing at him with his hands but Gregory head butted him on the nose and saw it burst with the blow. Gregory got up and stood back as Bailey cradled his face.

As Gregory stood over him he said, "Don't come back!" Bailey resumed his feet slowly and walked away shaking his head.

"I know where to get you," he said in return.

"No you don't, the spirit has allowed me to walk from my cell and I know where to find you. No lock will protect you now." Bailey shivered and shuffled off stanching the blood from his nose with his hand. Little was stunned still by Bailey's blow. Gregory scooped her up and carried her into his cell. He laid her on his bed and settled down beside her, cradling her in his arms. Without wanting it he felt himself grow hard against her. The wonderful soft femininity of her, even in her distress, worked its arousal on his body. She was shivering and shaking with the shock of it all and he enveloped her with his body. She turned for a moment and kissed his forehead. She hugged herself down into his arms. They woke at dawn and he let her out of the fire door.

Later in the morning the Dean came. "Bailey is of the opinion that you are some kind of demon now."

"The other way around I think."

"He tells me that he has seen you out of your cell - but I told him that if you got free you would be a million miles away by now."

"Absolutely."

"Strange, some of the pilgrims swear they have seen you out and about. It is an old sign of mysticism apparently to be able to transport yourself through space."

"Well your trust has not been misplaced," said Gregory and the Dean chuckled.

"Bailey is also indisposed, he fell on his face apparently. Broke his nose."

"I am sorry!"

"Don't be, nothing could improve his looks." Then changing the subject, "Things look bad. Did you know that war may be declared today?"

"Yeah."

"Pray for us."

"I do."

"One other thing - I know this is very old-fashioned but are your intentions towards my daughter honourable?" Gregory nodded. "Good," said the Dean. I have been invited onto the war cabinet. I don't know why maybe I am to get a second chance at politics, but..."

"But?"

"I would rather not now."

"Good for you."

"Yet I must."

"Yes, I meant your response is good for you - someone else -

maybe not."

"Hmm." The Dean wandered of whistling. He had not only mellowed but partly melted, Gregory thought.

Chapter 32

[D6] All human creativity is spiritual for it springs from the spirit or soul of humankind by the bounty of the divine spirit. The spiritual appears as a thread in the outworking of the providence of God's gift of human creativity. Yet not everything is holy and God sets apart some of the results of human creativity to be special to himself: as a patron chooses from a gallery the pieces that most interest him.

Within the Urban Landscape the Spirit has made holy, by his own choice, certain artefacts and areas.

Why should God always make obvious that which he has declared to be holy? It is the work of the Mystic to find them. He must search, as would a spiritual detective, for those pieces of holy ground and those artefacts that the divine spirit has endorsed, from the plethora of human creativity, to act as his holy things. In these the Spirit leaves his footprint within the urban environment to chasten, to encourage and to show us that he has been there and even now walks there. "Behold the sacred," he cries.

"I have seen it. I have felt it." declares the Urban Mystic.

The President dropped in later; he looked strung up and wild. "You are still a national treasure," he told Gregory, "and you need to be protected." He told Gregory that he would make alternative arrangements for him if he wished to be kept safe and guarded but Gregory declined and the President seemed relieved. Gregory asked if he could be released and let to live somewhere in the city to be a comfort to the people but the President refused categorically. It became clear that they wanted him to stay in the Cathedral: they were assuming his presence would protect it. "In fact," the President continued, "we are to post a guard here to ensure you do not escape or someone does not help you."

"Is that necessary? Surely my usefulness is over?"

"Not at all apparently, although the Cathedral at Persfeld fell out with you the people of St. Arburn's have not."

"It will be dangerous for the guard to be here at night in case there is another bomb or rocket."

"Arrh, but we have just the man for it." Then, as on previous visits, his mood seemed to change and he became quite obsessive for a few moments trying to cajole Gregory into making positive prophecies about the outcome of the war. Gregory had to deflect him and referred him back to his previous sermons. The President did not want to hear that and they parted in anger as on previous occasions. His parting words were. "As this is not a primary military target we cannot protect it you know?" He did not want a response and Gregory kept silent.

An hour later the sirens went off and an air strike began soon after. Gregory understood that he was to be left in the Cathedral to endure it on his own. He knew that at the sound of the siren the Cathedral would be evacuated and the staff taken to an underground catacomb nearby that had recently been prepared for such an eventuality. It had taken all Gregory's persuasion to make Little promise that she would also go to the shelter in the event of another air raid.

He heard the first crump of a bomb in the far distance and the sound of subsequent ones coming nearer, orchestrated by returning antiaircraft fire. Gregory felt very frightened. At first he sat on his pallet praying silently but he could not sustain it in the face of his own terror and he began to pace his cell. When he eventually looked out of his window he saw Bailey, in full fatigues standing staring wild eyed at him with an automatic weapon in his hands. He was clearly terrified as well. They were both sitting ducks. The explosions were coming nearer with each wave. A deep sick feeling overtook Gregory, he knew his time had come - either he would die under tons of rubble or Bailey would take this opportunity, in the crisis, to kill him. It was a bad moment. He tensed himself for the bullet. Bailey seemed under inordinate strain himself and appeared to be struggling with his own feelings. Gregory concentrated on him willing him to stay his arm. As he looked he saw that his nose was still broken. Nothing had been done to straighten it yet. He was breathing through his mouth as well. Then Gregory saw that some of his insignia was missing. Bailey had been demoted. Gregory felt exultant at this surmise. They both stood paralysed fighting their fear and staring hard at each other. Then Gregory had another insight, Bailey must be frightened of him, some primitive superstitious terror had him in its grasp. He had really believed that Gregory could walk through the walls. It became silent outside and the all-clear sounded. Bailey turned and ran away. Little came immediately to see him.

"Can I come in?" she asked straight away.

"I am sorry no," he said calmly, "I have thought about it and as much as I don't want to deny you, the risks are too great for the moment. I need to preserve the secrecy of it for a possible escape and my nocturnal work.

She came again later with the news; although St. Arburn's had not wanted to publicise the damage that had been done by Persfeld, it was impossible to stop the other City States reporting on the war or to stop the national or international TV stations getting through. There had been a huge amount of damage in the city and the provincial towns from the concerted air attack, however the ground war was going the way of St. Arburn's. Casualties were high on both sides but so was desertion from the armed services. Nobody liked the possibility of fighting in opposition to their own relatives in a neighbouring state. Little had saved the best bit of news until last: she told him that although Persfeld had aircraft and St. Arburn's didn't, Persfeld did not have the ordinance to go with it. One of the largest ammunition factories was in a neighbouring state and they had refused to sell any to Persfeld. There was of course the threat that Persfeld would fight them for it but this other state also had air power and was putting itself on alert. Little had no sooner said this than the siren went off again.

"Not run out yet," said Gregory.

"No." Little looked sad, her joy at the news had evaporated.

"Go now," he said, "and come back this evening. I have some news for you."

"Oh what?"

"Only if you go now to the shelter." She turned and ran off.

Bailey appeared within minutes and they went through their tense stand-off for another hour as bombs fell all around the Cathedral rattling and breaking the windows. Bailey had to duck as a rainbow of silica fragments fell around his feet from the stained glass windows above his head. A cool breeze stirred the curtains in Gregory's cell. He dare not move to put on his cloak for fear of losing his ocular grip on Bailey. Once more, as soon as the all-clear sounded, Bailey scooted off without a word.

In the afternoon Gregory prevailed upon his servant to fetch him a bunch of flowers. He returned with some primroses.

"There were none to be sold," the man reported, "but I found these in the Dean's garden."

"Splendid," said Gregory. Some men came to erect a scaffolding tower at the main window at the end of the Chancel. The Dean had used his clout to obtain help first. The men were old and slow and Gregory had no hope of a return of comfort for some time. The building had always been cold and there had always been draughts but now the wind whistled through the old Cathedral and rattled his door and eddied into his cell. He felt chilled and was glad it was spring now. Sometimes the air was slightly warmer, when the sun shone, but generally it felt as though he lived in a refrigerator. His ability to sustain this difficult environment was running away. He knew that some sort of conclusion was approaching in terms of his own resources to cope.

Little came very shyly to his window that evening. "Damn," he thought, "she knows." Women and their psychic powers for these things. She sat demurely on the chair and shivered a bit in the breeze.

"It's cold here now, are you all right?"

"No I'm cold." A silence developed between them. "Look," he said eventually, "I have got you some flowers."

"Went out and picked them yourself?" she asked saucily.

"No. You know I don't go out in the day. Look," he began again repeating himself and fumbling with the words.

"Yes," she said expectantly licking her lips. She was not going to help him. In the time honoured tradition he must get the words out himself.

"When you walk away from me to go to the shelter," he began, "it feels as though my heart would break."

"See," she said cheekily, determined to make it difficult for him, "I know I should stay with you."

"No that's not it, rather when you go you take part of me with you. I don't know what you see in me." He paused but she would not rise to the challenge, this was her moment. "But I think you are the most wonderful, intelligent, sexy woman I have ever met. I am deeply in love with you." He was getting into his stride now. "And I would be astonished and over the moon if you would consent to be my wife?" She sat still for a moment with her head down so that he could not see her face. Then in one fluid leap she sprung forward with an impish grin on her face and lunged through the gap to hold him and draw him to herself.

"Nine out of ten," she said humorously, "and of course. You should have asked me sooner. I thought you would never get around to it." She kissed him passionately on the lips and hugged the breath out of him. He was overwhelmed by the reaction. She was so excited. "Can I tell dad."

"Shouldn't I ask him?"

"Do you want to?"

"No."

"I'll tell him." They kissed and cuddled for a long time until the discomfort of the situation drove them to separate. She made him sing her praises over again and then they parted.

[F6] The Urban Mystic is best defined by what she is not. She is not there to write poetry, although what she writes may be poetic. Nor is she there to create literature, although in her discourse there may be stories. Neither does she have oil or water-colours before her, or clay or even a camera in her hand. Yet nevertheless within her beats the heart of an artist. She responds as strongly as any artist to what she senses before her. She endures as much pain to express it. Apart from the imprint in her own soul she is left with only the resources of her own words, the phrases of scripture and the similitude of conventional theology with which she resonates. The divine spirit stirs her, leaves her restless with an agitation to fulfil her vocation.

[G6] There would be no faith without mystery. Good theology enhances the mystery and does not disperse it.

Gregory did not feel he could go out that night in case there was an air raid and he was found missing. The next day the news showed that the ground war was gaining momentum and the air raids appeared to have come to an end due to lack of ammunition. However, that did not mean that they would not get more. The Dean and Mercy came to congratulate him but the Dean in particular seemed very preoccupied and did not stay long. "The loss of life the loss of life," he wailed at one point. It was ageing him.

Gregory waited until about 3 am until he went out. He could see and hear a great battle going on in the east by the glow in the sky and the sound of ordinance in the distance. He walked into the city. It was lit this night and the high street was changed. There were a lot of people about. Here and there were large craters where buildings had been. There was huge hole by the cinema which itself seemed undamaged and spot lights had been rigged up. There was a great crowd working in the declivity among the twisted steel and concrete. Debris was being passed out hand to hand. Gregory asked one exhausted man what was happening. Apparently there had been a shelter under the building and they were trying to release those who had taken refuge there. They could hear cries for help from underground but dare not use heavy lifting gear yet until the situation became clearer. He was all for helping but the spirit put his hand on his neck and urged him to walk on. The pattern was repeated down the street. For some reason the shopping centre seemed to have been the main target Gregory could see no reason for it except to demoralise everyone. Another intensive search was going on at the other end of the main street but here there was less hope as no noise had been heard. Gregory came to a halt by this second crater and began to weep. By this great hole there was a temporary morgue with a pile of body bags. Gregory remembered the words in his black book:

> *The sacred stones lie scattered*
> *at the head of every street.*

As he stood there he became aware of an elderly woman looking at him. She was covered in dust and her face was streaked with tears. She stepped towards him peering myopically up at him. He recognised her as one of the pilgrims that had come to see him a week before about her daughter. She took his hand and snuggled in close to him. "Praise the spirit you came," she said softly. He took her in his arms and wrapped his cloak around her.

In the following days the battle was bloody and close fought, the armies of both City States had made incursions into each other's countries and were besieging the towns. If it were not for the appalling casualties it would have been more like two equally matched children slugging away at each other without much hope of either becoming the victor. On the outskirts of the provincial town of Sylbent, Persfeld's heavy artillery was slinging high explosive shots into the centre but each time they tried to invade in the lull they were repulsed quickly. For although Persfeld had big guns they did not have the ground troops to compete with a local centre of St. Arburn's Militia. The newspapers and TV reports that continued throughout, which Little transmitted to him, were mesmerised by the conflict and jockeyed with each other to predict what the outcome would be.

What was clear was that both sides were becoming exhausted and destroyed. Then a journalist, in a newspaper editorial, suggested that both sides should revisit the original source of the conflicts. This simple thought became that actual news for the subsequent day and everyone held their breath. There was even a lull in the fighting. The Dean was the first to visualise what the implications might be.

Gregory had been going out regularly each night. Now that Little knew what he was doing he was able to go earlier while it was still light. In the warmth of the approaching summer he discarded his cloak and in some new clothes, given him by Little, and now clean shaven at her insistence, he walked around with a degree of anonymity. Only the pilgrims who had spent some time in his company and had actually paid him any attention recognised him or thought they did. Most of the pilgrims when they had been to see him were so distressed about themselves that they never really studied his face and the recent pictures in the newspaper had not been very clear. Nevertheless, here and there he was seen and appreciated. More as a ghost that a person.

With the good weather the homeless had gathered themselves into large family groups and cooked and shared their meagre resources. They were not starving, as other City States were sending in aid but there was no chance of normal life returning until the conflict was over.

Three days later the Dean came with Mercy and Little early one morning. He looked serious. "Look I have had a whisper of something," he said. "It was an idle thought from a junior officer but when he had spoken it there was no way to take it back. He said, 'why do we not destroy or take their Cathedral. Would not that be the decisive victory that would prove our superiority? Isn't that where it all began with these damn cathedrals squabbling over that ludicrous man.'". Gregory wished he had not been that explicit. "Nobody took it up but some heads were scratched." The Dean lent forward confidentially. "Of course it is not about that, more like power crazy politicians and mad ones."

"If we did that they might retaliate," Mercy spoke the words they were all thinking.

"Yes. And I don't think they would bother to take it," and the Dean spluttered a bit with the emotion and his voice went high, "I think they would just destroy it." There were tears in his eyes. "It could never be rebuilt." Little put her hand on his shoulder. "Anyway we must plan for the worst. They have no more rockets or bombs thankfully but if they were to pull up their big guns away from Sylbent then they could shell us from miles away. I don't know how much warning we will get. I am sending the staff, that still come, away."

"Dad what about Gregory?"

"Unfortunately Bailey has confiscated all the keys to your cell. He holds the only one now. I cannot get you out even if I should want to."

"There must be some other way?" Little's eyes sparked, she had to keep up the pretence.

"We will find a way. Oh dear I am so sorry," he looked at Gregory. This was the first apology he had had. But it seemed irrelevant now.

"Daughters you must go away into the country for safety."

"No way," they both said forcibly.

"Why did I think you would say that. However, at the last minute all three of you must go when they won't bother to pursue Gregory or bring him back. You must go and make new lives for yourselves."

"What will you do?" Gregory asked.

"My duty is to stay here. If the worse comes to the worst I will take the testimony of the old abbey ruins, they were reborn to this," he cast his eye to the ceiling of his beloved building.

"Maybe," said Gregory gently, "we don't need a building."

"I wish that were true - but at the moment I don't." Gregory nodded.

That afternoon the Dean came back alone. He said simply, "it is as I suspected - we are to go for their Cathedral - we can guess their response."

Chapter 33

The next day the newspaper reported a lull in the fighting and major troop movements on both sides. It was noted with interest that aerial photographs from the reconnaissance planes of other states indicated that the troops of both opposing sides were now retreating or advancing towards each other's cities. Gregory did not go out that night but sat long after dark savouring the dusty tranquillity of his home. Now he was at the point of his potential release he felt very calm about it all. All the old feelings of rage at his imprisonment and anxiety about trying to be a mystic had gone. With the black book open before him he mouthed the words of the fragments to himself. He knew the book by heart now, even down to which verse appeared on which page. They were his life, his food. His soul savoured and sucked on the nourishment of these frustratingly elusive words. He was quite alone from human company but the spirit seemed larger that night, more real than he had ever been. He was in Gregory's blood keeping beat with his pulse, warming his thoughts, inspiring him with further longings of hope and confidence. On top of all these present manifestations of God there was his own mystical experience; lodged so deeply in his mind he dare not even unpack it. There would come a time for that later. Inevitably it would become real enough if he were to die, such was his own acceptance of its veracity. And even if he did not die soon, then there would come a moment to relive and taste the power of it once more. As a result of that flash of rapture, that actual historical episode of communion, he felt the proximity of the divine more powerfully real than a memory, more like an incipient invasion of the sacred biding its time before it would burst like a holy whirlwind into his soul once again. Such thoughts were too much to contemplate at that time: he was so glutted that any holy hunger seemed a long way off. Gregory dipped his head and made himself return to earth.

Little had told him that there were to be no troops posted at the Cathedral itself. The army was so sure that the Cathedral would be a target that they were not prepared to lose lives in the building itself. They were to make their last stand some half a mile away ringing the city with their remaining troops and artillery. The rest had not been sent to press an attack on the Cathedral at Persfeld. They were at each other's goalmouths now. At 5am the siren sounded and Gregory got up from his pallet, where he had only recently lain and looked out of the window of his cell. A lovely beam of moonlight played down onto the presbytery floor from some broken window above. In it the dust particles whirled and danced for joy. He was mesmerised by the current of air in the vast ecclesiastical space. When, shockingly, into the spotlight stepped Bailey with a demonic look on his face. The strength of his emotions twisted his features, making the skin of his face tight with malevolence.

His nemesis had arrived for the last time. Gregory felt sad. Was it all in the end to come to nothing? Was his life in the world to be wasted? Was he to be denied a normal life after all? Did not the divine spirit have the power to protect him? Bailey raised his gun and pointed it into the cell. Gregory turned his face away from him and showed him his profile. He could not be bothered to run. He felt too tired. Do your best, he thought.

Then there were steps running up the Nave and into the Choir. Both Bailey and Gregory looked towards the sound. Bailey smiled when he saw who it was but Gregory had to wait until they appeared from his standpoint. It was the Dean and Little. The Dean was carrying a garden spade. "My god let's get him out," puffed the Dean.

"Please Bailey?" asked Little. Bailey was sweating. Gregory could see the perspiration on his forehead. He slowly gathered the moisture in his mouth and spat on the floor. The Dean, still breathing heavily with the exertion, was outraged by this desecration.

"Will I fuck!" Bailey said slowly. "It's time to kill him. Why have you changed your tune? It's because of him that they are coming to destroy your beloved Cathedral - you know don't you."

"Maybe in the beginning," the Dean said ambiguously. He was resting his hands on his knees now bending over with the spade resting against his side to catch his breath. When his breathing was more controlled he straightened once more . "You are not going to help then?" he asked Bailey. He was walking towards him with the spade in his hands again. Bailey shook his head in disbelief.

"No, I'm going to kill him," he held the gun up and shook it just in case they had not seen it. He pointed it again at Gregory. "Go away if you don't want to watch."

Gregory was shocked at what happened next. The Dean strolling nonchalantly just behind Bailey lifted the spade and brought it down with the flat of the blade on Bailey's head. It was only a glancing blow because Bailey must have seen it coming: he had begun to duck before contact. Nevertheless the blow felled him and his gun clattered onto the floor and slid away. Both the Dean and Bailey reached for it but the Dean had Bailey between him and the gun. Gregory stung himself into action. He raced for his door, tore at the bung and scrabbled with his trembling fingers at the door jamb. It wouldn't yield at first but, when it did move and just as he was coming through the doorway, a massive explosion thrust him back onto the stairs. As he picked himself up, his straining ears could make out the automatic gun firing. He raced down the south aisle and into the transept. Large chunks of masonry were falling at the west end of the Cathedral and a huge billowing cloud of dust was swirling up the Nave similar to the previous occasion. Other explosions followed, the blast of each one blowing him off course as he ran. The noise and the dust were horrendous. As he rounded the corner into the Choir he could see that Bailey and the Dean were still struggling. Little was pulling at Bailey's feet but he kicked her away brutally and she shot across the floor to the bottom of a pillar. The gun went off a second time and both men lay still. Then Bailey raised himself bloody but unbowed, the Dean lay still. Bailey tried to pull his gun from the Dean's grasp but his dead fingers would not release it. With a yell Bailey ran towards Gregory who braced himself for the shock of engagement. It never came, Bailey ran past him into the approaching dust storm. More stones fell above them and Gregory turned without thinking to chase Bailey. Ahead of him Bailey was limping. Pieces of ornamental carving, vaulting, wooden beams and slates were raining into the Nave. Moving with the jerking gait of a cripple Bailey dragged himself on into this hailstorm of debris. Gregory ran to catch him and at the point that Bailey threw himself into the dust storm Gregory propelled himself after. Into the hell of noise and flames Gregory, chasing through the choking fumes, caught Bailey by his coat and pushed him over. Then they fought like two madmen, clawing and scratching, viciously punching each other in the dark. Gregory could hardly see his assailant, the brick dust from the bomb blasts was making his eyes water copiously and he was choking for breath in the foul air. First

Bailey got himself behind Gregory and strangled him with the Chain of Office pulling it deep into his Adam's apple. In retaliation Gregory reached behind him to pull at Bailey's hair. A large junk came away in his hand. Then the old chain snapped and fell uselessly to the ground. With a twist and a struggle they faced each other. They had their hands around each other's throat grappling side by side on the new beach of dust.

Another huge explosion stunned them, the blast coming from the east of the Chancel and with it a strong sucking wind drew off the cloud for a few seconds. They looked like the survivors of a volcanic eruption. A singing from above made them both look up. Above them a huge section of the roof was sagging in and as it did so a stream of slates slipped of it into the Nave. The flat rectangles came scything down, shrieking and undulating in the breeze like some demonic harpies. One struck the floor by Gregory's head embedding itself deep in the wooden floor and scattering slate crumbs over them that stung and cut like shrapnel. Then others came winging towards them. Gregory stirred himself and heaving himself on top of Bailey applied pressure once more to his throat. The smog of dust returned, swirling around them, but the slates came unseen disgorging themselves from the broken roof high above. Gregory could barely see his hands. Then there was an awful pain as something sharp grazed his knuckles and he withdrew his hands as if stung. As the debris particles ebbed away again for a moment he could see Bailey lying broken under him. But now he had a new collar. A piece of slate from the roof had parted his head from his body slicing through just above where Gregory's hands had rested. Gregory hunched forward and looked over the slate. There was no blood just a silly look on Bailey's face. A large stone block landed and shattered near Gregory showering him with shards. He stood immediately and ran away back towards the presbytery. There he found Little kneeling over her dad trying to lift him. Gregory went to her and dragged her off. "Come away," he shouted above the din, "he's dead there is nothing you can do."

"I cannot leave him."

"You must it is too dangerous now. We will come back when this is all over."

"He is dead?"

"Yes." He lifted her to her feet and dragged her by the hand towards the cafeteria. A final bomb fell. It missed an impact with the roof, falling instead through a hole onto the Choir floor below. The explosion was enormous and it threw both Gregory and Little to the ground. But in that crushing blast a piece of shrapnel sliced a sliver from the large south pillar near to Little and sent it winging into her back. She felt it sting as she fell to the floor and later, when she got up again to go to Gregory, she felt the pain in her back like a strain and reaching up, under her clothes, wiped a smear of blood from where the needle of granite had pierced her. It was tender but it was the only blood on her. Later, outside they lay on the grass in the sunlight dusty ghosts cradling each other in their arms.

[H6] Human creativity cooks nature and prepares it for display. Is there not a seamlessness between nature and human creativity? Does God's judgement of goodness wear off the further away from him it is? The words, 'it is good,' sprung from an artist's heart. The divine spirit not only validates but also appreciates. In the same way that grass begets health and strength in creatures so we take all of nature to be food for our creativity. With some we make what is ordinary, with some we make what is to be holy. The artist processes nature to greater significance.

Chapter 34

Mercifully they were only a short time on the raft. Greg felt sorry for the sailor who had helped them because as he launched them, the raft had escaped from his grasp and the storm had blown them off before he could get in. Greg hoped he was safe. When they beached Greg carried the girl up the baking sand straight into the wood that lined the coast. His luck held: he quickly found a small stream of fresh water and, laying his precious burden on a grassy hummock, he carried water in his hands to her. This time the water roused her and she licked the moisture from her dry lips a few times before opening her eyes. Then she grimaced with some newly realised pain and gasped. Her hand went to her side. "There," noted Greg and she nodded. He gently pulled her blouse from her jeans and she winced as he did so. On her left side there was a black patch turning to blue as it spread towards her navel and down into the line of her knickers. "Have you hurt yourself," he said stupidly. She nodded.

"We saw you arrive," a voice called behind him. It was one of the sailors. "Are you all right?"

"No, we need medical help."

"I will fetch someone who knows first aid. He was gone ten minutes, during which Greg took the girl in his arms and soothed her by stroking her hair. This time two men returned and the second man looked at the bruise on the girl's side. She would not let him touch it. He nodded sagely.

"There is help coming," he announced.

"Soon?"

"Soon. Tonight."

"Do they have a doctor?"

He shrugged, "Too far for a helicopter." The men withdrew and spoke quietly to each other.

Greg heard one of them say, "I shall tell Mr. Kertz. The other laughed. They wandered of together.

One of them looked back. "Stay here it is cooler. We will come when it is time.

The day passed slowly. Greg held her in his arms for a while until she asked to be laid down. He made her as comfortable as he could and lay beside her. Every so often he would kiss her. Once she squeezed his hand; there seemed to be no need for words. Eventually she fell asleep and he could hear her snoring gently.

By the afternoon Greg was becoming frustrated that nobody had come to check on them. After ensuring that she was still asleep he returned to the beach. The sailors had lit a fire and were lounging around it obviously in good spirits. Mr. Kertz looked a bit crumpled and he was smoking a cigarette. When Greg came into their view they became quiet. "How is she?" the medic asked. Greg shrugged.

"How much longer?" One of the sailors held up a small emergency communicator.

"Two hours."

"She needs help now," Greg said pathetically.

"You can have her now," was the sharp response from Mr. Kertz. "I have finished with her." The men laughed. Greg walked away, he felt powerless and sad, and all the fight in him had gone. The woods were gloomier now the sun was hidden by some clouds. When he got back to her he was relieved to see she was still lying as he had left her. He stood over her for a few moments marvelling at her beauty. Then as he looked more intensely at her face he could see that the corner of her mouth had dropped. He knelt down and picked up her hand. It was cool, too cool. He touched her face and it was the same unnatural temperature. He began to weep and great drops rolled down his nose and on to her face. He kissed her on the lips.

A month later he was sitting drunk early in his flat late one evening when there was a knock on the door. "Go away!" he shouted but the knock came again more persistently. The door handle was tried and as it was opened somebody walked in. It was not until Greg looked up at the man, who now stood before him, that he saw it was Mr. Kertz. "What do you want?" he voice slurred.

"You're feeble, to be so sad over such a slut. Find another girl - I have."

"What do you want?

"Her sister told me that you have quite a treasure trove here." Greg looked stupidly at him. "The photographs! I want some to pay for the trip in my yacht." Greg staggered with difficulty to his feet.

"Are your minders here?"

"What, to deal with a lush like you."

"They are over here," Greg told him as he stumbled forward and pointed to a stack of portfolios leaning against the wall of his room. The man walked over and squatted down on his haunches by them. Mr. Kertz took the first and laid it on the floor before opening it.

"Yes, very nice," he mentioned the name of the photographer of the first print that presented itself to him. Mr Kertz bent further over the portfolio twisting his head to look at the subsequent prints which were in different orientations. "This will do." He meant the whole portfolio. As he turned his head he saw the paper weight in Greg's hand and was caught off balance by his crouching position. Instead of rising, as he tried to stand, he began to fall backwards. Greg threw the paper weight with all his drunken might at him. It caught Mr. Kertz on the forehead and crushed him to the ground where he lay still. Greg had never told the girl how much he loved her, although he had, and now he had not told her lover how he hated him either.

Chapter 35

```
[N6] I observe that humans are the only
creatures with the creative power to do more
than simply replicate themselves through
procreation.
```

Nobody recognised Gregory and Little when the city inhabitants began to gather. They all came to stand in stunned and mournful silence at the ruins of their great Cathedral. The glory had departed. Only the east end wall stood to its full height and only the cafeteria roof offered any protection from the elements. Behind the Cathedral the Deanery, untouched, stood proud testimony to the precision bombing of their enemy. Nobody spoke. People came and went but not one dared to venture inside.

Gregory pulled Little up from the ground, she rose stiffly holding her back. To his enquiring look she said, "I have pulled a muscle I think."

He smiled and wiping her mouth with his sleeve kissed her deeply on the lips. "Come with me," he commanded. He took her by the hand and they went into the cafeteria kitchen where they washed their faces and hair and ate some bread. Then leading her by the hand he took her into the ruins of the Nave and they picked their way up to the presbytery. When they found Bailey's body, impaled now by several slates, it did not stir their emotions. Entangled with his boot lace lay the Chain of Office which Gregory lifted and pocketed - it had become his property.

Her father was buried under a pile of masonry, only his feet stuck out. It would take lifting gear to free his corpse. Gregory's cell was destroyed, two interlocking beams had fallen through its fragile roof and crushed it. Gregory stepped inside the breached wall and tenderly lifted his black book from the dust. He nodded to Little that she should follow him further. They went and stood before the old altar rail and he prevailed on her to kneel with him. Gregory gave silent thanks for their survival while Little rested there. Then pulling her to her feet he took her in his arms again. He looked down into her eyes. "I pledge to you my life," he said gently, "for ever.

Whatever I become I want you to share in it and I want to share in your life also. Be my partner, my lover in all that lies ahead, good and bad for ever. Be mine."

"I am yours," she replied. "Be mine, be my friend and let me have your body as you have mine, may the Spirit make our lives fruitful. I promise my trust for ever." They kissed. Without a word they knelt again in the hope of a blessing and then walked out of the ruins hand in hand. That night they slept together in Little's bed in the Deanery and were gentle and tender with each other in their first consummation of their love. The next day they watched the news together. Both cathedrals lay in ruins and the destruction had proved cathartic in the war. St. Arburn's President lay critically ill in hospital injured by a hand grenade from an unknown assailant and the hawks had taken flight. Both armies declared a truce and held their position.

Few people attended the Dean's funeral as they had enough of their own relatives to bury. It was Gregory who dug the grave in the abbey ruins and later said a few words to the small crowd gathered there.

The following day the girl's cousin arrived from Persfeld and it was decided that Mercy should return with her. In the evening Little and Gregory said goodbye to them both and taking a few things in a rucksack drove off in the Dean's car. On the main road they turned north overwhelmed by an infinite sadness.

Printed in Poland
by Amazon Fulfillment
Poland Sp. z o.o., Wrocław